1971

252pp

New Theology No. 5

New Theology No. 3

New Theology No. 5

Edited by
Martin E. Marty
and Dean G. Peerman

The Macmillan Company, New York, New York

Collier-Macmillan, Ltd., London

Permission to reprint the following is gratefully acknowledged:

"New Left Man Meets the Dead God," by Steve Weissman, Copyright © 1967 by the Board of Education of The Methodist Church

"Man and His World in the Perspective of Judaism," by Emil Fackenheim, Copyright © 1967 by the American Jewish Congress

"Hope in a Posthuman Era," by Sam Keen, Copyright © 1967 by the Christian Century Foundation

"Appearance as the Arrival of the Future," by Wolfhart Pannenberg, © 1967 by American Academy of Religion

"Creative Hope," by Johannes B. Metz, Copyright © 1967 by Cross Currents Corporation

"God and the Supernatural," by Leslie Dewart, Copyright © 1967 by Commonweal Publishing Co., Inc.

"The Dehellenization of Dogma," by Bernard J. F. Lonergan, S.J., Copyright © Theological Studies, Inc. 1967

"The Absolute Future," by Michael Novak, Copyright © 1967 by Commonweal Publishing Co., Inc.

"The Future of Belief Debate," by Justus George Lawler, © 1967 by the Thomas More Association

"Christianity and Communism in Dialogue," by Roger Garaudy, Copyright © 1967 by Union Theological Seminary in the City of New York

"Evolution, Myth and Poetic Vision," by Walter Ong, Copyright © 1966 University of Maryland

Library of Congress Catalog Card Number: 64-3132

FOURTH PRINTING 1971

The Macmillan Company
866 Third Avenue
New York, N.Y. 10022
Collier-Macmillan Canada Ltd., Toronto, Ontario
Printed in the United States of America

Contents

1413

Christian Hope and Human Futures

One of the less attractive of contemporary expressions is "to pick brains." The phrase carries ugly anatomical overtones, suggests exploitation of other persons, hints at plunder or plagiarism. But unattractive though it may be, it aptly describes the technique with which each volume of *New Theology* is prepared.

Look at the brighter side: a compliment goes with the phrase. We assume that there are people with brains—people of intelligence and sensitivity, people on whom we rely to test our impressions and to compare the signals picked up on our own antennae. We encounter some of these people at parties, conferences, and seminars. For them the question, "What of significance is going on in theology?" is not a challenge to engage in teatime intellectual games; it is designed to break the ice, to stimulate a stream of consciousness that could be of benefit in what we consider to be a very serious enterprise: reporting to others.

Many of those whose brains we pick we do not meet in person; they are the editors of theological journals and their consultants. We know that their vocations call them to that combination of drudgery and discovery which belongs to journalism in its highest sense. They take on the tasks of editing because no one else cares to, or because they have a respect for the writings of others or a sense of responsibility in their discipline. Through the years they have learned that their success depends upon the acumen and skills they develop at selecting the representative and the best, and at serving as midwives in the painstaking work of bringing such writing to the printed page and to at least a part of the public.

This technique of brain-picking various editors in Europe

and America, in Christianity and Judaism, in Catholicism and Protestantism, has served us well. Now and then our reliance upon their journals turns out to put us so far in the advance guard that the timing of *New Theology* may seem a bit off: two years ago, following the journal editors' cue, we began to bury "death-of-God-talk" just before the public media gave it a second, wider cycle of prominence—and after which they and we scurried back to our galleys and took a second, more serious look at the phenomenon.

Aside from that venture in premature interment, we feel we have been generally successful at anticipating what would be discussed in a particular year because of the pioneering work of theologians, authors, editors, and those whose business it is to prepare agendas for theological discussion. This effort is not born out of an insatiable curiosity concerning "what's new" or a foolish pursuit of faddism and novelty. Much that is new is patently outrageous, ephemeral, and easily dismissible—and dismiss it we do. On the other hand, the Christian faith is conscious of its involvement with the new in history: the new birth, the new creation, the new life are familiar themes of the church at its best moments.

If Christianity (out of which most of this theology flows) numbers some 900 million adherents in the world and a few hundred million in northwest Europe and Anglo-America— the terrain on which we keep our own eyes most steadfastly— should it not each year generate a new idea or two? Can the community of memory and hope live only on rehash of memories? In a time when competition over the future is most intense, would it be wise for that community to abandon the future to others by refusing to probe and push into it with provocative—and sometimes mistaken—ideas and views? Should not its professional thinkers—men and women who devote their lives to theology—be able to come up with enough grist to sustain a small anthology dedicated to newness?

This year we have allowed ourselves this brief soliloquy or duoloquy for a particular reason: *New Theology No. 5* is even more devoted to the new, the *novum*, the not-yet, the pull of the future, than were the earlier volumes in the sequence. It is true that most of us are a bit nervous when attention to the future is expected of us. If Christianity is a community of hope, it is also one of memory, demanding due regard for the past. If it is an eschatological movement, devoted to an End time or a last time, it is preeminently a historical religion. The desperately urgent issues—people often call them "eternal"—are confronted in the temporal sphere, and they have their roots in promises from a past. In a time when faddists treat memory, history, and the past cavalierly, serious people do not want to contribute to such casual disregard of the historic.

Yet talk about the future, about hope, about the new, we do. For those whose brains we have picked and those on whom we rely have begun to concentrate on these themes, and they strike us as representing much of the most creative work in theology today. Whether the "theology of hope" will turn out to be a well-defined and serious movement, we cannot now determine—let the unfolding future take care of that. But that the "theology of hope"—to which most of the selections in this volume are in one way or another directed— has served as a magnet to attract people of vastly differing approaches is already clear; if not a movement, then at least a tendency or trend is present. Now is the time to begin to define and clarify it and to expose it to criticism.

When this series was initiated in the early 1960s the theological mood differed considerably from that which now prevails. Each year it seemed to us that one book more than others received attention, caused a stir, inspired reviews, generated a follow-up. *Honest to God, The Secular Meaning of the Gospel,* and *The Secular City* were the first three such titles; despite their authors' notable differences, these books belonged to a single movement or mood or style. They suggested that most people in Western, technological society— including Christians—had moved into a post-religious era; their lives were characterized by a pragmatic, empirical temper. The new man might very well be the serene, man-in-control agnostic, the productive political urban animal who did not welcome metaphysics or myth, ritual or religion, or anything in life which mattered very much. God, the old problem-solver, the old "x" in the human equation, the old symbol for what went on behind the curtain of human ignorance, was evaporating from human consciousness.

New Theology No. 4 had as its theme the title of a book that, to our knowledge, has not been written but which was called for by David L. Edwards: *Beyond the Secular*. The passing of twelve months has convinced us of the propriety of that choice. Some reviewers and friends at first thought they detected in the chosen theme a kind of new conservatism in the authors (or the editors); was the reintrusion of religious motifs into theology a sign of a failure of nerve, a reckoning that twentieth century theology, having taken a fateful turn into mere modernity, was now turning back, regressing into the more congenial and cozy environment of supernatural spheres?

By now, however, it has become clear that to talk about "beyond the secular" and the reappraisal of religion (see *New Theology No. 4*, pp. 12f.) does not mean comfort, conservatism, return, or regress. The "theology of hope" and the futuristic humanism with which it carries on conversation are far from being conservative. In their own way they are more radical than the secular-bent modern theology they bid fair to displace.

Perhaps Hegelian historians in particular will enjoy watching the dialectical progress of theology in our century. Two generations ago the giants in the earth who pioneered the theological recovery (and they *were* giants: Barth, Brunner, Bultmann, Berdyaev, Buber—and we are not yet past the "B's" to the Niebuhrs and Tillich) were often regarded as existential pessimists. Self-consciously rejecting nineteenth century liberal progressivism, shaken by World War I, shaped by biblical judgment and apocalyptic despair, their probings sought to go behind modern technology and politics in a concern for persons and community.

The generation which followed World War II and which prevailed for two decades (from Bonhoeffer to Cox and

Hamilton) seemed to be the antithesis of the mood and mode their fathers had represented. Not simple-mindedly optimistic, the new generation *was* optimistic; open to the possibilities of technology and politics, it shared the secular style of contemporary nontheological thought and action and rejected existential doubt and despair. Experiencing the absence of God but feeling liberated by the model of Jesus Christ, it wished to become an advance guard in the secularization of the world, but also to bring to the world some sort of biblical perspective.

Whether the "theology of hope" described in this book is a synthesis of the two generations' thought, we do not know. If it becomes the new "thesis," we venture to predict that it will be anything but stable. It is a "vibrating needle"—a characteristic built into the task the new theologians have defined for themselves. Devoted to the "not-yet" and the pull of the future, they must deal with the divergent dimensions of man that have come to the fore in our century. As Paul Ricoeur—one of the profound mentors of the new thinkers—has put it: "The modern world can be viewed under the twofold sign of a growing rationality along with a growing absurdity." Ricoeur sees in the proclamation of the death and resurrection of Christ "the surplus of sense over nonsense in history. . . . Being a Christian means detecting the signs of this superabundance in the very order that the human race expresses its own designs." While the Christian devotes himself to the past and to the Scripture in which Christian history takes root, the pull of the future is strong: "He will never finish the task of spelling out and forming a complete picture of this inner meaning."

The current theologians, then, are trying to deal with past and present without the commitment to the pessimism which people saw in neo-orthodoxy, or to the optimism which people saw in its successor, secular theology. They can appreciate both of these generations and are probably more positively related to them than they were to each other (most of the giants of the first generation lived through most of the second!). The new theologians differ from their predecessors in that, whereas eschatology was a postscript or minor motif in neo-orthodoxy and a matter-of-fact element related to prediction of the future in secular theology, it is the organizing and even the integrating principle of the theology of hope. Eschatology, prophesy, future-talk, hope: these are not postscripts or last words or subthemes but first words and dominant notes in the new theology.

If one book title this year were to supply our organizing and integrating theme, it would be Jürgen Moltmann's *The Theology of Hope*. However, influential though the German original has been, the English translation appeared too recently for review in the journals on which we depend; it can wait for a future year—if there is a future year (or another *New Theology*)—for it is hard to imagine hope theology's losing momentum quickly. Instead, in this volume we are exploring the themes of and the reaction to the most discussed recent work in North American theology, Leslie Dewart's *The Future of Belief*.

We do not here need to go into detailed analysis of *The Future of Belief* or the controversy surrounding it, since both are dealt with in some of the articles we have included. Some accents stand out, suggesting the work's typicality and the problems it raises. A Spanish-Cuban-Canadian, Dewart is alert to the meaning of future-orientation in the social and political revolutions of our time. Not much of those influences is apparent in the book, but Dewart has elsewhere spoken of them and has been shaped by them. We mention this fact because it points to a first dimension of the theology of hope—its interest in revolution, a word that has become so "in" in theology that one might guess that it is on the verge of becoming "out." That these theologians are open to dialogue with Marxism and are involved with change in "the Third World" was evidenced in one of the main religious events of the year we are covering: a conference on Church and Society held at Geneva, Switzerland, which was dominated by laymen, people from revolutionary or developing nations, and political radicals. Do not look for new political conservatism in post-secular theology!

It should be noted, secondly, that Roman Catholic Dewart was somewhat reckless in his dismissal of the main line of previous Catholic thought. Jaroslav Pelikan took him to task for this recklessness in a major review in *Theological Studies* —appearing tandem to one by Bernard Lonergan (in this volume). Like many of the newer theologians, Dewart reacts to "Hellenism," to scholasticism, to conventional churchly thought without always being mindful of the contexts in which they originally appeared and of the potential which they retain. Sometimes the theology of hope comes close to being a cult of the future. The Lonergan essay raps Dewart for this tendency, and we will let it speak for us, since we possess the credentials of neither a Dewart, a Pelikan, nor a Lonergan for entering the fray.

A further note: Dewart's thought is "post-ecumenical." That is, he goes about his business as one who is responsible to an emerging Christian-humanist community in which Protestant, Orthodox, and Catholic boundary lines are no longer meaningful. For the coming generation, many of the ecclesiastical issues of the ecumenical movement are of little consequence. However those issues might be decided, the outcome would have no effect on the way they do theology or on the themes they choose. Their dialogue is with Marxists, revolutionaries, radicals, representatives of world religions, university colleagues, and men in the street, without regard to denominational proprieties. One gets the impression that if Protestants federalized or conciliarized or merged themselves into brave new worlds, these thinkers would yawn. While organic union between Protestants and Catholics would, we must surmise, be greeted with an element of surprise or at least decent notice, a step-up in conventional dialogue would mean little. These communities are already wholly exposed to each other and highly interdependent.

The earlier volumes of *New Theology* reflected an ecumenical age; we editors were Protestants on the prowl for essays which portrayed Catholicism on the move, articles which spoke across the falling ghetto walls. But a Catholic article was self-consciously introduced and constituted a rarity. This year less than half the essays, chosen without denominational considerations in mind, were written by Protestants. Some of them were written by non-Christians and nonreligious people who deal with the same themes Christians have dealt with in the past.

We have accented three contextual features of Dewart's work (revolutionary, post-historic, post-ecumenical), but the most important is its bearing out of our theme of last year: "the post-secular." *The Future of Belief* calls for Christian theology in a context which neither reverts to *homo religiosus* nor relies on secular man, and for a new anthropology in theology, for the development or recognition of a new stage of human consciousness. Such a call is prominent in the work of Catholics like Bernard Lonergan and Johannes Metz (who are represented in this volume) and Karl Rahner and Edward Schillebeeckx (who are not but who well might be). Dewart's book includes the hopeful note we ought to associate with a theology of hope and a concern for the future of belief: "We should not place any *a priori* limits on the level of religious consciousness to which man may easily rise. In the future we may well learn to conceive God in a nobler way" (p. 185).

In his essay herein, Dewart speaks for himself and condenses his thought on the central theological focus today, the "problem of God." Those who have read this book will be interested in seeing him press still further. However, owing to the condensation, his piece is difficult, as is the Lonergan commentary. Newcomers to the issue or to Dewart's thought might do well to turn first to Justus George Lawler's survey of the controversy; Lawler is an editor of Dewart's work and himself a stimulator of this kind of theology.

To clear the scene for the discussion focusing on Dewart, two of the book's sections review the immediate past of theology and then generalize about the theology of future and hope. In the first section we revisit the still durable secular theology. In its final resolution this brand of theology was called "radical" or "death-of-God." Because its representatives wanted to be in touch with non-Christian radicals, they invited a New Left spokesman, Steve Weissman, into their circle for a chat. A secularized Jew, an agnostic, an activist influenced by Marx, Weissman might have been expected to show enthusiasm for *au courant*, secularizing, ethics-oriented theology. However, as his essay suggests, his enthusiasm proved to be moderate at best, and his trenchant criticisms serve as reminders of the barriers radical theologians face when they remain within the Christian or theological or "Jesus-focused" community. Weissman reminds them of some things Jesus was not—and today, for him, *is* not—and wishes the theologians well, but not too well, as he parts company with them.

A religious Jew, Emil Fackenheim, enters cautionary note against secular theology. Here again is a Canadian voice—quite fitting, surely, in the year of the Canadian centennial and as a kind of corollary of the Dewart work, also originating in Canada. Extrapolating on the basis of the "secular theology" implicit in the brightly humanistic Expo '67, the world exhibition held at Montreal, Fackenheim looks at "Man and His World" and registers a few demurrers concerning theologians who draw their first, middle, and last words therefrom.

Also in this backward glance at the still dominant theology is a piece by another Canadian (though an English "import"), R. F. Aldwinckle. At first glance his question, "Did Jesus believe in God?" might seem both impious and unpromising. But he concentrates on what constituted the central problem for secular theologians and what will preoccupy Christian theologians of hope: who is Jesus Christ, who is Jesus Christ *for us*, and how does he relate to God, to transcendence? This essay in biblical theology well summarizes the present state of the issue and sets the stage for the book's second section.

In that section Sam Keen, a young and consistently promising philosopher of religion, discusses the phenomenological side of the hope issue. We feel particularly at home with this article; for the first time in five years we have had the audacity to include something from *The Christian Cen-*

tury, in which we have a share in editing. In other words, we picked our own brains for this one. *The Christian Century* is edited for a public which includes many nontheologians and is not a professional journal of the discipline; hence Keen was asked to address himself to a broad audience, and he does so. While elsewhere he can be as arcane as the next man in discussing Ricoeur or Gabriel Marcel (who also has influenced the hope theologians), his article here is to be recommended as a starter for readers who want to know from the word "go" what the hope issue is all about.

Equally helpful is the overall introduction to the new future-oriented theology by Carl Braaten, himself a participant-observer in its development. However, his essay is more than an introduction; while he surveys the field, he also pushes toward new resolution. One of the thinkers he mentions, Wolfhart Pannenberg, is represented in this section by a difficult philosophical and theological treatise on "appearance as the arrival of the future." Pannenberg is now being translated; with Moltmann, he is the most influential of the European Protestants manifesting concern with the future. We are particularly interested in his work because of his knowledge and awareness of the Christian past; his writings on Christology and the resurrection deal with questions many avoid because of the contextual and substantial difficulties involved. In another article, Pannenberg's Roman Catholic counterpart, Johannes Metz, speaks of the creative aspects of hope.

New Theology No. 5 closes with some follow-through pieces. Harvey Cox, who seems to be successfully negotiating the move from secular theology to the theology of the future (see his essay in *New Theology No. 4*), introduces the grand guru of the movement, Ernst Bloch, a unique kind of latter-day Marxist. Cox and like-minded Protestants are not alone in their desire to employ philosophic insights such as those of Bloch in order to carry on dialogue with Marxists. In both Europe and America Roman Catholics have taken advantage both of the dialogical interest of some Marxists and the urgent situation of a world in revolution to call for a theology that deals with Marx, revolution, and change, all under the rubric of "the future." In fact, American Catholic philosopher Michael Novak, in his article "The Absolute Future," suggests that the pull of the future will necessarily alter some historic Catholic Christian God-concepts, moving them away from the accent on dependence and toward emphasis on freedom.

Roger Garaudy, a somewhat more orthodox Marxist than Bloch, helped to further the now-urgent Christian-Marxist dialogue by visiting North America during the year past; his essay is one dividend—if we may be permitted such a capitalist-sounding word!—from that visit. Finally, Walter Ong—who has been influenced by Teilhard de Chardin, whose evolutionary thought parallels Bloch's "pull of the future" as impulse for hope theology—exercises his remarkable literary gifts by delineating some of the humanistic implications of Christian evolutionary symbolism.

As participant-observers ourselves in writing, editing, and enjoying the theology of the times, we have a commitment to the theology of hope that is—as was our relationship to secular theology—hopeful yet critical. Editors have to measure all the winds of doctrine without being carried away by any of them. The theology of the future and of hope raises many questions. Is this theology as original as its advocates claim it to be? The eschatological note of the New Testament has been repaired to again and again at times of upheaval like our own. Does it replace the part for the whole? Eschatology is a strong motif (Bloch: "The true genesis is not at the beginning but at the end") but not the only one in biblical and Christian theology. It may be an integrating factor or an angle of vision, but can it replace concern for creation, incarnation, and other major themes? Will it be understood in a sick society which confuses hoping with a craving for things—the second car, the first boat, more chloresterol in which to wallow? Most of all: is its doctrine of God ("I will be who I will be"), with its temporal transcendence in place of spatial transcendence, an evasion, an elusive way of keeping theology going without saying much of anything at all? We would not be so rude as to raise these questions were it not the case that many of the thinkers represented in this volume are themselves raising them, working toward answers, and—here and there, now and then—beginning to provide answers. Read and see.

M.E.M. and D.G.P.

New Theology No. 5

New Left Man Meets the Dead God

Steve Weissman

To some observers at the Conference on Radical Theology held on the University of Michigan campus in October 1966, the conference seemed to toll the death of the death-of-God theology—at least, the proponents of that point of view seemed to be running out of steam (or, if you will, embalming fluid). One speaker who did spark some life into the proceedings was atheist Steve Weissman, who gave the radical theologians "what for." In particular, he admonished them for what he saw as their lack of value-standards by which to judge what goes on in the secular world. Their emphasis on "the specific, the idiosyncratic, the personal" (words of William Hamilton, one of their own) are inadequate, Weissman argued, to indict the "irrational whole" of the established society. An adherent of the New Left, Mr. Weissman was at the time of the conference on the staff of Ann Arbor's Radical Education Project, an experimental program sponsored by Students for a Democratic Society. At present a graduate student in Latin American Studies at Stanford University, he is the editor of *Beyond Dissent*, a collection of political essays scheduled for publication this year. His conference speech was first published in the January 1967 issue of *motive*.*

ALTHOUGH the "death of God" did chase the New Left off the nation's feature pages, radical activists have paid scant attention either to radical theology or to radical theologians. At most, the news that "God is Dead" brought forth snide remarks about the 1968 elections or pallid reflections of the mockery which Nietzsche's madman suffered at the hands of the unbelieving townspeople. Equally signi-

* P. O. Box 871, Nashville, Tenn. 37202.

ficant, neither God nor his demise is even mentioned in the insufferably long list of cosmic concerns and worldshaking questions which the Students for a Democratic Society Radical Education Project has outlined as the intellectual agenda of our generation. All of which seems to punctuate William Hamilton's observation that "there is no God-shaped blank in man."[1]

This state of innocence was breeched only recently when Hamilton, one of the most prominent "Death of God" theologians, asked that someone from the New Left speak to the October 27–29 Conference on Radical Theology at the University of Michigan. Rather by chance the invitation came my way, and spurred only by faith (and a nice honorarium), I set out to discover whether or not there was actually anything "to enter into dialogue" about. Six weeks later— after I had built up a rather sizable bedside stack of books and articles by Hamilton, Thomas Altizer, and Harvey Cox— my faith seemed justified.

As an activist, I remained somewhat wary of what seemed an overly psychological concern with exorcising guilt from individuals. As an atheist, I shared little of the passion involved in losing and then replacing a once believed-in God. And as a Jew, I was uneasy with the Jesus language, which had replaced the transcendence- or God-language so conscientiously avoided by the radical theologians. But for all that I was deeply impressed by the insistence that the human community was "where it's at," a theme most forcefully expressed by Hamilton. "We must learn," he wrote in *Playboy* (Aug., 1966),

. . . to comfort each other, and we must learn to judge, check and rebuke one another in the communities in which we are wounded and in which we are healed. If these things cannot now be done by the human communities in the world, then these communities must be altered until they can perform these tasks and whatever others, once ascribed to God, that need to be done in this next

[1] Thomas J. J. Altizer and William Hamilton, *Radical Theology and the Death of God* (New York: The Bobbs-Merrill Co., Inc., 1966). Unless otherwise noted, all subsequent quotes from Hamilton and Altizer are also from this source.

context. In this sense the death of God leads to politics, to social change, and even to the foolishness of utopias.[2]

Common ground for dialogue and political agreement are, of course, two very different animals. To be productive, any continuing dialogue must concentrate more on what separates than on what unites the thinking of New Left people and that of the radical theologians. And nothing separates the two groups more than the questions about ideology which are discussed in this paper.

———Is there, in the absence of some metaphysical transcendence, a need for some ideologically consistent standard of criticism and self-criticism?

———Can a critically transcendent, yet strictly rational, historical, and earth-bound standard be found in the implications of present-day technology?

———Is there an ideological contradiction between the celebration of man's freedom in history and the figure of Jesus as a guide to "revolution" *and* the "Freedom Now!" thrust of the Negro revolution?

These questions are significant even for those who know little of the radical theology and care less for the New Left. For radical theology, as defined in the writings of Cox, Hamilton and Altizer, seems little more than another variant of "the end of ideology," proclaimed by Daniel Bell in a 1960 book of that name. Certainly the radical theologians carry with them little of the pessimism and exhaustion of the 1950s, a mood well mirrored in the earlier book. But today, even sociologist Bell is more optimistic. His pragmatic, nonideological problem-solving politics has been taken up by celebrants of "the new technologies," of "the exponential growth of knowledge," of "the professionalization of reform," of "the managerial revolution," and similar slogans of the post-political Establishment ideology. And by the same token, it seems likely that, without radical change, the present radical theology will fit the "religious" needs of the newly powerful technocrats and managers—and through

[2] Hal Draper, "In Defense of the 'New Radicals,'" *New Politics*, Summer 1965, p. 8.

them the continuing *status quo*—in much the same way that Niebuhrian pessimism served the wielders of power during the Eisenhower years.

This conclusion and the questions and answers which lead up to it are the burden of the present essay. But having already "entered into dialogue" at the Conference on Radical Theology, I'm somewhat dubious that any radical change will be forthcoming, at least from the theologians most closely identified with the "Death of God" controversy. Even more disturbing, I've lost faith that dialogue with the radical theologians is important. For beyond a few of the younger participants, themselves political activists, and some of the more theologically conservative older men, the conference evidenced little seriousness about the intellectual, let alone ethical, responsibility due "the human community." Significant questions (not just my own questions, by any means) on Christology and ethics, and even psychology, were never honestly confronted. Intellectual fads—everything from psychoanalysis to Marshall McLuhan—were accepted more for their novelty than for an understanding of their content. Many participants seemed more concerned about making it with their "wife, kids, and mortgage" than about making meaningful sense. And there was throughout a shabby commercialism. The sponsorship of the conference by Bobbs-Merrill caused the theologians to see themselves as smalltime Fausts who, having lost their souls along with their God, were now compelled to trade their wit for a steak dinner and the prospect of a publisher's piddling advance.

This is not to deny the presence of real anguish and a real sense of loss. It was as if the conferees had too long accepted Dostoevsky's dictum that "If God is dead, all things are possible." But even without a Father, there was still guilt over his death, and many at the conference were somewhat horrified by their own potential for a theologically undefinable but nonetheless real evil. "He is dead!" they seemed to shout. "He is *really* dead: all things are not only possible, they are perhaps necessary."

Thus it seems far more useful to readdress this essay, not

to the radical theologians, but to those laymen who have confronted the problem of faith and politics, less eruditely, but with more earnestness. For whatever the state of the other-world, believer and non-believer alike are finding it increasingly difficult to create a human life for the human community, a life which allows *men* to overcome their powerlessness and share in the freedom of *Man*.

In his *The Death of God*, Gabriel Vahanian says of the Puritans:

The City of God meant for them that no earthly city could be self-sufficient, since the rule of God, which actually provided the principle of criticism and self-criticism, always stood in judgment over men's judgments and decisions.

Vahanian contrasts this recourse to a transcendental standard of criticism against current syncretic religiosity which promotes "the hope that better societies will be born when better cars are built and more gadgets (material and spiritual alike) inundate our lives." The Puritans, however, offer an equally intriguing contrast with the more honest immanentism of radical theology.

Out of "a sense of the loss of God," writes William Hamilton, Death-of-God Protestants say "yes" . . . "to the world of technology, power, money, sex, culture, race, poverty and the city." Into this world with them, probably ahead of most, goes the radical theologian proclaiming the secular world as "normative intellectually and ethically good." Hamilton continues,

Theological work that is to be truly helpful—at least for a while —is more likely to come from worldly contexts than ecclesiastical ones, more likely to come from participation in the Negro revolution than from the work of faith and order.

Death-of-God theologians, then, along with secular theologians like Harvey Cox, have agreed that the heavenly kingdom should be brought down to earth. And, having moved heaven, they now seek to move earth. This redirection should certainly be applauded, but the applause should not be allowed to obscure one fundamental hang-up. Just as mass-tailored religiosity in the absence of some metaphysical transcendence becomes swamped by the crassness of the secular world, a change-minded theology faces similar dangers in the absence of some secular standard by which this particular intellectually normative and ethically good world might be judged.

Certainly Cox and the Death-of-God theologians are willing to ignore Christ's caveat to judge not. Cox, whose God is not dead but only hidden (*deus absconditus*), seeks a theology of social change and uses the word "revolution" so much that one would think it was going out of style. Hamilton and Cox both seem particularly impressed with the Negro revolution and with the criticism of the *status quo* inherent in it. And the more mystical Thomas Altizer finds the particular vocation of American theology precisely as a negation of "the very emptiness of the American present," and of the "shallowness and barbarism of life in America." Yet in all these judgments one finds little evidence of any systematic standard of criticism and self-criticism. Only Altizer seems concerned with holistic thinking. "Today the task of thought," he writes,

. . . is the negation of history, and most particularly the negation of the history created by Western man. . . . Nor can true negation seek partial or nondialectical synthesis; it must spurn a twilight which is merely ideological (ideology, as Marx taught us, is thought which is the reflection of society). In our time, thought must hold its goal in abeyance; otherwise it can scarcely establish itself, and is thereby doomed to be a mere appendix to society.

Hamilton insists upon the ethics of "ultimate concern for the neighbor." This fairly simple statement of values probably is sufficient on basic questions of segregation and discrimination. As Hal Draper wrote of the civil rights involvement of the New Left, "You don't need much of an ideology to feel deeply about it." On more complex questions of foreign policy and economics, however, Hamilton, whose major concern is the ethics of radical theology, suggests little basis for judgment. Indeed, he shies away from any generalized and fundamental critique which seeks to explain the interrelationships between, and the basic causes of, the particular ills of secular society. Borrowing the phrase of Philip Toynbee, Hamilton seeks rather "to leave the general alone and to concentrate all our natural energies and curiosity on the specific, the idiosyncratic, the personal."

Cox, in *The Secular City*, offers a highly detailed set of political likes and dislikes. He is, however, less concerned with the mode of secular involvement than with convincing Christians that "secularization arises in large measure from the formative influence of biblical faith in the world." Gospel, he argues, is "an invitation to accept the full weight of this world's problems as the gift of its Maker." Cox's argument is a *tour de force* of Christian sources, theories, and analogies, interspersed with urbanity and social science. Unfortunately, he seems to think that he can slip social revolution into the thinking of his Christian readers without their noticing the change. Thus the reader senses the same inauthenticity as in efforts to present "Communism as Twentieth Century Americanism" or to wrap the New Left in the American Flag.

If Cox does favor a certain mode of involvement, it is much like "the specific, the idiosyncratic, the personal" espoused by Hamilton. Cox speaks highly of the pragmatic and particularized thinking of the functional approach (how does it work?). Secular man, he points out, "approaches problems by isolating them from irrelevant considerations, by bringing to bear the knowledge of different specialists. . . ." Cox does warn of narrow "operationalism," which ignores those aspects of a problem that have not been isolated for special attention. He also urges a broadening of the concept of usefulness to include artistic beauty and poetry. But he clearly opposes what he terms ontological thinking (what is something?) and seeks no greater unification of analysis than that which comes from solution of specific human problems. "It is a mark of unbelief in the ontologist," Cox writes, "that he must scurry about to relate every snippet to the whole fabric."

To be sure, the New Left is also non-ideological; that was the whole point of Draper's comment. Moreover, there remain many in the New Left who are as anti-ideological as Cox, Hamilton, or the image of "the idealistic young activist" conjured up by sympathetic journalists. Still, the New Left is probably best defined by its *rejection* of "end of ideology" thinking and by its *search* to relate at least the important "snippets" to a coherent and fundamental critique of society. Thus it is precisely on the need for ideology that any dialogue with radical theology must focus.

The significance for radical theology of this *rejection* and *search* can be illustrated best by an unfortunately overlooked episode from Berkeley. During the summer of 1965, before the Senate doves had articulated the widespread distaste with the Viet Nam War, Berkeley's Viet Nam Day Committee organized a campaign of massive civil disobedience. Our purpose was "to strike at the invisibility of evil in this war."[3] The much-publicized stopping of troop-trains; the sit-in against General Maxwell Taylor, whom we most uncivilly branded a war criminal; and the marches which the Oakland police and the Hell's Angels stopped short of the Oakland Army Terminal were thus calculated efforts to break through complacency and make a public issue of the war.

At the same time, the VDC attempted to get beyond conventional explanations of the war, as well as of the other issues which concerned us: the American South and the multiversity. All three we felt to be "mirrors" of what Altizer terms "the shallowness and the barbarism of life in America." Looking back, the tentative arguments of the VDC seem hardly ideological. Using the research of Robert Scheer, Foreign Editor of *Ramparts* and later a nearly successful Congressional candidate from Berkeley-Oakland, VDC members traced the origins of the war to liberal anti-communism. We pointed to the similar lack of democratic principle in America's effort to direct the development of the haveless nations. We condemned the fact that in the American South and the multiversity "the inhabitants are prevented from participating in the decisions that shape their lives." Finally,

---

[3] A full account was published in *Liberation*, September 1965. All quotes are from that issue.

we discerned in the Viet Nam policy "the insensibility of America to the suffering of colored peoples." We noted that while the killing of the white Reverend James Reeb helped to create a "Selma," even among liberals the killing a week earlier of Jimmie Lee Jackson, a local Negro, had gone almost unnoticed.

Of course, our desire for new answers and our feelings of outrage were not born of academic calculation. We were still living in the wake of the atrocious behavior of the Berkeley administration during the Free Speech Movement. We had just grasped the failure of the civil rights movement to meet the needs of the Negro poor. And the February 1965 escalation of bombing into North Viet Nam had ended whatever innocence we might have retained. But no matter how unstudied the inspiration, our beginning analyses were sound. As the nationwide demonstrations in October and the Thanksgiving March on Washington proved, our civil disobedience did hold promise of catalyzing anti-war response among moderate groups.

One of the first moderate responses, however, was an open letter which vented its spleen more on the VDC than on the war. It was signed by a group of eminent faculty liberals, whose expressed opposition to the war was limited to "grave reservations about its conduct." The letter concluded that "the good your committee can do for peace in Viet Nam is limited; but the harm it can do the values of the university is quite certain." The reasoning behind that conclusion bears directly on the question of ideology.

First, the faculty liberals misread the phrase "invisibility of evil" and accused the VDC of believing in the "indivisibility of evil" and of viewing the war "as the logical projection of some all-pervasive moral and social iniquity in American life." Whether the professors actually believed themselves witness to the Manichaen heresy remains unclear. What they definitely found heretical, however, was the willingness of their students to go beyond a "legitimate national self-criticism" which identifies itself with the personal dilemmas of a liberal President; which views Viet Nam, Guatemala, and the Bay of Pigs as "tragic ambiguities" and "counterbalancing errors" in a generally benign foreign policy; and which, in the words of the VDC, finds "the napalming of children balanced by the passage of medicare." To the VDC, the balancing and the moderation implicit in "legitimate national self-criticism" actually seemed to support the continuation of the war. For they bolstered the Johnson government by preventing the development of a determined and knowledgeable anti-war constituency.

The second heresy cited by the open letter was the refusal of the VDC to participate in the very anti-communism which we felt responsible for the war. Unlike the faculty liberals, VDC refused to accept the idea that "the desirability of containing communism" could ever justify American intervention against an indigenous social revolution. On the contrary, the very enunciation of such a policy *desiderata* seemed an invitation to further interventions, as in Santo Domingo, and to further involvement in rationalistic calculations about the cost-effectiveness of various anti-revolutionary stratagems.

Finally, the faculty liberals faulted the student group for undermining the ideal of the rule of law "through a heedless civil disobedience." Here the liberal professors implied that social legislation and legal processes (e.g., The National Labor Relations Act and Supreme Court decisions) were more significant for change than the social movements and social disruption that forces changes through those channels. They also evidenced real fear that disrespect for law by the left would aid the warhawks and hinder stability and progress by strengthening the hand of the Ku Klux Klan, the Minutemen, and the neo-Nazis. The incipient analysis of the VDC, however, contrasted progress and stability. Moreover, we saw the spectre of the "right wing" chiefly as an immobilizing myth which made change difficult by directing attention away from the real base of power in the corporate liberal center.

These three heresies against liberal orthodoxy reject dependence upon the pragmatic and "the specific, the idiosyncratic, the personal." Incomplete as it might be, there is rather a search for generalized *critical thinking* which would transcend the affirmative content of "legitimate national self-criticism," of liberal anti-communism, of the spectre of the right wing. For without that transcendence, criticism of the specific might well become affirmation of the whole. As Herbert Marcuse writes in *One Dimensional Man*, the acceptance of the blunders, crimes and ambiguities

. . . is part and parcel of the solidification of the state of affairs, of the grand unification of opposites which counteracts qualitative change, because it pertains to a thoroughly hopeless or thoroughly preconditioned existence that has made its home in a world where even the irrational is Reason.[4]

Despite its horrors, the war in Viet Nam, which occasioned this search, is still but a small part—and perhaps a rational part—of the overall irrationality of a society which binds man by armpit and genital to production for warfare and waste. This is not to suggest that radical theology take up the tired plaint against mass society or renew "the chronicle of middleclass hypocrisy," which, in Hamilton's view, "may well be complete, with no more work on it necessary." It is rather a plea that we come to grips with the structure rather than the superficialities of the world as it is. Here Marcuse's sharp summation will suffice:

The union of growing productivity and growing destruction; the brinksmanship of annihilation; the surrender of thought, hope, and fear to the decisions of the powers that be; the preservation of misery in the face of unprecedented wealth constitute the most impartial indictment—even if they are not the *raison d'être* of this society but only its by products: its sweeping rationality, which propels efficiency and growth, is itself irrational.

The pragmatic, "the specific, the idiosyncratic, the personal" never can indict adequately this irrational whole. Without some standard of what ought to be, without a standard which transcends the quite possibly rational parts of the irrational whole, thought is swallowed up by "the oppressive

[4] Herbert Marcuse, *One Dimensional Man* (Boston: Beacon Press, 1964). All subsequent quotes from Marcuse also are from this source.

and ideological power of the given facts," by the given frames of reference, by the intellectual norms and ethical goods of the established society. The problem, then, is not how to say "yes," but how to say "no," how to find a transcendent secular standard when the kingdom of God has come home to roost.

The problem of finding a principle of criticism and self-criticism is in no way limited to radical theology. Just as the critical dimension of the heavenly kingdom has been deflated by the disappearance of the hand of God from history, the critical potential of revolutionary political theory has been enfeebled by the fact that the proletariat in advanced industrial society—if not dead as a revolutionary force—certainly remains hidden. Unprecedented affluence, an omnipresent technology, and a masterful communications system have so "satisfied" the working class that the concept of class conflict takes on a Disneyland ring. No one really knows whether the concept will regain its dignity through the demands of the underclass of white and Negro poor or through the dilemmas of urban rot. But more likely than not, conflict will be contained and the quantitative changes dragged from the system will if anything strengthen its coherency and cohesion. Finally, although a few Leninist theoreticians and most international businessmen believe that domestic affluence requires imperialism, there is as yet little promise that revolution in the underdeveloped world will reduce affluence here and thus lead to increased domestic conflict.

The demise of the working class as a revolutionary force has, to be sure, occasioned a search for some new agency of social change. Many have looked to the vastly expanded white-collar work force, the teachers and social workers, the bank clerks and computer technicians. These groups, however, have hardly reached trade union, let alone revolutionary, consciousness. Other observers, chiefly students, have seen students and youth in general as the new proletariat. On their side is the growing importance of the university to the national economy and security, and the enormous expansion of youth and student population, both absolutely and relative to the population as a whole. Nonetheless, radical fervor does seem to decline with age, much as our elders explained, though without the vicious conservatism of the older generation of ex-radicals. And even if we could organize the intellectual workers to close down the knowledge industry, which so far remains a wet dream, universities and schools are just not as important to the day-to-day functioning of the system as are the automobile factories and the airlines.

Finally, there are those who see a radical transformation of the society coming from the wholesale disaffection, disaffiliation, and social disorganization which plagues Darien, Connecticut, every bit as much as Berkeley or the Bowery. One has a vision of the masses of junior executives, bolstered by their third martini, all on a given day placing chewing gum in the office postage machine. But most of the spiritually dispossessed aren't even that close to the levers of the machine, and even if they were, what will bring them out of themselves, out of their *anomie*, to engage in sustained and united activity?

Demands that an ideology be created—for example, the demand which brought SDS to establish the Radical Education Project—often tend to ignore these facts. But while the theorist of social change, the revolutionary intellectual, can ignore God, he cannot ignore the secular reality; he cannot from his armchair call into being an agency of social change; he cannot ascribe to social forces in the present context the potential for overcoming that context, if in fact no such potential exists. At the same time, however, he must not—but too often can, and does—abandon the critical standard which would demand revolutionary change. The difficulty of such a stance is obvious: "In the absence of demonstrable agents and agencies of social change," explains Marcuse, "the critique is thus thrown back to a high level of abstraction. There is no ground on which theory and practice, thought and action meet."

Nevertheless, the responsibility for critical thought remains. Perhaps a parallel is the waiting for the dead god found in Hamilton's writing. "Thus we wait," he explains, "we try out new words, we pray for God to return, and we seem to be willing to descend into the darkness of unfaith and doubt that something may emerge on the other side."[5] In any case the commitment to critical thinking seems in at least some sense to be religious. But the revolutionary intellectual hasn't the guarantees of either gospel or science, which earlier prophets enjoyed, and even his opportunities for martyrdom are marred by the suspicion that he's doing something quaint. He remains the Christian in Pagan Rome, the Jew in a Gentile world. But his now uncertain faith confronts the promise that the technology of the presently constituted, irrational society, if nudged, can remedy the visible evils without in any way qualitatively affecting the basic irrationality of the whole. And more threatening than this promise, there is always the nagging fear that the technologically omnipotent society will so shape his categories of thought and pervert his consciousness that the unremedied evils will, even for his sensitive eyes, become invisible. (In which case, I suppose, he gets a foundation grant to become a social critic.)

Much like theologians who have abandoned the metaphysics of an other-worldly kingdom of heaven, the revolutionary intellectual must anchor his standard of criticism in the realm of man's history. Critical standards, to be verifiable, must stay within the universe of possible experience. There is, however, a difference between remaining in the universe of possibilities and saying "yes" to this particular secular world. As Marcuse makes clear, "This universe is never co-extensive with the established one but extends to the limits of the world which can be created by transforming the established one with the means which the latter has provided or withheld."

Critical thinking, then, must explore the historical alternatives which haunt "the established society as subversive tendencies and forces." It must settle upon the specific alternatives available for the reorganization of intellectual and natural resources to provide "the optimal development and satisfaction of individual needs and faculties with a minimum of toil and misery."

---

[5] William Hamilton, "Questions and Answers on the Radical Theology" (mimeo.), p. 5.

This formulation accords well with both the "ultimate concern" of Christological ethics and the experience of many young activists. First one discovers the discrepancy between the "what-ought-to-be" of the dominant value system and the "what-is." ("Negroes don't get equal rights.") Then one discovers the gap between "what is" and "what-could-be." ("Cybernation makes poverty unnecessary.") Finally—and this is the difficult step—a new standard of "what-ought-to-be" is constructed on the basis of "what-could-be." In the present period this standard would be based on the technological capabilities of society.

The idea of a standard which transcends the present use of technology differs significantly from judging "what-could-be" on the basis of the already existing standard of judgment. Thus, it is important to note that Cox, who is much impressed by the possibilities of technology, never arrives at the need for a transcendent standard. Rather, he sees the gap as "between the technical and political components of technopolis." He continues, "The challenge we face confronts us with the necessity of weaving a political harness to steer and control our technical centaurs." No doubt such a challenge exists. But the weaving of a new political harness would in no way offer fundamental criticism of the way in which the technical centaurs presently serve to *prevent* "the optimal development and satisfaction of individual needs and faculties with a minimum of toil and misery."

Some people have read into *One Dimensional Man* a rejection of technology as being incompatible with the norm of optimal human development. Nothing could be farther from Marcuse's thinking. Marcuse does oppose the present "technological project," the subordination of technology's productivity and growth potential into a cultural, political and social system which "swallows up or repulses all alternatives," and "which stabilize(s) the society and contain(s) technical progress within the framework of domination." Marcuse also rejects the notion of the "neutrality" of technology:

Technology as such cannot be isolated from the use to which it is put; the technological society is a system of domination which operates already in the concept and construction of techniques.

Nonetheless, he clearly states his belief that the technological base must be preserved, albeit with a new "technological rationality":

If the completion of the technological project involves a break with the prevailing technological rationality, the break in turn depends on the continued existence of the technical base itself. For it is this base which has rendered possible the satisfaction of needs and the reduction of toil—it remains the very base of all forms of human freedom. The qualitative change rather lies in the reconstruction of this base—that is, in its development with a view of different ends.

Marcuse's discussion of transforming technological rationality brings the argument full circle. He sees the transformation as a "reversal of the traditional relationship between metaphysics and science." As in Puritan society, metaphysical concepts traditionally have provided a critical dimension by posing "a discrepancy between the real and the possible, between the apparent and the real truth." With the development of technology there is a vast expansion of the universe of possibilities by which the "truth" of metaphysical concepts may be verified. "Thus, the speculations about the good life, the Good Society, Permanent Peace obtain an increasingly realistic content; on technological grounds, the metaphysical tends to become physical."

Marcuse stresses that he "does not mean the revival of 'values,' spiritual or other, which are to supplement the scientific and technological transformation of man and nature." Rather he argues that "the historical achievement has rendered possible the translation of values into technical tasks," and that science can now proceed to "the quantification of values."

For example, what is calculable is the minimum of labor with which, and the extent to which, the vital needs of all members of a society could be satisfied—provided the available resources were used for this end, without being restricted by other interests, and without impeding the accumulation of capital necessary for the development of the respective society. In other words; quantifiable is the available range of freedom from want. Or, calculable is the degree to which, under the same conditions, care could be provided for the ill, the infirm, and the aged—that is, quantifiable is the possible reduction of anxiety, the possible freedom from fear.

Whether or not one accepts the specifics of Marcuse's quantification of values, his examples provide a sharp contrast to the segmental rationality of the present technological project. Marcuse is not talking of the highly rational manpower planning, which promises to keep unemployment low while providing workers for the degrading assembly line production of immediately obsolescent automobiles. Nor does his discussion include the application of cost-effectiveness studies to the creation of counter-insurgency strategies. "The technological redefinition and the technical mastery of final causes," he tells us, "*is* the construction, development, and utilization of resources (material and intellectual) *freed* from all *particular* interests which impede the satisfaction of human needs and the evolution of human familities." This, then, is far more than the political harness which Cox proposes for the technical centaurs. Indeed, it is qualitatively different.

The overall thrust of Marcuse's argument, moreover, suggests a way of transcending the present world while remaining firmly within it. Like Hamilton, Marcuse affirms the value of technology. Unlike Hamilton, however, he proposes a standard of criticism and self-criticism which, while based on the existence of that technology, is not shaped by technology's present uses and rationality. Thus he offers a hope that man's age-old aspirations, as expressed in metaphysics, need not be sacrificed to the irrationality of the present. Would it not be a sad irony for radical theology, at a time when the metaphysical *can* become the physical, to discard the content of metaphysical standards along with the form?

Insistence on a rational historical standard for criticism should in no way be considered value-free. Marcuse makes clear that his thought assumes that "human life is worth living, or rather can and ought to be made worth living." Less intellectually, perhaps, the New Left also affirms life and values; indeed, much of our time is spent struggling against the scientistic "value-free" orientation which rests like a fog upon the groves of academe.

The key value and demand of young activists is, of course, "freedom." Thus it is gratifying to learn that radical theologians are so largely concerned with "Man's freedom." There is a problem, however—perhaps a paradox. Hamilton affirms the moral centrality of the Negro revolution. Yet at the same time he is as concerned as either Cox or Altizer with optimistically asserting Man's freedom to act in history, now that "God is Dead" and "all things are possible." And, far more than Altizer or Cox, he insists on following the ministry of Jesus, on being guided by "the kind of thing he did, the way he stood before men, the way he thought, suffered, and died." The problem is that both the celebration of an historical freedom and the example of Jesus' ministry seem diametrically opposed to the "Freedom Now!" of the Negro revolution.

"Freedom"—under the weight of the "Now!" mood—has in the process of the Negro revolution become a cover for a multitude of good things. That multitude, unfortunately, will never be accommodated by a traditional or etymologically proper definition of terms. Listen to the opening lines of a poem written by Liz Fusco, a white freedom worker in Mississippi:

> Waiting
>   for rain
> and for freedom
> and for something to do
> to take away
> the way it is.[6]

This is the world of freedom schools, freedom trains, freedom budgets, freedom parties (big "D" democratic and otherwise), freedom unions, and freedom highs. Here the demand for "freedom," for "rights," also is a demand for quality education, de facto mobility, jobs, control of the police force and of public schools, and the right to do politics independently—all *Now!*

[6] Liz Fusco, "Poems From the Delta" (mimeo), p. 1.

The young German playwright Peter Weiss, also influenced by the Negro revolution, places this expanded sense of freedom into political focus. In Weiss' play "Marat/Sade," the revolutionary Paris crowd beseeches Marat,

> Marat we're poor and the poor stay poor
> Marat don't make us wait any more
> We want our rights and we don't care how
> We want our Revolution NOW

The cry of the poor—whether in revolutionary Paris, Watts, or Viet Nam—does share in what Hamilton terms "an increased sense of the possibilities of human action, human happiness, human decency, in this life." Revolutionary movement, by its very nature, cannot be pessimistic. *But neither does the dogged determination of the poor to have their Revolution NOW, to be free, reveal the optimism which Hamilton read into the Negro revolution.* "That there is a gaiety, an absence of alienation, a vigorous and contagious hope at the center of this movement is obvious," Hamilton writes, "and this optimism is the main source of its hold on the conscience of America, particularly young America." There is gaiety, perhaps; and young white Americans, struggling themselves to overcome the cultural straitjacket of Anglo-Saxon culture, are caught up by the discovery that "Ye need not suffer to be righteous." But Hamilton seems wrong—and we shall see, dangerously so—in finding optimism in either the Negro movement or the student activism which it has inspired.

The last time that I personally heard any optimism in the singing of "We Shall Overcome" was at the nicely middle-class March on Washington in August of 1963. Perhaps the optimism there reflected the fact that a March originally planned to demand jobs had been sidetracked into a Civil Rights freedom sing. Since that time, at any rate, optimism increasingly has become the stock in trade of "Negro Leaders," who in return for national influence seem willing to prevent the development of a political movement that might explore the expanded sense of the necessary which Hamilton mistakes for optimism. "Freedom" must be explored, and for the poor who make up the majority of the Negro population, that means far more than the equal rights and poverty programs which the established leadership seeks. "Freedom" means a total reorientation of national priorities and of the power centers which depend on the present orientation. And it most certainly means a rediversion of national resources from foreign war to domestic peace.

The "Negro Leaders," with all their optimism, admit that they do not speak for the Negro poor. Even the advocates of "Black Power" fail in this respect, though it is certainly to their credit that they seek to organize the poor to speak for themselves. Until the poor *are* organized, optimism is impossible; there is only the dogged determination of Watts, where one might well hear another stanza from "Marat/ Sade" aimed directly at the "Negro Leaders" from whom too many whites take their cue:

> Why do they have the gold
> Why do they have all the power
> Why do they have friends at the top
> We've got nothing always had nothing
> Nothing but holes and millions of them

Beyond the enticement of optimism, there are also difficulties in the identification of "Freedom" with the philosophic question of Man's freedom in a godless universe. "All things *are* possible." For the poor that has already been established, even without Ivan Karamazov's aid. The question is not whether Man *can* have dominion, but which men *will* have dominion. Similarly, the cry of the poor shows little concern with the cosmic implications of the suffering of children. In *The Great Fear in Latin America*, the journalist John Gerassi tells of a conversation with a pregnant woman in the favelas, the hillside slums of Rio:

My first two babies died within a few months of their birth. Now I hope that this one will be a boy and that he will grow up to be strong so that he can avenge his dead brother and sister.

I asked her who she thought was responsible. Her answer was blunt:

You!—and all the others like you who can afford those shoes and that suit.

I think just the money you paid for that pen could have saved one of my children.

If one seeks to support the poor in their struggle for dominion, the celebration of the new freedom probably remains spurious. The real question is one of power, of "which side are you on?" I say this not to be anti-intellectual, or to denigrate the importance of ultimate questions. But radical theology itself seems convinced that it is time to get beyond *Weltshmerz*, beyond existentialist preoccupations. Many in the New Left would agree. Camus was terribly important in helping us break through the immobilizing pessimism of the fifties. Now there is a fear that his philosophy can too easily become a pose, as it seemed in his own inability to move beyond nationalism and deal with the admittedly unpleasant realities of the independence struggle of the Algerians. My concern, however, is that the forward motion away from pessimism and its existential antidote might well lead to a demobilizing optimism.

Choosing up sides, however, is only half the battle. Jesus, whose ministry Hamilton would use as a guide, clearly sided with the poor and the meek. In addition he warned the rich of the difficulty of their entering the kingdom of heaven. Thus many have pictured Christ as a revolutionary. Phil Ochs, in *Ballad of a Carpenter*, sings:

> He became a wandering journeyman
> And He traveled far and wide;
> And He noticed how wealth and poverty
> Lived always side by side.

> So he said come all you workingmen,
> Farmers and weavers, too;
> If you would only stand as one
> This world belongs to you.

Tempting (and useful) as this image might be, radical theology would do well to find better revolutionary leaders than Jesus. To begin with, revolution is political and must aim at the levers of power. As C. Wright Mills said of the social scientist, the task of the revolutionary is to "translate personal troubles into public issues." Christ made his appeal public, but he advocated a withdrawal from public or political issues, and directed attention away from those who would prevent the workingmen, farmers and weavers, too, from exercising their claim to this world. Like LSD, Christ might have offered important pre-revolutionary insights. But opposition, political opposition, is what must be rendered unto Caesar.

Secondly, Christ was less a political organizer than a demagogue. In a thoughtful discussion of the "Legend of the Grand Inquisitor," Hamilton writes that "Dostoevsky's Christ is the idea of freedom," which "is precisely the reason why this Christ cannot be identified with Jesus Christ of the New Testament record." Following D. H. Lawrence, Hamilton reminds us that "the rejector of miracles still performed them, the rejector of authority claimed it from man, and, we might add, the rejector of mystery came proclaiming the mystery of the Kingdom of God." Miracle, mystery, and authority—which Dostoevsky ascribed to the Grand Inquisitor—are no less damnable in the hands of a Christ than in those of a benevolent despot. Nor are they beneficial in the building of a political movement, for as with Jesus, they lead not to political consciousness but to almost religious dependence on a single leader. Of course, freedom also presents problems for movement, and like Berdyaev (to whom Hamilton refers), many present day organizers preach (but usually don't practice) the notion that "the principle of freedom cannot be expressed in words without some form of authority being suggested." Nonetheless, Black Power militants and Frantz Fanon probably have better things to say on these sticky problems than either the biblical or the Dostoevskian Jesus.

Finally, there is the Christian admonition to "Love Thy Neighbor." Christian theologians cannot easily ignore the very rich concepts of harmony and peace among brothers found in the New Testament. Cox, for example, speaks of the diakonic or healing function of the Church. Unfortunately, he finds diakonia very specifically in efforts to strengthen existing movements toward centralization in metropolitan areas. Here Cox is reading the Good Samaritan into the balance-of-tension theory presented by Edward C. Banfield and James Q. Wilson in *City Politics*. Quoting Banfield and Wilson, Cox argues that the give-and-take organized groups on which city politics depends is threatened by racial, ethnic, political, and center city-suburban cleavages. This is certainly the case, but like most theories of premature pluralism, *City Politics* overlooks the fact that certain interests—specifically the Negro poor—remain unorganized and therefore out of the give-and-take. Their organization, moreover, would probably further polarize a metropolitan area, in part—but only in part—because organization will probably necessitate at least some recourse to racial consciousness (e.g., Black Power). Conversely, the centralization of metropolitan government, while probably necessary for a whole score of good reasons, will not only reduce polarization, but will also reduce the potential political power of any group of the inner-city Negro poor.

To be fair to Cox, he does parallel his support for the healing power of centralization with a concern for the *powerlessness of certain groups in the city*. His model here, however, is Saul Alinsky's The Woodlawn Organization. This Chicago group can be criticized seriously for its lack of democracy, its dependence upon its financial contributors, its failure to represent the interests of the truly poor who are not in churches or other formal organizations, its refusal to make significant (and disruptive) demands upon the Daley machine, etc. This is not the place to rehearse those criticisms, but neither should Cox suggest such a specific *political* strategy without offering a more complete *political* justification. The point is that neither Jesus nor the Christian sources can provide much of a guide to questions of political strategy. Whether Alinsky or Black Power is better, whether non-violence actually retards organization in the ghetto, the question of electoral politics versus direct action, the problems of tax base and governmental centralization—all those important problems need a coherent analysis far more comprehensive than Christian sources. To use those sources is to engage in the mystery-miracle-authority approach, which can only keep the poor in a state of dependence.

Though radical theology, in its insistence on the pragmatic and the particular, seeks to eschew ideology, there is some indication that at least Cox and Hamilton have settled nicely into the "twilight" of ideological thinking. Cox presents his ideological world-view quite succinctly. He suggests that "a titanic struggle" is now going on in "the organization," a struggle whose outcome

. . . will shape the countenance of America and of the world for decades to come. It is a duel to the death between the rising new technically educated class and the old class of zealous business barons.

Cox seems to believe that the "seizure of power" by technology has taken place already, evidently preparing the base for a victory of the technically educated classes. Cox does not make a fetish of technology; indeed he condemns the "technological utopians" for being "bogged down in the metaphysical and religious stages of human development." Nonetheless, he, along with Hamilton, provides strong ideological support for the technically educated in their social ascent. Both men eulogize the pragmatic, problem-solving approach; both emphasize technology without challenging the assumptions which govern that technology and both exude the optimism, the insistence on maturity, and the revolutionary rhetoric which has come to mark the new managers.

The difficulty with this managerial ideology is that it doesn't tell what's happening. For rather than a duel to the death, one finds more an incestuous marriage between the upwardly mobile new technologists and the owners of capital. This marriage is evidenced by the willingness of the technologists to subordinate their rationality to the wholly irrational priorities of the present economy, and by their willing perpetuation of the elite patterns of control usually associated with the "zealous business barons," but so much more subtly practiced by their personnel managers. Thus, like the middle class of the underdeveloped world, the new managers might engage with the capitalist in family squabbles over the distribution of the household privileges and responsibilities, but they have settled down with him into an acceptable routine of family life.

The best example of this process can be found in the very activity which radical theologians would most sympathetically support—the reform efforts of the public sector. Daniel Moynihan, one of the architects of the War on Poverty, explains that the initiative for the anti-poverty program "came largely from within," and was based "on essentially esoteric information about the past and probable future course of events." This he sees as "an example of the evolving technique and style of reform in the profoundly new society developing in the United States." This "professionalization of reform," found also in the Alliance for Progress, involves

. . . precisely the type of decision-making that is suited to the techniques of modern organizations, and which end up in the hands of persons who make a profession of it. They are less and less political decisions, more and more administrative ones. They are decisions that can be reached by consensus rather than conflict.[7]

When all was said and done, however, the administrative decisions in both programs were made within a continually narrowing framework of political considerations, shaped in large measure by what Cox would see as zealous business barons. No doubt there was squabbling, as over the Mississippi Child Development Group, the maximal feasible participation of the poor, the intervention in Santo Domingo, and the support for military dictatorships. But the technocrats continued to man their desks and computers, and in both programs even developed highly sophisticated rationales for why their original rationality could not work. Which perhaps explains why *Fortune*, the magazine of the most zeal-

---

[7] Daniel Patrick Moynihan, "The Professionalization of Reform," *The Public Interest*, Fall 1965.

ous and businessy of barons, now celebrates the expansion of the public sector and the professional approach to problem solving as "creative federalism."

Cox, of course, seems much more committed to a technocratic and managerial ideology than does Hamilton. Hamilton's support is more one of tone and of unquestioning and apolitical support for the technology and its problem-solving "operationalist" approach. Altizer, on the other hand, though rarely involved with the specifics of politics, provides a possible antidote to this unhappy trend. For his warning against thought's becoming a mere appendage to society closely parallels Marcuse's injunction against "the premature identification of Reason and Freedom, according to which man can become free in the progress of self-perpetuating productivity on the basis of oppression." Hopefully an understanding of the need for thought to hold its goal in abeyance, to establish itself as a negation of the society, will prevent any yes-saying to this particular society. Only our "no" can provide a qualitatively different society, which affirms man's worth in place of perpetuating his oppression. And to maintain that "no" as a critical standard, the radical thinker must identify with those who are oppressed, with those whose interests are represented by neither the technocrats nor the barons of business.

Man and His World
in the Perspective of Judaism

Reflections on Expo '67

Emil L. Fackenheim

Utilizing Expo '67—Montreal's international exposition marking Canada's centennial—and its secular-humanist theme as a starting point, Emil L. Fackenheim first discusses the inadequate responses to secularism that Jews and Christians have made in the past—rejection, retreat, accommodation. Then, drawing on Midrash teaching, he affirms that an aspect of secularity is implicit in biblical faith itself: "It is the primordial event of [God's] Presence which both destroys the idols and hands over the earth to the children of man." At the same time, Fackenheim avers that the biblical man has the task of distinguishing between types of secularity; with some varieties he must welcome the risk of mutual dialogue, but the kind that presumes to abolish heaven he must oppose, for it is but an ancient idol in modern guise. The author of such books as *Metaphysics and Historicity* and *Paths to Jewish Belief*, Dr. Fackenheim is Professor of Philosophy at the University of Toronto. His paper—reprinted from *Judaism** (Spring 1967)—was originally delivered at Temple Emanu-El, Westmount, Montreal, in the series "Man and His World," in observance of Canada's centennial year and Expo '67.

I

As a community of Jews and Christians, how should we welcome the more than seventy nations preparing to gather in Montreal for the great International Exhibition

---

* 15 East 84th Street, New York, N.Y. 10028.

known as Expo '67? The theme under which they assemble—"Man and His World"—is a truly challenging one. Indeed, not many themes pose so great a challenge to this present generation of Jewish and Christian believers.

In a world full of strife, the gathering nations will meet in amity and concord. Yet although Judaism and Christianity preach amity and concord, it is not religion which makes this meeting possible: many of the assembling nations are non-Christian, and some avowedly atheist. And whereas to Jewish and Christian believers God is either all-important, or else of no importance, the theme of the gathering is the world of man, not that of God. Man "the Creator," "the Explorer," "the Producer," "the Provider," "Man and His Community"—these are all sub-themes of the overall theme which represent varieties of human, man-made culture; and if religion appears among them—for there will be religious pavilions—it is as but one of these varieties. It is secular culture, then, which has produced such unity among the nations as has made this meeting possible; and religion is allowed a place among them only because this culture is variegated enough to generate a spirit of pluralistic tolerance.

How then shall a believer in the Biblical tradition respond to this gathering and to its guiding theme? This question may well seem to pose a fatal dilemma. On the one hand, we dare not accept on behalf of our God reduction to one or two pavilions among many others: can the all-important God of Israel or the Church be reduced to a mere religious "contribution" to human culture? On the other hand, to repudiate this gathering, on the grounds that it makes God marginal, would be both religiously perverse and historically reactionary. Religiously perverse, because our God, the Father of all men and the Lord of Peace, is present wherever men meet in peace; historically reactionary, because it is on secular terms, and on secular terms alone, that in modern times those international bonds will be created without which the human race will not long survive. Ancient Roman internationalism could unite all pagan gods in a pantheon. Medieval internationalism could unite the European nations under the banner of Christianity. The world-wide internationalism which is so desperately needed in the modern age, and which we hope is coming into being, can only be secular. For Jews or Christians to turn against this internationalism, on the grounds of its inevitable secularity, would be religiously unthinkable; and it would also be utterly futile. How then shall we cope with this dilemma?

II

Implicit in the dilemma just stated is a question which has been with us for a long time—in the West, since the rise of the modern world. For it is the modern world which gave birth to the idea of radical secularity. Radical secularity means human autonomy; and the idea of human autonomy permeates all those modern activities which are distinctly modern. All science seeks rational knowledge; only modern science rests on the idea of rational self-sufficiency. All technology seeks rational control of nature; only modern technology—there is hardly a pre-modern technology worth mentioning—is fully rational. Every state is a system in which man governs man; only modern states eliminate kings ruling by divine right and wholly recognize that political power is human, and human only. In short, the modern-secular world is, as the Expo '67 theme so clearly indicates, a strictly human world. How shall the Biblical believer—Jew and Christian—respond to it?

Four responses have been tried and found wanting in the past. The first is to ignore or simply to reject the modern-secular world. This response, most obvious in such forms as the nineteenth-century fundamentalist attacks on modern science, was all along foredoomed to failure. It might conceivably still win the odd victory, such as the demonstration that the theory of evolution is debatable. But victories of this kind are bound to be short-lived. The advance of modern science will not be stopped, even if some of its theories should turn out to be mistaken: for science will not conceivably repent of its basic idea of rational autonomy.

The second response—this, too, harking back to the nineteenth century—may be described as the fundamentalism of the intellectuals. These latter cannot deny or reject the claims of modern science. They are able, however, to shrink from the plebeian-democratic aspects of the modern world with an aesthetic aristocratic horror. This occurs in religious romanticism, which longs for past medieval glories. But these glories, if glories they ever were, are gone beyond modern recovery; and they are presently alive, if at all, only in the minds and hearts of a self-styled aesthetic aristocracy. But no Biblical believer, Jew or Christian, may flee from the real into an aesthetic world, afraid lest he dirty his hands—all the less if the aesthetic world in question is fit for no one but reactionary aristocrats.

No more is another flight an authentic Jewish or Christian possibility—from the modern secular world into an unworldly mysticism. To be sure, mysticism has always been an authentic possibility within Christianity. Judaism, though less prone to mysticism, has its Kabbalistic tradition; and of Hasidism, the last great mystical movement within Judaism, Martin Buber was able to say that it would be indispensable for any foreseeable Jewish religious renewal. But mysticism-in-general is one thing, a mystical flight from the world is another. This latter is unacceptable for any Jew who believes that God has made the world for man to live in, not to flee from. And today Christian thinkers generally hold that such a flight is unacceptable for Christians as well.

The above-mentioned three responses all fail because they ignore, reject, or flee from the modern-secular world. This is not true of the fourth response which must be noted—nineteenth-century religious liberalism. This sought to come to terms with the modern-secular world; and this was a merit to the extent that it was motivated, not by the spirit of easy compromise, but rather by the perception of the good in modern secularity. Enlightenment, liberty, progress—these are all ideals which, to religious liberalism at its best, were not alien forces to which to surrender, but rather friendly and indeed Biblically-inspired forces which deserved Jewish and Christian approval; and religious liberals were apt to accept them in a spirit of optimism and hope, not in a spirit of defeat.

And yet, nineteenth-century liberalism *was* shot through with the spirit of compromise, and this was its fatal weakness. The great symptom of this weakness was that it approved the modern-secular world indiscriminately, blind to those features in it which are neither good nor, by any stretch of the imagination, compatible with Biblical faith. (Thus in 1914, the year which brought the nineteenth century to an end, liberal religion in every European country surrendered to militant nationalism, and the shock of this phenomenon, as much as anything else, provoked the neo-orthodox protest against religious liberalism.) And the weakness itself was the spirit of "me-too-ism" with which religious-liberalism approved the modern-secular world. There assuredly was nothing wrong with the approval, in the sphere of theory, of the search for scientific truth; and in the sphere of practice, of the search for greater human liberty and greater social justice. What was wrong, or at least a sign that there was something wrong, was the apologetic reaction to the fact that the secular forces could do nicely without religious approval. The reaction should have been that the modern earth, as much as any other, is, despite everything, the Lord's. Instead, there was retreat. The modern-secular world was handed over to secularism, and religion, once all-pervasive of life, became a mere segment of it. There was science, technology, secular morality and politics, all of which were, or ought to be, devoted to the amelioration of the human lot. And then there was "religion," which made its own "contribution" to human betterment and had a sphere of its own.

Much effort was given to defining what this sphere was. But this was in the end of little moment: whether the religious sphere was the Unknowable which science could not know, or the Uncontrollable which technology could not control; whether it was at such limits of the human condition as death and guilt which, despite doctors and psychiatrists, will always be with us, or a "numinous" feeling present in religion alone and nowhere else. For the crucial fault was that "religion" was limited to one sphere among others, a fact which predetermined that the sphere reserved for it would diminish as the forces of secularism advanced. And as religious liberalism retreated under their impact its retreat revealed its basic weakness—a total loss of Biblical radicalism. Ever since smashing the idols, the God of Israel has been the Radical who would tolerate no idols, and demanded total commitment in the center of life. Nineteenth-century religious liberalism, in contrast, reduced Him to a mere contribution at the margins of modern secular-liberal culture. Under these circumstances, it was natural that doubt should arise as to whether this contribution was still necessary, and to what it was "relevant."

III

It is an impressive sign of religious vitality that religious radicalism should have reappeared in authentically twentieth-century Jewish and Christian thought. For it is dissatisfaction with liberal compromises, and a search for the roots, which characterizes the great so-called neo-orthodox thinkers of this century, such as Karl Barth and Reinhold Niebuhr among Christians, and Martin Buber and Franz Rosenzweig among Jews. Radicalism is characteristic, too, of those present thinkers, mostly Protestant, who seem temporarily to have eclipsed their immediate neo-orthodox predecessors. Whatever one may ultimately think of these present thinkers, one must certainly listen to them. For in theological matters, unlike in many others, it is radicalism—including mistaken and indeed perverse radicalism—which is the road to truth.

These present thinkers may be called neo-liberals. What distinguishes them from their nineteenth-century predecessors is precisely their radicalism. Thus from one quarter we hear that the Biblical faith must be demythologized; and the demythologization demanded seems to include, not only ancient views of the world, but also the ancient God who is its

Creator. From another quarter we hear the demand for so total an identification with the secular city and all its works as would involve the surrender of all attempts to speak in that city in a language different from its own. Going further, some thinkers assert that religious language has become meaningless; that, in the twentieth century, the word "God" is dead. The climax in radicalism is reached with the assertion that atheism is not a modern phenomenon which Biblical faith must confront, but rather its own final consummation. "Christian atheism" is said to be not a contradiction in terms but, on the contrary, the result aimed at from the start by the Christian, if not the Jewish, faith. If it is radicalism that is wanted from theologians, we have, today, no cause for complaint.

As has been said, since in theological matters even wrongheaded radicalism is an instrument to truth, it is necessary for us, Jews and Christians, to listen to the radicals whose thought has just been sketched. And the service they perform is to confront us with a challenge which we have too long avoided. No longer can we behave as though the modern-secular world were no different from any other, i.e., ignore or soft-pedal the unprecedented challenge of its secularity. And no longer can we react by confining our faith to a mere department of life, hoping for safety in it. Not only is there no such safety; we also act un-Biblically when we seek it. In Biblical times, the God of our faith was in the midst of life, where the action was. If there is any one genuinely Biblical motif in the neo-liberal radicalism, it is the wish to be where the action is today—in the struggle against poverty and for racial justice, and in the concern with world-wide peace which overshadows, or ought to overshadow, all our other concerns. Today, the four above-criticized religious responses to the modern world are all dead.

The "radical" new theology teaches us two lessons. One is found in what it preaches, the other in the fate it suffers. It preaches that we, Jews and Christians, must be in the midst of the modern-secular world, radically self-exposed to its secularity. The fate it suffers is total dissipation into secularism. For, despite all protestations to the contrary, there can in the end be no real doubt that a theological radicalism of the present neo-liberal sort must finally lead to wholesale surrender. This is still not quite certain when the radicalism is not itself quite radical, such as when we are bidden to forsake the past voice of our God, and yet to hope that He who will speak with a wholly new voice will be the same God. All doubt is removed when it is asserted that the very word "God" is not meaningful to enlightened present believers, i.e., that its past use was a mere superstitious mistake. As for a "Christian atheism"—can it be taken seriously? At least to a Jew it must be clear that He who is the God of Israel and the Church appeared in history smashing all idols. And he must ask: Can those claim Christian warrant who now declare that this God Himself is, and was all along, a mere idol? The question is seen in the full extent of its absurdity when it is remembered that the modern world in whose name the Biblical God is rejected has brought forth, not only modern science, enlightenment and democracy, but also Auschwitz and Buchenwald.

IV

We must then conclude that the present "radical" theologians have sharpened for us the dilemma with which we are concerned throughout the present discourse. Is the dilemma, then, unresolvable? Do we, Jews and Christians, have but the choice between surrender to secularism and half-hearted compromises doomed to increasing irrelevance? If so, we are in sore straits indeed; for both alternatives amount to a despair of the Biblical God, who is sought, found and obeyed in the very midst of the world.

When in such straits, a believer always does well to consult his classical sources, open to the possibility that they have the power to speak. On my part, I have been accustomed, for a quarter of a century, to consult Midrash; and I have time and again found unexpected light where I had previously thought there was none. Midrash, the work of the

Talmudic rabbis, is the profoundest and most authentic theology ever produced within Judaism; and it is more rather than less profound and authentic for the fact that it is written, not in the form of system—final, air-tight, and fully spelled out—but rather in the merely fragmentary and suggestive form of story and parable.

The Midrash which will be my text for the remainder of these reflections is the following:

> When God created the world, He decreed: "The heavens are the heavens of the Lord; but the earth He has handed over to the children of men" (*Ps.* 115:16). Yet when He was about to give the Torah, He rescinded the first decree and said: "Those who are below shall ascend to those on high, and those who are on high shall descend to those that are below, and I will create a new beginning," as it is said: "And the Lord came down upon Mt. Sinai" (*Exod.* 19, 20), and later "And unto Moses He said: 'Come up unto the Lord' " (*Exod.* 24:1).
>
> (*Exodus Rabba,* XII, 3)

V

All Midrash is symbolic. The first thing to be understood symbolically in the present Midrash is the idea of a temporal sequence in which the past has vanished from present reality. If creation, and the "decree" made at creation, were of the past only, they would be of no religious significance: creation is a religious reality, affirmed by faith, only because it is a present reality also, forever re-accepted and appropriated. Hence the subsequent "rescinding" of the decree made at creation is of a special sort. The second decree supersedes the first; yet it so wholly presupposes the continued reality of the first that it would lose its own meaning without it. The Rabbis would never have thought of God as literally changing His mind; such a notion is at odds with their belief in the divine eternity and perfection. Yet so deeply were they impressed, at once with the reality of both decrees and the clash between them, that they dared speak of God as though He changed His mind.

The first decree, then, is still a present reality, so much so that on its basis alone is the second possible. What does it establish? In the words of the 115th *Psalm*, "the heavens are the heavens of the Lord; but the earth He has handed over to the children of man." This tremendous passage, which incidentally figures prominently in Jewish literature and liturgy, with one stroke demythologizes the world. For mythological religion the world is "full of gods" (Thales). For Biblical man—and hence for both Jew and Christian—the world is radically emptied of the gods because it is the work of God. Mythological man is subject to all sorts of demonic powers. Biblical man is radically liberated from these. Mythological man worships nature, or defies parts of nature. Biblical man worships the God who is wholly beyond nature because He is its Creator. As for nature, Biblical man subdues it; for he is bidden to rule the earth which is handed over to him. It is God Himself, then, who demythologizes the world, and His act of doing so is the primordial act of grace.

In the light of this truth, one must be extremely puzzled by the contemporary talk about the need to demythologize the Bible. One can readily admit that there is some important truth to this talk; for what scholar nowadays denies that the Bible borrows much of the imagery of contemporary culture? And who can affirm that this insight of Biblical scholars is fully assimilated even by theologians, not to speak of the man in the street? Yet this truth must under no circumstances obscure the far more important truth that the Biblical God Himself stands in no need of contemporary demythologizing. He is demythologized from the start. It is the primordial event of His Presence which both destroys the idols and hands over the earth to the children of man.

It is, therefore, necessary to assert that an aspect of secularity is implicit in the Biblical faith from the start. The philosopher A. N. Whitehead rightly connects the rise of modern science and technology with the modern Protestant return to the Bible. So long as man worships nature he will not "torture" it by means of scientific experiments; hence the Greeks, as well as the medievals still vitally affected by the Greeks, merely contemplated nature. Only a demythologization of nature—the maxim to subdue the earth rather than worship it—could have made the time ripe for modern science, for technology, and indeed for the modern secular world as a whole.

But what if *modern* secularity implied a radicalism which is in necessary conflict with the Biblical faith? What if it made imperative the conquest of heaven as well as of earth? And what if to shrink from the former task were the result of mere medieval cowardice? It is true that there is no lack of heaven-stormers in the modern world; despite the infatuation of present theologians with Marx and Nietzsche, one wonders whether in the light of Biblical faith these men must not ultimately be characterized as at best misguided and at worst idolaters. But the view that there is a *necessary* conflict between modern secularity and the Biblical faith is due to a tragic misunderstanding among secularists and believers alike. "The earth" handed over to man by no means includes our planet only; it includes the universe. The skies are not barred to our conquest, either in scientific understanding or technological control; for the skies are not heaven. The Biblical God places no limitations upon the exercise of human reason; His gift of the earth to man is radical.

But what if the unlimited exercise of this human reason implied the *abolition* of heaven? What if it rendered superfluous the "hypothesis" of creation, and hence the Creator Himself? In the Biblical faith, creation is not and never has been a scientific or quasi-scientific hypothesis. It is, and always has been, the gift of existence—the world's and his own—to the man who in faith accepts it. And it is for this reason not an occurrence which took place once and for all in the past; creation is a gift which is renewed whenever there is human acceptance of it.

Such an acceptance is not at odds with secularity, modern secularity included; on the contrary, it makes inescapable the acceptance of its burden. We say "burden" even though it is a liberation also, and even though many present "radical" theologians are intoxicated in its celebration. Secularity *is* a burden. For to live a secular existence is to be responsible for the world. And indeed, so great is the burden of this responsibility in our own time that many among both the "religious" and the "irreligious" are in full flight from the world into a variety of fancies. The Biblical believers—Jew or Christian—may not join their number. For this God bids him stay with, and assume responsibility for, the secular world. And if such an existence is, today, often solitary, it is the Biblical God who makes this solitariness inescapable.

VI

But, according to our Midrash, God "rescinds" the first decree by means of a second. Like the first, this second decree is not a past event only but also a present reality, forever newly received. And since it forever rescinds the first decree, which yet remains forever real and presupposed, a "new beginning" occurs whenever such reception occurs; so new is the beginning as to produce radical surprise. The first decree has distinguished between the God who dwells in heaven and the man who has been given the earth. It is radically surprising that this God should, nevertheless, descend on earth; and that this man should, nevertheless, be commanded, and hence enabled, to ascend to heaven.

There is no parallel for this new beginning or this radical surprise in mythological, i.e. pagan, religion. Here the world is full of gods as a matter of course; and it is a matter of course, too, that man communes with them. Such communication, however, is not revelation. The Biblical believer dwells, not in secure possession of the Divine, but in holy insecurity.

It is in this holy insecurity that the Jew experiences the joy of the Torah. For there is joy in a grace which in its heavenly power needs neither man nor the earth handed over to him, and which yet in its heavenly love chooses to need both; and which, having handed the earth over to man's profane possession, yet commands him, and hence enables him to have a share in its sanctification. And as in this joy the Jew speaks and listens to the Christian, he discovers common ground.

However they differ in their understanding of revelation, they share the knowledge of a "first decree" which has set apart heaven and earth; and of a "second decree" by virtue of which heaven descends to earth, and man may ascend to heaven.

For this reason, there exists the possibility of a joint Jewish and Christian testimony against ancient mythology. There exists, too, the possibility of a joint stand toward modern secularism. In the light of Biblical faith, one may, indeed must, discriminate between different kinds of secularism, although doubtless these are less sharply distinguished in life than in thought. There is a modern secularism which presumes to destroy heaven; one which asserts that heaven is in principle inaccessible; and one which bears witness to being in fact cut off from heaven. The stance of Biblical faith toward these three cannot be the same.

How can man on earth presume to destroy heaven? Only if, to begin with, he has failed to distinguish between them; that is, if he remains pagan. A secularism destructive of heaven remains bound to mythology even while it imagines itself to be its sworn enemy. It destroys the gods; yet in seeking to destroy God it deifies its own earthbound, and not wholly demythologized, powers. Today, we see on every side the ancient demons of the earth resurrected, however modern their guises. Such demons as blood, soil, race and the capitalized Unconscious are not called gods; they are even given scientific or pseudo-scientific names: this serves but to augment their power. The Biblical believer—Jew and Christian —must detect the ancient idols underneath their modern guises. And he must fight them with all his might.

In this fight he may well be joined by the second secularist. For in asserting heaven to be inaccessible to earth this secularist is free of the temptation to deify earth. His quarrel with the Biblical believer is otherwise. The issue between them is whether or not, heaven and earth being divorced, revelation can take place.

How may the believer confront this second secularist?

Open to all possibilities of the earth, this secularist is closed to the possibility that heaven may enter into it. Against such a dogmatism of earth, the Biblical believer dare not pit a dogmatism of heaven, as if heaven could be his secure possession. He must, rather, testify against this secularist security with his own holy insecurity; against a control of earth immune to surprise with his own vulnerability to radical surprise. Could it be that this secularist's fear of error is, ultimately, a fear of truth?

What, finally, of the third secularist? He does not idolatrously presume to destroy heaven, nor does he dogmatically assert its inaccessibility. Like the believer, he has made himself open, insecure and vulnerable. But what he has experienced is that heaven does not enter into his modern earth, and that all his modern attempts to ascend to heaven have come to grief. And in this experience he has discovered a fact of modern life.

For this reason, the believer may not bear witness against this third secularist one-sidedly. He must, rather, accept the discipline of mutual dialogue. And its mutuality, like all mutuality, involves risk; in this case, the risk is that, having listened to the testimony of this secularist, he, the believer, may himself be reduced to silence. He dare not shrink from this risk; for if indeed heaven still descends to earth this must be the modern earth. Yet he need not surrender to the fear that this risk is destructive of faith; for it but extends the range of its holy insecurity. And since revelation marks a new beginning whenever it occurs, he may stubbornly hope for the possibility of such a beginning, even today, even in the midst of our secular world.

How then shall we, Jews and Christians, welcome the international gathering in Montreal, and the secular theme under which it stands? We must welcome both wholeheartedly, unreservedly, and indeed do so with the knowledge that this secularity puts us to shame. Yet this knowledge must not mislead us into an indiscriminate admiration of secularism, let alone surrender to it. For while the earth is handed over to man, he may not erect idols upon it. And while earth is set apart from heaven, it is yet incumbent upon us to bear witness to a grace which may descend upon this earth and command us to have a share in its sanctification.

Did Jesus Believe in God?
Some Reflections on Christian Atheism

R. F. Aldwinckle

Perhaps the answer to the question which R. F. Aldwinckle
deals with should be obvious, but to certain radical theologians
it is not obvious at all. Indeed, some of them traverse a tor-
tuous route in the hope of arriving at a negative answer, for
they seem to believe that it is impossible to affirm both the
world and a God who is the transcendent Creator and Sustainer of the world; somehow God must, for them, "become
wholly identified with existence in the body here and now." In
countering the radicals Aldwinckle first "rehabilitates" the Old
Testament, indicating that there was nothing escapist about
the Hebrew people's ultimate realization that God's purpose
cannot be achieved completely in the present order. Then,
moving to the New Testament, he shows that—the radical
theologians to the contrary notwithstanding—the biblical evidence leaves no doubt that Jesus took for granted the basic
Hebraic convictions concerning the nature and character of
God. Dr. Aldwinckle is Professor of Systematic Theology at
McMaster Divinity College, Hamilton, Ontario. The *Canadian
Journal of Theology** published his critique in its January
1967 number.

DID JESUS BELIEVE in God? No doubt this
question will strike many readers as odd, if not fantastic. To
the ordinary Christian it will appear to answer itself. The unbeliever will see in it another evidence of the peculiar pass to
which modern Christian thinkers have come. To the sophisticated theologian, nurtured in the two-nature doctrine of Chalcedon, other problems may suggest themselves. If Jesus is
truly God, as the creeds assert, then is not the question
badly put? Does it mean that Jesus believed in himself since

* University of Toronto Press, Toronto 5, Canada.

God can only believe in God? But what can it mean to talk of God in this very anthropomorphic way as believing in himself?

It would obviously be unprofitable to get ourselves involved at the start in subtleties of this nature. Since the two-nature doctrine, as John McIntyre has pointed out, is only one, albeit time-honoured, theological "model"[1] attempting to do justice to the New Testament witness to Jesus Christ, it would seem desirable, as well as theologically correct, to start with the New Testament itself. The soundness of this approach is not affected by the fact that the New Testament has to be interpreted. The creeds and confessions of the Church, which emerged from the worshipping community, may be important pointers to an adequate hermeneutic. The fact remains that such creeds do not stand alone. They only make sense as attempts to articulate the meaning of the New Testament and the experience of the Church as the worshipping community which acknowledges Jesus as Lord.

However, for the purpose which we now have in mind, it would be legitimate to practise the detachment or the "suspense" advocated in other connections by the philosophical phenomenologists, and leave on one side for the time being technical problems of Christology and the validity of the credal confessions. Our question could be rephrased to ask: Does the New Testament show us a Jesus who took for granted certain affirmations about the nature and character of God, rooted in the Hebraic and Jewish tradition? To this question only certain alternative answers seem to be open to us. Either Jesus accepted and built upon the foundation of Judaism or he did not. If he did, then the further point may be raised as to whether the Jewish understanding of God is possible for modern men. If he did not, then he must either have repudiated the Jewish concept of God root and branch, or have modified it beyond recognition, or have obtained an idea of God from some other source. That idea of God either came from the religious, philosophical, and cultural environment of the ancient world or

[1] Cf. J. McIntyre, *The Shape of Christology* (Philadelphia: Westminster Press, 1966).

he evolved it out of his own peculiar self-consciousness without any reference to outside influence of any kind, whether Jewish or non-Jewish.

Until recently, it would have been accepted by the overwhelming majority of biblical scholars that Jesus built upon the religious and theological assumptions of Judaism. Whatever his view as to his own role in the working out of the purpose of God, or whether the theological "models" used to interpret his Person in the New Testament were influenced by the mystery religions, or Hellenistic philosophy and religion, or even indirect Oriental influences, few questioned that Jesus stood fairly and squarely within the Jewish faith and accepted its basic premise concerning the transcendent Creator-God. The radical theologians, with their attack upon transcendence, are at least gnostic to this degree, that they raise again the question of whether the Old Testament has any significant place in the thought of Jesus, and therefore in any modernized version of the Christian faith. Their attack is directed, not only against classical Christian theism but against the Old Testament understanding of God which lay behind it. It is important to be quite clear about this, for there have been many criticisms levelled against Christian theism on the grounds that in some of its historic expressions it represents an illegitimate fusion of biblical and philosophical ideas of God. Those who have attacked it for this reason have usually done so in order to free the biblical idea of God and to present it again in its purity undisturbed by an alien metaphysic. The radical theologians are obviously going beyond this position. They are not only questioning this hybrid theology composed of biblical and philosophical elements. They are questioning the fundamental doctrine of God which is Judaism's legacy to Christianity, and which Jesus himself shared. Any adequate reply to them must involve a rehabilitation of the Old Testament at this point.

It is just conceivable that someone might even try to show that the Old Testament does not speak of the transcendent God, but this is obviously not a very promising line of approach. The radical theologians do not try to argue that the Old Testament does not teach the transcendence of God, but only that the radical self-emptying involved in the career of Jesus makes such a belief no longer desirable or compelling. However, in order that nothing may be taken for granted, let us raise the question again: Does the Old Testament faith in Yahweh really depend upon his transcendence, and what precisely does this latter signify? To answer this question we are compelled to consider the subject of creation, and even to ask whether the Old Testament has a "doctrine" of creation. "When early Christianity speaks of the relation of God and the world, it begins with the ideas and concepts of later Judaism. . . . The God of the New Testament is neither in the world nor outside the world, but above the world."[2] The modern philosophical analyst will no doubt immediately want to know precisely what significance is to be given to the prepositions in, outside, and above, with their spatial connotations. There seems little doubt, however, that the intention is to assert a basic difference between God and the totality of heaven and earth which depends upon him for its existence but is not to be identified with him. "Transcendence means, and always has meant, *difference*; God's transcendence means that his being cannot be simply identified with the being of the universe. God's transcendence opposes pantheism, not intimacy."[3] That the faith of Israel is not content with the mere assertion of transcendence is obvious. God's presence and his activity within history are everywhere stressed. It is, however, somewhat misleading to state with Mr. Jacob that "faith in God the creator holds a less important place than that of God the saviour, and the God who made the heavens and the earth is less often and less directly the object of faith than the God who brought his people out of Egypt."[4] In so far as this language implies a repudiation of a merely metaphysical doctrine of transcendence, not rooted in the living and redeeming God of Israel's historical experience, then there is no reason for dissent. It is obvious,

[2] G. Kittell (ed.), *Theological Dictionary of the New Testament*, III, ed. and transl. by G. W. Bromiley (Grand Rapids: Eerdmans, 1966), p. 116.

[3] A. A. Vogel, *The Next Christian Epoch* (New York: Harper & Row, 1966), p. 78.

[4] E. Jacob, *Theology of the Old Testament* (London: Hodder & Stoughton, 1958), p. 136.

however, that Yahweh could not have brought his people out of the land of Egypt unless he had been in effective control of natural forces, and this implies his transcendence of such forces as well as his immanent activity in and through them. That the Jew interpreted the activity of the mysterious God who created the world in the light of his covenant purpose may be accepted without demur. It may also be true that the full implications of God's transcendence were not fully articulated until the time of the Exile and Second Isaiah, and even then not in what would today be called metaphysical terms. This, however, does not mean that there are not important metaphysical implications in such language as:

> The creator of the heavens, he is God,
> The former of the earth and its maker, he established it;
> Not chaos (*tohu*) did he create it, for dwelling did he
> form it (Isa. 14:18).

The significance of the Old Testament history for this matter has been well summed up as follows: "The creation is so closely linked to conservation and control that all dualistic deism is irrelevant, whilst there can be no pantheistic absorption of such a Person in the immanent energies of Nature."[5] The important point for our discussion is that this is the underlying assumption from which Jesus himself started. Whatever additional factors need to be added in the light of later apocalyptic and eschatological development or Jesus' own unique self-consciousness in relation to the Father, God in this sense is assumed. Jesus prayed to "Our Father, which art in heaven," addressed him as "Father, Maker of Heaven and Earth," and interpreted his own role as that of the bringer of the realm and rule of God among men.

On what grounds, then, would it be possible to argue that the significance of Jesus can be understood apart from belief in such a God? The options would appear to be limited:

(*a*) The basic Hebrew and Jewish intuition as to the nature and character of God was mistaken; (*b*) Jesus accepted the

[5] H. Wheeler Robinson, *Inspiration and Revelation in the Old Testament* (Oxford: Clarendon Press, 1950), p. 21.

Old Testament teaching about God and was mistaken in so doing; (c) Knowledge of the "mind" of Jesus of Nazareth is so limited or infinitesimal that we have no means of knowing how much or how little he accepted of his Jewish heritage. (a) or (c) would seem to be crucial; (b) is simply a logical consequence of (a). The only question to be asked is whether, if Jesus was mistaken on a point as fundamental as this, he can really be trusted on other matters. In any case, could such a Jesus be seriously offered as the object of adoration and worship, or made a central figure in any religion of the future still claiming to be Christian?

Let us, then, turn to (a) and the Hebrew and Jewish conception of God. It could be maintained that this conception is true because it is the teaching of the Bible, and the Bible is authoritative. This is a widely held view, not confined to literalists and fundamentalists, but equally assumed by those who claim full freedom of literary and historical investigation. "Yet it is not sufficient to declare that the Old Testament is a book *about* God. It would be more correct to say that the Old Testament is the book through which God speaks and reveals His will. Thus we note that this fact renders a discussion of whether God is, both academic and pointless."[6] It is not easy to be sure what exactly Professor Knight wishes to imply by this statement. Perhaps he simply wants to affirm that there is something self-authenticating in the biblical disclosures of God's reality, nature, and purpose which does not require any buttressing from natural theology or philosophical theology of any kind. He does not appear to assert this on the basis of a doctrine of verbal inspiration, but would presumably maintain that a critical approach to the Scriptures does not destroy the reality of the biblical history or the revelation of God disclosed in and through certain events and persons there described. If one asks to whom the biblical understanding of God is self-authenticating, then the answer again must obviously be, not to the unbeliever, but to the man of faith in whom the Holy Spirit has made possible the kind of

[6] G. A. F. Knight, *A Christian Theology of the Old Testament* (Richmond: John Knox Press, 1959), p. 17.

response which can discern the presence of God in the biblical history. This is the thesis so brilliantly defended by Helmut Gollwitzer. While theism is a suspect term because of its metaphysical associations, Gollwitzer nevertheless admits that the Bible is theistic to an unprecedented degree,[7] that the Christian must not be ashamed of his theism, even though he must never forget that his is the theism of the personal God of the Bible, not of the highest being of the metaphysician. Faith must confess that God is, even if his existence must not be treated as that of an object which can be grasped by man's scientific or philosophical reasoning. Faith may question metaphysical arguments for God's existence but cannot deny his reality. There is no transcending of theism in the sense of "going beyond" or "leaving behind" the living God of the biblical revelation. Karl Barth speaks in similar terms. Knowledge of God is not given and cannot be given apart from biblical revelation, and when thus given, it is human knowledge. But this knowledge, by virtue of its source, is given to us "in insurpassable and incontestable certainty."[8] "Given to us" means, given to those of us who have faith, and its source guarantees its certainty because it comes from God, and the Bible is by definition and canonical authority the medium of God's revelation. Thus, the truth of God's transcendence is guaranteed both by the authority of Scripture and the insight granted to faith. We can leave on one side for a moment the question whether the Bible itself is hostile to any knowledge of God not mediated through history and apprehended by faith.

Why is it that the radical theologians have reached their negative conclusions about the transcendence of God in the biblical theistic sense? Presumably Scripture is not self-authenticating to them, at least on this point. Shall we go a step further, therefore, and say that they lack faith, that they lack the humility before the Word of God which alone could make possible their true understanding of God? This is a searching question which can hardly be avoided, even though one rightly shrinks from giving the impression that one is substituting

[7] Cf. H. Gollwitzer, *The Existence of God as Confessed by Faith* (London: S.C.M. Press, 1965), p. 42.

[8] K. Barth, *Church Dogmatics*, Vol. II/1 (Edinburgh: T. & T. Clark, 1957), p. 180.

abuse for theological argument. It is far from our intention to defame the character of the radical theologians in order to discredit the sharpness of their criticisms. Nevertheless, the question has to be asked, not only of them, but of countless modern men. If the Old Testament does speak of the transcendent Creator, and if Jesus built on this foundation, then why can modern men not come to accept its truth? Are the reasons scientific, moral, metaphysical, existential, or what have you? Or are the roots of the modern attitude to be found in moral failures and sin? Or is it our technological society which has for the time being obscured modern man's awareness that neither he nor his world is self-created or self-sufficient?

In fact, all these influences have contributed to creating that peculiar modern inhibition against the recognition of transcendence. In the case of the radical theologians, and of Dr. Altizer in particular, the primary factor is the passionate demand for a form of Christianity which will be relevant and effective in every sphere of human activity. They desire to escape from the stuffiness and timidity of "church" Christianity, to share to the full the doubt, fear, bewilderment, and religious perplexity of modern men, to claim the whole baffling realm of man's life in this present world and transform it by agape-love into a significant, positive affirmation of existence here and now. Nothing human is alien to them. The barrier between sacred and profane must be broken down and the secular must become the area where holiness and love again gain their triumphs. It is hardly possible to question the legitimacy of the motives here at work. Even orthodox Christianity has never denied that God sent his Son, not only to save the church, but to save the world. Jesus himself was a layman and a man among men. The question raised by these thinkers, however, is whether it is possible to have this creative approach to human life in its totality and still accept a transcendent God. Is not the only way to achieve this "worldly" holiness to be found in a doctrine of radical immanence which finds God wholly and completely in our present form of human existence?

As a matter of historical fact, it would be difficult to show that the early Hebrews combined their faith in Yahweh with a negative approach to human life here and now. It has often been pointed out that a belief in an after-life worth the having was a comparatively late development in the Old Testament. The Hebrews evidently found it possible to combine the affirmation of the reality, holiness, and steadfast love of the transcendent God with the conviction that this life was the only existence man had. Altizer accepts this claim that early Hebrew faith was world-affirming and only capitulated to yearnings for personal immortality after the Exile.[9] This world-affirmation of early Yahwism, however, gave way in course of time to a world-denying ethos, and at this point biblical religion approximates to the radical Indian rejection of the claims and values of "reality," that is, of present human existence in this world.[10] When the prophets pronounced doom upon their contemporary society, and demanded obedience to the will of an absolutely holy and righteous God, they logically implied, even if it took some centuries for the full implications to be made plain, that this present world must in the end give way to a supra-mundane existence where alone such ideals of perfect justice and love could be realized. In being committed to a new creation, they were impelled to disvalue the present created order, and man's life within it. Altizer would seem to regret this development, and would prefer to build upon the world-affirming character of early Hebrew faith. He is convinced, however, that this can only be done by getting rid of Yahweh as a transcendent Creator and Sustainer of the world. Somehow he must become wholly identified with existence in the body here and now.

If the radical theologians wish to accept the full implications of this position, so be it, but it is worth pointing out the consequences. Their natural affinity would appear to be with some kind of modernized millennianism which hopes for a permanent establishment of the rule of justice and love on this earth, but a millennium without God in the transcendent sense.

[9] Cf. T. J. J. Altizer, *Oriental Mysticism and Biblical Eschatology* (Philadelphia: Westminster Press, 1964), pp. 57ff.
[10] Cf. *ibid.*, pp. 67f.

The eternity of the world, and in some form of this earth, is required to give substance to this hope. It is interesting to note in passing how closely this view approximates to the secularized Marxist eschatology of a perfect community on earth when the dialectic of history reaches its inevitable goal. This revival of optimism is an astonishing psychological fact at a moment of history when mankind's confidence in its future on this earth has been so badly shaken. William Hamilton has left us in no doubt at this point:

This is not an optimism of grace, but a worldly optimism I am defending. It faces despair not with the conviction that out of it God can bring hope, but with the conviction that the human conditions that created it can be overcome, whether these conditions be poverty, discrimination or mental illness. It faces death not with the hope of immortality but with the human confidence that man may befriend death and live with it as a possibility always alongside.[11]

What these thinkers never seem to have seriously considered is whether it is possible to accept the essential incompleteness of existence in this world with a relative optimism about our future prospects, together with the conviction that God is real and transcendent to all earthy reality, though actively interested and present within it. As against their absolute valuation of present existence, Christians have no option but to accept the charge of otherworldliness. This world, and human existence, is not for the Bible a final and eternal good, even though the latter may be experienced here and now in some significant sense. "This is eternal life, that they know thee the only true God, and Jesus Christ whom thou hast sent" (John 17:3). Dr. Manson has rightly pointed out that whenever a living faith in a righteous, holy, and loving God is brought up hard against the facts of human experience, some sort of eschatology must emerge if men are to retain their faith.[12] The resolution of the conflict between what is

[11] T. J. J. Altizer and W. Hamilton, *Radical Theology and the Death of God* (New York: Bobbs-Merrill, 1966), p. 169.
[12] Cf. T. W. Manson, *The Teaching of Jesus*, 2d ed. (Cambridge: University Press, 1935), pp. 245ff.

and what ought to be can only be met in three ways: by sheer naturalism which denies that human moral and spiritual aspirations can ever be fulfilled, by the argument that the conflict between the ideal and the real is illusory and that, properly viewed, all is already reconciled, or by an eschatology which affirms that what ought to be will be. The last is the biblical view. When the Old Testament Jew finally realized that ultimate fulfillment of God's purpose cannot be achieved completely in this present order and demanded an eternal dimension, he was not indulging in escapism. He was recognizing the facts of the situation and following the true logic of his faith. He was able to do this with confidence, however, because he already believed that God, though active in, was also "above" the process of becoming and the tragedies of human history. Without this faith he would have despaired, and this consequence still holds true, whatever the radical theologians say.

There is, however, more to be said if justice is to be done. If we recognize, as late Judaism and Jesus himself did, that our true home is in the eternal dimension with God, does this mean a complete disvaluation of present existence? The radical theologians fear this conclusion, and can point with some degree of justification to certain expressions of Christianity in the past, which are so preoccupied with heaven after death that the present life is reduced to a pale shadow and emptied of any positive significance. It is worth observing that Teilhard de Chardin is also deeply concerned with this same problem. How is it possible to reconcile the transcendence of God and the Kingdom with a positive attitude to human life on this planet and all its finest cultural achievements? Is the proper stance of the Christian to wait with resignation for his translation to a transcendent realm, or can he work wholeheartedly for a future on this planet? Teilhard believes, in my judgment, rightly, that these two can be combined. However, he differs from the radical theologians in preserving the transcendent reference. The fulfillment of God's purpose in and through physical evolution and human history is taken up at the parousia or omega-point into the eternal realm where

God will be all in all. Whatever may be thought of the details of Teilhard's vision, there can be no question that it is closer to the biblical view than the position of the radical theologians. The latter will find it increasingly difficult, without the transcendent God, to avoid falling into the naturalism which confines man within purely this-worldly horizons. It could be argued with Bertrand Russell that this is the only option for modern man. It can hardly be claimed that it deserves the name of Christianity. If, then, the radical theologians have not successfully made their point on this question of transcendence, the question can be posed again in real seriousness: may not the Old Testament offer us the truth after all about God and his relation to the world?

However, other objections, of a more strictly metaphysical character, could still be raised. Has not our scientific knowledge of the world made it both impossible and undesirable to seek "explanations" which compel us to assume a reality of some kind "beyond" the natural process or sum total of events as science investigates them in the here and now? Dr. Altizer does not appear to be concerned directly with this aspect of the problem, though he may very well have it in the back of his mind as a support for the position which he has already reached on other grounds. Such contemporary thinkers as van Buren are quite obviously influenced by empiricism and philosophical analysis in so far as these appear to lead to a denial of transcendence in the biblical and theistic sense.[13] The essence of his position is to be found in the assertion that we have no option in the contemporary secular world but to take a non-cognitive view of faith.[14] Simple literal theism is wrong and qualified literal theism is meaningless.[15] The Christian faith only has meaning when referring to the Christian way of life interpreted as action controlled by agape-love. It is not a set of cosmological assertions.[16]

If these assumptions are accepted, then it follows that the

---

[13] Cf. P. M. van Buren, *The Secular Meaning of the Gospel* (New York: Macmillan, 1963).

[14] Cf. *ibid.*, p. 97.

[15] Cf. *ibid.*, p. 99.

[16] Cf. *ibid.*, p. 101.

Old Testament understanding of God must be repudiated, as well as Jesus' dependence upon the Old Testament at this point. The astonishing thing about van Buren's book is the implication that a particular contemporary philosophical approach is normative for modern man and will remain so for future generations. This is obviously not true even for the present situation, since one can find many notable philosophers who still defend the idea of a transcendent God—e.g., H.D. Lewis and the late Paul Tillich (in his own special way). The latter does not repudiate transcendence, even if his "God" beyond theism leaves many Christians dissatisfied.

Professor Langdon Gilkey raises the question of why the classical Christian doctrine of creation *ex nihilo* has not received either the attention or the approval it deserves in the last century and a half. In so far as this doctrine was wrongly interpreted as an attempt to give a scientific answer to questions concerning physical origins (and was coupled with a literal interpretation of Genesis) it naturally fell into disfavour when nineteenth-century science had increasing success in suggesting plausible answers to purely scientific questions. However, Dr. Gilkey rightly points out that scientific hypotheses and statements are by definition about "relations between finite things in space and time."[17] The doctrine of Creation, on the other hand, is concerned with the more fundamental question of why there is a universe at all, whatever scientific account be given of the processes of that universe. If it is accepted that our experience both of ourselves and of the world is one of continued change and process, then men are driven inexorably both by their existential frustrations and by the mind's restless search for intelligibility in the world to seek to find some permanent and enduring reality behind the everlasting flux. This is a human quest, not a peculiarly Christian search, though it might be argued that this profound aspiration after the transcendent in some form or other bears witness to man's affinity with God. Certainly it is a feature of Buddhist experience, as we have already seen in our discussion

[17] L. Gilkey, *Maker of Heaven and Earth: A Study of the Christian Doctrine of Creation* (Garden City, N.Y.: Doubleday, 1959), p. 25.

of Altizer's treatment of Oriental mysticism. The sharp reaction in the present against the transcendent springs in part from past philosophical efforts to reach the ultimate One in a spirit of cool intellectual analysis. The transcendent thus reached seems to be a bloodless abstraction, far removed from the actual day-to-day needs of men. Furthermore, it seems to lack those "personal" characteristics which alone make worship of God with heart as well as head possible. This judgment is true, but only partly true. Certainly there is an apparent coldness about Aristotle's handling of these problems, but in Plato and Plotinus, in Hindu and Buddhist metaphysics, there are obviously profoundly personal motives behind their investigations, which give to their thinking an "existential" quality, despite the apparent abstractness of their language and concepts.

It is certainly true, as Dr. Gilkey goes on to insist, that the Hebrew mind did not arrive at the transcendent God by following a metaphysical urge to discover the enduring unity underlying multiplicity. It started from the familiar personal awareness of bodily limitation, weakness, and death, the moral and spiritual failures and frustrations of each individual life, and the large-scale tragedies of social groups, written large in the history of the Jewish people. It sought a firm standing ground amid such realities and found it in the transcendent God. It found such a secure base, not "from a careful scientific or metaphysical analysis of the general experience of nature and of finite experience, but rather from the illumination that comes from special encounters with God in revelatory experiences."[18] We must not, however, immediately jump to the conclusion that the philosopher's quest for intelligibility in the world is a hopeless and futile quest, or that he has nothing in common with the religious man's quest. Indeed, in some men both quests may be present and both may demand their proper satisfaction.

The conclusion to be drawn from this somewhat lengthy digression is that the Old Testament teaching about the transcendent God cannot yet be safely written off as impossible for

18 *Ibid.*, p. 41.

a modern man. The fact that Jesus himself did not write it off must also make us hesitate to dismiss it. The same fact makes it extremely unlikely that Jesus can be properly understood apart from this fundamental assumption about God, which governed all his thinking and action.

In claiming that Jesus took for granted the Jewish faith in a transcendent God, it is assumed that we have enough reliable knowledge of the "mind" of Jesus to be able to make such a statement. Here again, after stripping away all the extraneous issues, the basic issue can be simply stated. Such reliable knowledge of Jesus' thought about the nature of God is either attainable or not attainable. In the former case, the mind of Christ must presumably be taken seriously by anyone claiming to be his follower. If, on the contrary, such knowledge is not attainable, then there would seem to be no point in trying to establish a religious position in which Jesus would have a central place. It is no answer to this problem to insist that we still have the "faith" of the church. Either the faith of the church has some foundation in the mind and intention of Jesus or it has not. If it has, then it is logical to claim that the "faith" of the church is not self-created or simply the mythopoeic activity of the worshipping community, but derives in the last analysis from an understanding of the "mind" of Christ reliably known. On the other hand, if the faith of the church is not rooted in any knowledge of the mind of Christ, and the thought and intention of Jesus must inevitably remain a mere x, then the church is no longer bound, morally, intellectually, or spiritually, to its past or to Jesus, and can develop its contemporary spiritual life in complete freedom. The Church might continue to use the term "Christ" to denote the Christ-idea or some constellation of spiritual ideas and ideals, but these would have no necessary connection with Jesus of Nazareth. Once again it could be argued that biblical criticism has left us with this option alone, but it must be asked whether the result would still be Christianity in any intelligible and recognizable form.

It must be confessed that, in the present state of New Testament study, there is ample reason for confusion on the part of believer and unbeliever alike. It is difficult to establish any point by a simple appeal to the consensus of New Testament scholarship, for it is always possible to list some learned scholars who will dissent. Nevertheless, the absence of unanimity does not mean that in this field there is a free-for-all, where any one position is just as plausible as any other. Furthermore, the fact that New Testament study today has to be carried on in an ecumenical context has made the idea of a real consensus of Christian minds less utopian than it might have appeared not long ago. The constant reiteration in recent years that "the quest of the historical Jesus" has failed is one of those oversimplifications which can seriously mislead the uninitiated. If it is simply the claim that it is no longer possible to penetrate behind the New Testament documents to a purely human Jesus who by definition could not be the "Christ of faith," then the point is well taken. But it is possible that the authentic Jesus of history was never such a figure stripped of all supernatural claims. It might just be the case that the Christ to whom the apostolic witness testifies was in fact the real Jesus of history. At least, this is a thesis not to be cavalierly dismissed without serious consideration.

However, the question which concerns us at the moment is not the defence of the whole faith of the church in respect to the Incarnation. It is whether we have enough reliable information about the mind of the "Jesus of history" to enable us to say that he shared the Jewish belief in the transcendent God. Professor John McIntyre makes the valid point that our inability to give a modern psychological account of how Jesus developed from childhood to manhood, or to write an official two-volume biography in the best Victorian style, does not mean that we are completely ignorant of the mind of Christ, "of how he thought about the Father, about his own death, about men and women."[19] He goes on to assert that, if we are unable to speak in any sense at all of the personality of Jesus, then we are really forbidden by the nature of the case to talk of Jesus in any meaningful sense. One cannot escape the conclusion that many who speak of the failure of the quest of

[19] McIntyre, *The Shape of Christology*, p. 124.

the historical Jesus do not wish to go this far. Usually they go on to speak as if they knew with reasonable certainty a good deal about Jesus' thought, and in particular about the Jewish belief in God which he took for granted and everywhere presupposes in his teaching. Of course, it is still possible to argue that Jesus was a Jew of the first century, and therefore shared the Jewish belief in the transcendent God, but that he never made claims for divinity and that the church was wrong in making such claims on his behalf. This argument, however, raises the whole Christological problem and the question of the correct interpretation of the total New Testament witness—and with these issues we are not concerned here. Our concerns *vis-à-vis* the radical theologians has been to point out the New Testament presuppositions about God. Without these, the New Testament could never have developed whatever Christology its pages contain. It could not have said that "God" sent his Son, or that "God" was in Christ reconciling the world unto himself.

All this seems like flogging the proverbial dead horse or underlining the obvious, but when the obvious is no longer admitted, it is necessary to affirm it again clearly and unambiguously. Our conclusion, then, is that Jesus believed in God, in that he accepted the basic Jewish convictions on this point whatever he said or did not say about his own special relationship to the God of Abraham, Isaac, and Jacob. Jesus was not an atheist either in the ancient or the modern sense.

Hope in a Posthuman Era

Sam Keen

Can a religious style of life exist in the acid soil of the promethean view of man which characterizes contemporary secular thought? Such is the question to which Sam Keen addresses himself—and though his answer is hedged about with the "epistemological humility" which the intelligent theist shares with the humanist and the skeptic, it is affirmative nonetheless. Essential to any religious life-style, contends Keen, are the abdication from pretensions of omnipotence and the positing of a ground for hope; hope—which is not to be confused with illusion-induced optimism—"begins with the realization that human experience is finally inadequate to deal with all the possibilities that reality harbors." A young man "on the rise" in the theological world, Dr. Keen, Associate Professor of Philosophy and Christian Faith at Louisville Presbyterian Seminary, is the author of a book on the thought of Gabriel Marcel and a forthcoming book titled *Apology for Wonder*. His article first appeared in the January 25, 1967, issue of *The Christian Century*.*

But what is the philosophy of this generation? Not God is dead, that period was passed long ago. Perhaps it should be stated death is God. This generation thinks—and this is its thought of thoughts —that nothing faithful, vulnerable, fragile can be durable or have any true power. Death waits for these things as a cement floor waits for a dropping light bulb.

Herzog, by Saul Bellow.

WESTERN CULTURE is undergoing a fundamental crisis in its understanding of what it means to be human. In the past there have been periods of crisis and re-evaluation—the breakup of the Greek city-state, the emergence of Christianity, the Renaissance, the Reformation, the

* 407 South Dearborn Street, Chicago, Ill. 60605.

79

industrial revolution. All previous periods, however, have shared a consensus about human life which today is widely questioned and rejected.

This consensus has been twofold. First, there has been virtual agreement in the Western tradition that there are certain built-in limitations with which every man must reckon if he would lead an authentically human life—the necessity for labor, the inevitability of disease and tragedy, the brutal fact of death—and that in spite of these limitations man has experienced life as a gift because his world has been a meaning-full and value-full arena within which he might act responsibly. Second, previous ages assumed that man lives in a cosmos governed by a mind or minds more potent and enduring than his. Man has until now thought of himself as belonging not only to the relativities of history but also to an order of reality not subject to the law of destruction and tragedy that rules within history. Because he has understood himself as an "amphibious" creature, belonging to both the profane and the sacred, the earth and the heavens, traditional man has conceived of the authentically human life as one lived in full awareness of both the limitations and the transcendent destiny of man. To be human has involved combining the virtues of realism and hope.

In our time this traditional view of man is called into question at both points. The idea of human limitation has come under attack both practically and theoretically. In the first place it has become obvious that some of the limitations previous cultures regarded as basic to the human condition are giving way before the advance of science. Cybernation promises to eliminate labor for most people in some not too distant future. Disease after disease is being conquered, with the result that life expectancy is twice what it was in the Middle Ages. Recently it was hinted that even the frontier of death may not be impervious to scientific advancement. In the future those suffering from incurable diseases may be quick-frozen and later thawed when a cure has been found. While this possibility does not seem imminent, that it can be seriously discussed reveals something important about the 20th century mind: it is offended by the suggestion that there are any a priori limits to the human condition. Even death itself must not be considered a limit with which scientific man may not negotiate!

Awareness of death has been repressed in our culture, much as the Victorian era repressed awareness of sex, because we are unable to accept the idea of built-in human limitations. Saul Bellow is right in suggesting that the underlying philosophy of our generation is "death is God." But Dietrich Bonhoeffer is also correct in saying that death is no longer experienced as a border-situation by most people in our culture, because they have ceased to fear it. A repressed awareness may give rise to anxiety but not to fear.

The New Anthropology

More and more, modern man is also rejecting the traditional notion that human life has only limited creative potentialities because the world into which man emerges already has meaning and value. In spite of the sense of expanding limits and the greater promise of modern life, contemporary man increasingly experiences life not as a gift but as a burden, and the world not as a place filled with value, to be wondered at, but as a morally neutral arena of blind physical laws. In this neutral world man must assume the responsibility for creating meaning. The clue to the mentality which is increasingly dominating Western culture is the fact that the process Feuerbach longed to see has taken place: the predicates traditionally assigned to God have now been reclaimed by man.

No one has articulated this new anthropology with more clarity and power than Jean-Paul Sartre. Man exists, according to Sartre, in a world that, objectively, is devoid of all meaning. It is therefore up to man to do what God was once thought to do—to create *ex nihilo*, to improvise value and meaning out of unlimited freedom. The current of meaning and value now flows only one way—from man to the world. Man is a giver, a creator of meaning, not a recipient.

The second area of the traditional consensus has fared no

better. Modern man understands himself as belonging totally to the flux of history. Since he can believe only in what he can experience and think, and since his modes of thought are empirical, pragmatic and operational, he finds himself increasingly cut off from the possibility of relating in hope to any transcendent reality. The ancient, amphibious character of man is denied. Modern man lives a profane life, in a secular city, in a bungaloid world. We may expect him to be realistic, but the growing testimony is that the virtues of faith and hope are impossible for him.

It would not be too extravagant to say that the fundamental thesis of the new view of man which is coming to dominate the 20th century intellectual is that modern man has become posthuman. To be a "modern man" is to recognize that one is discontinuous with traditional man. It is to join in the refrain "Nothing like us ever was." Somehow, because we belong to the 20th century, we are supposed to be freed from the limitations that governed past human beings and also to be incapable of believing in the reality of anything that transcends the testimony of sense and experience.

Acceptance of the Secular

The dominant tendency of modern theology is to adapt Christian faith to the presuppositions of the 20th century mind. Bonhoeffer set the mood in suggesting that the "religious premise" of traditional man is no longer valid for the man who has "come of age"; the Christian must learn to live in the secular world. The death-of-God theologians have followed this lead in maintaining that there can be a Christian style of life which is not informed by the traditional Western understanding of the limitations and transcendent destiny of man. In the view of William Hamilton, for example, the Christian theologian of today is "a man without faith, without hope, with only the present and therefore only love to guide him" ("Thursday's Child," *Theology Today*, January 1964). When Paul van Buren accepts the principle of empirical verification and thus is forced to reduce the rich New Testament language about God and the eschatological destiny of man to the principle of "contagious freedom," he also compresses the Christian life into the present moment. Thomas J. J. Altizer achieves the same effect by limiting theology to an Incarnate Word which can be known only as we are open to the experience of the moment before us. In accepting the working assumptions of the secular mind, modern theology has more and more come to concentrate upon the present moment, has given itself over to the categories of what Marcel has called "established experience," and consequently has been unable to articulate an adequate doctrine of faith or hope.

My concern here is to question whether a religious style of life can exist in the acid soil of the promethean view of man which characterizes secular thought. I would maintain that there are two movements which belong essentially as well as historically to any theistic style of life. I call these the abdication from the pretensions of omnipotence and the positing of a ground for hope. If these two movements are essential to a religious style of life, Christian theology will have to be far clearer than it now is about where it is to say Yes to the secular mind and where it is to say No.

Abdication of Omnipotence

The movement toward religious faith begins with the realization that the self is not God, is not absolute in power, knowledge or responsibility. A friend of mine described this experience by saying, "I decided to hand in my resignation as manager of the universe. I was surprised to find how quickly it was accepted."

Perhaps this comment seems a little silly, an insult to common sense; isn't it obvious to everyone who has ever lived, experienced pain, observed his own failure or contemplated death that no human being is omnipotent? Astonishingly enough it is not! A growing body of opinion and evidence suggests that most people harbor illusions of immortality and omnipotence. Sartre argues convincingly that the whole project of human consciousness is directed toward becoming God.

Karen Horney makes a similar point in psychological terms. She shows that the key to neurosis lies in an effort to actualize an idealized, godlike image of the self rather than devoting the energies to realization of a realistic set of goals. The neurotic says to himself, "Others might have to struggle for success, but it should come easily to me; others may fall prey to disease but not me. I am insulated from misfortune by my unique gifts, my position, my potentialities." The neurotic's working assumption is that he is an exception to every cosmic rule. We need only to remind ourselves that the neurotic search for glory is an aspect of every personality.

This hidden pretension of omnipotence is nowhere more clearly seen than in the illusions of immortality we all harbor. Tolstoy in "The Death of Ivan Illych" graphically illustrates the destruction of such illusions and the shock which comes to a man when he discovers he is mortal.

Ivan Illych saw that he was dying, and he was in continual despair. In the depths of his heart he knew he was dying, but not only was he not accustomed to the thought, he simply did not and could not grasp it.

The syllogism he had learnt from Kiezewetter's Logic: "Caius is a man, men are mortal, therefore Caius is mortal," had always seemed to him correct as applied to Caius, but certainly not as applied to himself. That Caius—man in the abstract—was mortal, was perfectly correct, but he was not Caius, not an abstract man, but a creature quite separate from all others. He had been little Vanya, with a mamma and a papa, with Mitya and Volodya, with the toys, a coachman and a nurse . . . What did Caius know of the smell of that striped leather ball Vanya had been so fond of? Had Caius kissed his mother's hand like that, and did the silk of her dress rustle so for Caius? . . . "Caius really was mortal and it was right for him to die; but for me, little Vanya, Ivan Illych, with all my thoughts and emotions, it is altogether a different matter. It cannot be that I ought to die. That would be too terrible."

We are always ready to ignore our limitations—which, I suspect, accounts for American funeral practices, as well as for the slight revulsion we all feel in the presence of the poor, the crippled or the seriously ill. We do not want to be reminded of our mortality! But theology must constantly remind man of his mortality, for hope becomes a possibility only where there is a vivid awareness of the tragic limitations of human existence. Omnipotent beings have no need of hope, for they are not threatened by extremities.

I fear that Bonhoeffer has done modern theology a disservice in suggesting that death and the other boundary situations of human existence should not be central considerations of theology. One looks in vain among the radical theologians for any concerted effort to deal with the problem of death. Theology has escaped from the extremities and turned them over to pastoral psychology. And yet, much as we would like to forget, we cannot. The malevolent trinity of suffering, tragedy and death has yet to be dethroned. Lucidity demands that we deal with human life in light of its limitations.

Desirable Disillusionment

Let us consider the abdication of the hidden claims to omnipotence from another perspective.

To give up such claims is to become disillusioned, in the best sense of the word. It requires a considerable amount of energy to harbor an illusion. When we abandon our claims to omnipotence we stop nourishing the illusion that the world is as we would like it to be. With great relief we are finally able to declare that "things are what they are." When Margaret Fuller wrote to Carlyle, "I have decided to accept the universe" (Carlyle is reputed to have replied, "By Gad, she'd better!"), she articulated a sentiment which may be linguistically odd but which is psychologically and religiously profound. To lose our illusions and accept the rules of the game of life is a prerequisite to human freedom and responsibility. As long as we harbor claims and illusions of omnipotence, we judge both our successes and failures, our responsibilities and limitations, by fantastic standards which we inevitably fall short of. But once we accept the limitations that constitute the human condition we become free to explore the possible.

To accept the rules of the game is not equivalent to mere

resignation. Rather, it is to live in an attitude of wonder. Once we are able to confess that we are not the center of the world, we perceive things in an altogether new way. We are set free to admire rather than possess, to enjoy rather than exploit, to accept rather than grasp. In the attitude of wonder we experience life as a gift. G. K. Chesterton has expressed this beautifully. There are, he says in *Orthodoxy*, two convictions that grow out of the experience of wonder. "First, that this world is a wild and startling place, which might have been quite different, but which is quite delightful; second, that before this wildness and delight one may well be modest and submit to the queerest limitations of so queer a kindness." In wonder we perceive that it is not the case, as Sartre contends, that we are condemned to a neutral world in which human freedom must create all meaning and value. Merleau-Ponty has more accurately stated that "we are condemned to meaning." When we abandon our fantastic claims we find, as traditional man always knew, that our power to create meaning is limited on the one hand by the fragility of human life and on the other by the givenness of the world into which we emerge.

Positing a Ground for Hope

We come now to consider a second aspect of religious faith. Seemingly, the world of the spirit loathes a power vacuum no less than does the political world. When realism prevails and we acknowledge that our infantile strivings to have dominion over all things are doomed to failure, the question of God inevitably arises. If I am not the source of a deathless and victorious power, is there any such power? If I am not God, is there a God? Is there any force, mind or person working at the heart of things to accomplish what I desire but cannot achieve; to bring order out of chaos, meaning out of contingency, triumph out of tragedy? Or is human history "a tale told by an idiot"?

The question of God is not the question of the existence of some remote infinite being. It is the question of the possibility of hope. The affirmation of faith in God is the acknowledgment that there is a deathless source of power and meaning that can be trusted to nurture and preserve all created good. To deny that there is a God is functionally equivalent to denying that there is any ground for hope. It is therefore wholly consistent for Sartre to say that human beings "must act without hope," or for Camus to warn that hope was the last of the curses which Pandora took from her box. If God is dead, then death is indeed God, and perhaps the best motto for human life is what Dante once wrote over the entrance to hell: "Abandon hope, all ye who enter."

The concept of hope has been so little examined in our time that it is frequently thought to mean the same thing as optimism or illusion or mere agnosticism about the future. There are, however, crucial differences. Optimism is based upon illusion—in the Freudian sense—in that it arises out of a drive for wish fulfillment which ignores contrary evidence. The optimist conspires to ignore the facts because they suggest an interpretation he does not want to make. Contrariwise, the believer's affirmation of a ground for hope is made in the knowledge that by all realistic calculations human history is ultimately tragic. It is in light of this certain knowledge that the believer sets himself to examine his experience to determine whether there is any basis for hoping that what is penultimately the case is not ultimately so.

Affirming the Unknowable

It is important to realize that the believer is clear that experience renders an ambiguous verdict. In both the inner world and the outer world it is as Ecclesiastes has told us: there is both building up and tearing down, creating and destroying. And if the life force seems ingenious in circumventing all that threatens life and growth, it is nevertheless true that finally death wins. Thus the question of hope becomes the question of the adequacy and the finality of the categories of human understanding.

Hope begins with the realization that human experience is

finally inadequate to deal with all the possibilities that reality harbors. We might say that to hope is to take experience seriously but not to absolutize it. Gabriel Marcel says (in *Homo Viator*) that at the basis of hope is the realization that "the more the real is real the less does it lend itself to a calculation of possibilities on the basis of accepted experience."

This is not yet, however, the full meaning of hope. The humanist and the skeptic share with the believer an agnosticism about the adequacy of human categories of thought and experience to comprehend the limits of the real. Such agnosticism is merely epistemological humility. But we confuse the issue if we identify faith with mere agnosticism. Faith and hope arise out of agnosticism, but they go on to proclaim an affirmation about the unknowable.

There is a leap of faith which can be taken only as an act of courage in which a man says, "Although the categories of experience yield evidence that is at best ambiguous and is sometimes indicative of the finality of death and the triumph of evil, I *nevertheless* decide to trust that there is a deathless source of human life in which the meaning created within human history is conserved and brought to fulfillment." It is in this positing of the trustworthiness of the ground of life that we find the essential element of the religious consciousness.

Surely William Hamilton and the other radical theologians are wrong in suggesting the possibility of a form of Christian life in which faith and hope have been eliminated. Hamilton seeks to describe the Christian theologian and Camus's rebel with the same formula; echoing the previously quoted description of today's theologian, he says of the rebel: "Faith is abolished for the rebel; hope is quite absent. But love remains; 'rebellion cannot exist without a strange form of love' " ("The Christian, The Saint, and the Rebel," in *Forms of Extremity in the Modern Novel*, edited by Nathan A. Scott, Jr.).

Although I have the greatest admiration for the heroic spirit of Camus, I do not think we should confuse the style of life he recommends with any form of religious or Christian faith. *He* did not. Religious faith involves a movement in which the believer goes beyond the categories of present experience and posits a metaempirical ground for hope. This is precisely the movement Camus refused to make. He wished to live in the certainties and to live without appeal. To eliminate the movement beyond the certainties of the present moment of experience is not to make Christianity palatable to the empirical and secular mind of the 20th century. It is to eliminate the religious option.

Religious faith, in any of its theistic varieties, involves essentially those virtues of realism and hope that it has involved historically. In many ways modern technology has changed the face of the earth and the texture of human life. We can perhaps realize a security and abundance of life which to traditional man would have seemed utopian and in this sense become posthistorical. Yet as we savor the bittersweet taste of life which is always accompanied by tragedy and as we face the mystery out of which life arises and into which it speeds, we remain *merely human*, indistinguishable from the man of the first or the 31st century. Perhaps in the face of this mystery we are able to be most fully human and free when we have the courage to be both lucid and hopeful.

Toward a Theology of Hope

Carl E. Braaten

Counting himself among those who view the new theology of hope as being "on the right track," Lutheran theologian Carl E. Braaten maintains that it provides, in its affirmation of change and openness to the future, a point of contact between modern man and the radical eschatology that is central to the biblical message. The previous debates by biblical scholars on the subject of eschatology have failed to go beyond the historical question, What did Jesus or the early church happen to hope? The new apocalypticists, however, are seeking to determine "in what way eschatologies from the past may be addressed to man today." And, says Braaten, while such theologians profit from attention to such non-Christian future-oriented thinkers as the Marxist Ernst Bloch, it is knowledge of the Christ event which prevents hope from being merely utopian. Associate Professor of Systematic Theology at Chicago's Lutheran School of Theology, Dr. Braaten is the author of *History and Hermeneutics* and co-editor (with Roy A. Harrisville) of *The Historical Jesus and the Kerygmatic Christ* and *Kerygma and History*. His essay is from the July 1967 issue of *Theology Today*.*

IN HIS *Critique of Pure Reason*, Immanuel Kant stated: "The whole interest of reason, speculative as well as practical, is centered in the three following questions: (1) What can I know? (2) What ought I to do? (3) What may I hope?"[1] Modern philosophy since Kant has preoccupied itself almost exclusively with the first question, the epistemological question, to a much lesser extent with the second, the ethical question, and hardly at all with the ques-

* P. O. Box 29, Princeton, N.J. 08540.
[1] Immanuel Kant, *Critique of Pure Reason* (London: J. M. Dent & Sons, 1934), p. 457.

tion of hope, the self-transcending movement of man towards his future. If this is generally true in philosophy, it is nearly equally the case with modern theology. Theology since Kant has been exhaustively methodological; the introductory section of dogmatics usually called *Prolegomena* became a lengthy effort to give the Christian faith proper epistemological credentials. Karl Barth's *Prolegomena*, running to over 1,300 pages, must be seen as a thoroughgoing theology of *revelation* that answers the acute epistemological concerns that the nineteenth century refined. Paul Tillich also wrote his *Systematic Theology* to a great extent in light of Kant's first question: What can I know? Its controlling purpose was apologetic.

Whenever it appeared that theology was not succeeding in making a good case for itself at the level of Kant's first question, there were those who came forth to suggest that religion in general and Christian faith in particular have nothing to do with the question of *knowledge*. Religion or faith arises in connection with Kant's second question: What ought I to do? Religion is reduced to the practical level of ethics. In fact, Kant himself was perhaps the chief stimulus behind the Ritschlian tendency to interpret religious statements as judgments of moral value. At the present time this translation of religious language into ethical propositions has won some new advocates, notable among whom are William Hamilton and Paul van Buren. Christianity is basically an expression of what those who are somehow or other stimulated by Jesus of Nazareth intend to do.[2] Since Christianity is now transformed into the practical issues of moral existence, it is relevant to secular man even though the living God of the Bible is dead.

[2] R. B. Braithwaite, a philosopher of language analysis, tries to interpret religious statements as a declaration of loyalty to a certain set of moral principles. Religious statements are not only emotive (A. J. Ayer) but conative as well. He believes that a conative explanation of religious assertions is in fine accord with the spirit of empiricism. In the light of the theology of hope that we describe in this essay, it is precisely such an accord which spells its death as an interpretation of religious statements. R. B. Braithwaite, "An Empiricist's View of the Nature of Religious Belief," *Classical and Contemporary Readings in the Philosophy of Religion*, edited by John Hick (Englewood Cliffs, N. J.: Prentice-Hall, 1963), p. 429.

I

With all these past and present theological investments in Kant's first and second questions, what has meanwhile happened to his third question? Post-Kantian philosophy has not bothered much with it. Kant's doctrine of the immortality of the soul, which provided the answer to his own question about hope, has been disregarded as a case of bad philosophy and bad theology. Most modern philosophers would say of a fellow philosopher who would still teach a doctrine of "life beyond death" something similar to what Goethe once said of Kant's doctrine of radical evil: "Even Kant, who, throughout a long life, has tried to cleanse his philosopher's cloak from various disfiguring prejudices, has now deliberately allowed it to be stained with the shameful idea of radical evil, in order that even Christians will be drawn to kiss the hem of his garment."[3] However, it isn't only Kant's peculiar version of immortality from which philosophy has "cleansed" itself; no doctrine concerning the hope of man for a future beyond death has survived. Even to assert the *meaningfulness* of asking the question about hope for an "absolute future"[4] or total fulfillment may be one of those "disfiguring prejudices" or "shameful ideas."

Modern theology has not treated Kant's third question with much more respect than philosophy. When the doctrine of the immorality of the soul was fumbled away by philosophy, theology attempted to recover the fumble by falling on the biblical idea of the resurrection of the body. But when it came to stating what "resurrection of the body" really means, we were not so well instructed. The idea of "resurrection of the body" has functioned most successfully in parochial theological polemics, that is, when budding theologians armed with "the resurrection of the body" (with Bible in hand, plus Hebrew categories) have taken the offensive against poor pas-

[3] Quoted from Emil Brunner, *The Mediator*, trans. by Olive Wyon (Philadelphia: The Westminster Press, 1947), p. 128.
[4] Karl Rahner's expression; Ingo Herman, "Total Humanism," *Is God Dead?* Concilium, Vol. 16, edited by Johannes B. Metz (New York: Paulist Press, 1966), p. 162.

tors and professors over fifty who still believe in the orthodox —but unbiblical—doctrine of "the immortality of the soul." But what have these biblical theologians themselves meant by "the resurrection of the body"? Has it not been demythologized and therefore interpreted existentially to mean that Christians, like the Hebrews, place a high value on the physical body in this life? It is an anti-Manichean statement; it was meant to counteract the gnostic depreciation of the material body. It may also be taken as a statement against the Hellenistic body/soul dichotomy. That is all well and good. But is that what "resurrection of the body" meant? Is that *all* it means? If that is the case, the teaching has been taken out of its eschatological context, and has been reset in the framework of the doctrine of creation, with certain strong ethical implications for this life. But then it no longer functions as the Christian answer to Kant's question, What may I hope? It is more a roundabout way (a long detour indeed!) of speaking about how Christians ought to regard the body as an integral part of the whole man created by God, and what that ought to mean for Christian life. The content of eschatology is rendered intelligible by translating it into a non-eschatological framework, and Kant's third question goes a-begging.

My observation that theology has not done well by Kant's third question may be challenged, it would seem, by citing the decades of debate on eschatology in the New Testament since Johannes Weiss and Albert Schweitzer traced the apocalyptic passages in the gospels back to the historical Jesus. Many word studies on "hope" and books and articles on biblical eschatology have been written, and in the course of all this research we have learned interesting things about what Jesus or Paul or John or this or that community in the early church believed about the future. I would not say all this has been much ado about nothing, only next to nothing, unless it is shown how one can make a transition from an historical observation to an existential concern. What do the eschatological ideas in the Bible have to do with my existence, that is, with my hope concerning the future, especially with the inevitable future of death's annihilating power? How can it concern me existentially whether it was first Jesus or Paul or anyone else who formulated a certain teaching about the future, unless it is also shown how such a teaching corresponds significantly with a structural element in human existence? So the debates that have gone on between Schweitzer, Cullmann, Bultmann, Dodd, Jeremias, etc., have not yet yielded an answer or answers to Kant's third question: What may I hope? —but only answers to the historical question: What did Jesus or the early church happen to hope? They have not taken up the question of what it means for man to hope at all, whether to be human is to have hope, and therefore in what way eschatologies from the past may be addressed to man today, offering him the ground, guidelines, and goal of his inevitable hoping. Perhaps the sole exception here is Bultmann, who does take from biblical eschatology as much as he thinks is existentially relevant. Bultmann is right in doing that. He is the one who has taught us that biblical theologians cannot postpone indefinitely the hermeneutical question. That is the question of how to move from what it *meant* to what it *means*.[5] The question, however, to address to Bultmann is whether his dependence on Heidegger's existentialist system of philosophy has not overly restricted his view of what may be relevant in the biblical eschatology. In other words, is his reading of the dynamics and scope of hope in human existence adequate?

Just when it seemed that the Bultmannian existentialist translation of New Testament eschatology was to rule the day, a new movement towards the re-eschatologizing of theology was launched a few years ago in Germany. The leading bearers of this movement are Wolfhart Pannenberg and Jürgen Moltmann. They are grafting on to the rediscovery of eschatology at the turn of the century through the research of Weiss and Schweitzer. At the same time they are trying to overcome the "sterility" of this rediscovery. There has been no lack of

---

[5] Cf. Krister Stendahl's use of this distinction in his article, "Biblical Theology," *The Interpreter's Dictionary of the Bible* (New York: Abingdon Press, 1962), p. 430.

talk about eschatology in contemporary discussions. It may therefore strike us as rather tedious that still another effort will be made to activate the meaning of eschatology, or to rescue it from its dissolution in existentialist analysis. But if Pannenberg and Moltmann are right, we will have to endure the tedium, and try once again to understand the eschatology of the Bible, because without it there is nothing that remains that deserves to be called "the biblical message."

II

It is doubtful that just another attempt to describe the contents of biblical eschatology would be any less free of that "sterility" which has characterized all other recent efforts without some point of contact in contemporary culture or modern philosophy. The reason for the validity of Bultmann's program is that it had a point of contact (namely, modern existentialism) which the efforts of others, for example, Cullmann, Dodd, and Jeremias, seriously lacked. In the case of Schweitzer and his school, the postponement of the parousia meant a complete refutation of New Testament eschatology. While eschatology was central to Jesus and primitive Christianity, it is incredible to modern man. We have to build on other foundations. Few theologians have agreed with Schweitzer. Somewhat piously they have assumed that what is so central to the New Testament must still somehow be relevant to our time. It is as if they have had their hands on a cord attached to a powerful electrical generator, but haven't found where to plug it in. That is what we mean by the need for a cultural point of contact. Otherwise theology is done in the isolation of its own ghetto with no power to convince or interest anyone outside its circle. A non-theological point of contact for Pannenberg and Moltmann, not exclusively but significantly, is the philosophy of hope sketched out by the eighty-one year old Marxist, Ernst Bloch, who after his flight from East Germany has been teaching at Tübingen. His major work is entitled *Das Prinzip Hoffnung*, which he wrote between 1938 and 1949 while he was in exile in America from Nazi Germany. It was published in West Germany only as recently as 1959, and since then has stimulated the new dialogue between theologians, both Protestant and Roman Catholic, and Marxism.[6] Moltmann's exciting book, *Theologie der Hoffnung*, is itself a theological parallel to *Das Prinzip Hoffnung*, as its title hints.

For Ernst Bloch the key to human existence is to be found in the hopes which man holds for the future state of humanity and the world. What fires man's spirit in the present is the radiation which emanates from "the promise of a 'transcendental' homeland where all who now suffer, labor, and are incomplete will find their true identity. In the 'radiation' from this utopian state, an attempt is made to discover the ultimate meaning of human existence. This radiation derives from an unshakable confidence that there will be a new life or *novum ultimum*."[7] Bloch, a Jewish-Marxist atheist, draws much of his understanding of man's directedness toward the future from the prophetic history of the Bible. He says, "Man is indebted to the Bible for his eschatological consciousness."[8] As Moltmann puts it, Bloch accepts the "major objects of hope in the Bible" without belief in the transcendent personal God of Judaism and Christianity. It is a "hope without faith," or a "humanism without God." What is significant is that Bloch's view of man provides a point of contact for the

[6] Cf. the following articles by theologians: J. Moltmann, "Ernst Bloch: Messianismus und Marxismus. Einführende Bemerkungen zum 'Prinzip Hoffnung'," *Kirche in der Zeit*, 1960, pp. 291–295; Moltmann, "Die Menschenrechte und der Marxismus. Einführende Bemerkungen und kritische Reflexionen zu E. Blochs 'Naturrecht und menschliche Würde'," *ibid.*, 1962, pp. 122–126; Moltmann, "Das 'Prinzip Hoffnung' und die christliche Zuversicht," *Evangelische Theologie*, 23, 1963, 537–557; Moltmann, "Die Kategorie *Novum* in der christlichen Theologie," *Ernst Bloch zu ehren*, ed. by Siegried Unseld (Frankfurt: Suhrkamp Verlag, 1965), pp. 243–263; Moltmann, "Hope Without Faith: An Eschatological Humanism Without God," *Is God Dead? op. cit.*, pp. 25–40; W.-D. Marsch, "Eritis sicut Deus. Ueber das Werk E. Blochs als Problem evangelischer Theologie," *Kerygma und Dogma*, 7, 1961, 173–196; W.-D. Marsch, *Hoffen worauf? Auseinandersetzung mit E. Bloch* (Hamburg: Furche-Verlag, 1963); Gerhard Sauter, *Zukunft und Verheissung* (Zürich: Zwingli Verlag, 1965); Fritz Buri, "Ernst Blochs 'Prinzip Hoffnung' und die Hoffnung im Selbstverständnis des christlichen Glaubens," *Reformatio*, 15, 1966, 211–225; Wolfhart Pannenberg, "Der Gott der Hoffnung," *Ernst Block zu ehren, op. cit.*, pp. 209–225.

[7] J. Moltmann, "Hope Without Faith: An Eschatological Humanism Without God," *op. cit.*, p. 26.

[8] *Ibid.*, p. 26.

biblical promise of the kingdom of God. Man as such is open-ended toward the future; this openness is evident in his hopes. Bloch makes the categories of possibility, of the new, of futurity, fundamental in his "ontology of not-yet-being."[9]

Theologians who have entered into dialogue with Bloch see that his categories of hope and the future correspond to the biblical picture of man as one who lives within the framework of promise and fulfillment. The arrows in the biblical conception of reality as history are always pointing toward the future. The tremendous emphasis on remembering the past is due precisely to the fact that it contains the promises which articulate our hopes for the future. Bloch's philosophy of hope is being hailed as a secular confirmation of the fact that biblical eschatology deals with what is central in human existence; man's hopes burst open his present, connect him with his past, drive him toward the horizons of the not yet realized future. Moltmann says, and here we pass on only a few testimonies from theologians on Bloch's relevance, "As scarcely any other philosophy *Das Prinzip Hoffnung* is suited to help in activating and elaborating the Christian doctrine of hope . . . *Das Prinzip Hoffnung* can in the present situation of Christian theology give us courage to try a new interpretation of the original Christian hope. . . ."[10] Pannenberg in similar vein states, "Perhaps Christian theology will have Ernst Bloch's philosophy of hope to thank if it regains the courage to return to its central category, the full concept of the eschatological. What remains decisive in this is the outlook on the future which is to be temporally understood. Bloch has taught us to understand anew the overwhelming power of the still open future and of hope which anticipates that future, for the life and the thought of man as well as for the ontological quality of all reality. He has recovered the eschatological thought-pattern of the biblical traditions as a theme of philosophical reflection, and also for Christian theology."[11] Wolf-

---

[9] Ernst Bloch, *Philosophische Grundfragen. Zur Ontologie des Noch-Nicht-Seins* (Frankfurt: Suhrkamp Verlag, 1961).

[10] J. Moltmann, "Die Kategorie *Novum* in der christlichen Theologie," *op. cit.*, pp. 243, 244.

[11] W. Pannenberg, "Der Gott der Hoffnung," *op. cit.*, p. 213.

Dieter Marsch, in his book *Hoffen worauf? Auseinander-setzung mit Ernst Bloch*, says, "Evangelical Christians can find in him a worthy partner in the discussion so urgently needed today about the basis, content, and goal of Christian hope—a hope in a God who is coming—especially when so many of the leading images of the 'good old order' as well as of an otherworldly fulfillment have become so questionable."[12]

In our situation Harvey Cox has enthusiastically endorsed this new direction in German theology in his "Afterword" of *The Secular City Debate*: "I am now pursuing the hints, perhaps misleadingly, of two vagabonds on the periphery of theology, Pierre Teilhard de Chardin and Ernst Bloch. . . . Though there are many differences, both Teilhard and Bloch discuss transcendence in terms of the pressure exerted by the future on the present. They both see that his future is the key to man's being, and they recognize that an authentically open future is only possible where there is a *creature* who can orient himself toward the future and relate himself to reality in terms of this orientation—in short, *a creature who can hope*."[13] Then with an intuition that here I can only applaud, Cox states, "I believe that Bloch's massive *Prinzip Hoffnung* . . . supplies the only serious alternative to Martin Heidegger's . . . *Sein und Zeit* as a philosophical partner for theology."[14] The basis for Cox's judgment is that Heidegger's vision of man shuts him up within a finitude whose core is anxiety and whose boundary is death (*Sein zum Tode*), whereas Bloch sees hope as the kernel of existence pressing on toward a future world that overcomes the limitations of the present, toward a "still unpossessed homeland."[15]

It would be perhaps gratuitous to observe that the crux of the theological dialogue with Ernst Bloch is the question whether the living God of the Exodus and the Resurrection is not the only guarantor of a future that corresponds to the

[12] W.-D. Marsch, *Hoffen worauf?* op. cit., pp. 91–92.
[13] Harvey Cox, "Afterword," *The Secular City Debate*, ed. by Daniel Callahan (New York, Macmillan Co., 1966), pp. 197–198.
[14] *Ibid.*, p. 200.
[15] Bloch's expression, quoted by Harvey Cox, *ibid.*

highest hopes of man. The dialogue with Bloch affirms the humanism of his hope, but grounds it in the "power of the future" who has revealed himself as the "God of hope"[16] in the eschatological event of Jesus' resurrection. The attempt is made to show that Bloch's atheism is right to the extent that it is a protest against a divine hypostasis who obstructs the freedom and the future of man, and instead guarantees the prevailing forces in nature and society. The God of orthodox churches has usually been pictured as one most at home in the past, as relating to the present only through the churches, and keeping his distance from those revolutionary tendencies in society which accept responsibility for the future and somehow threaten the social status of Christianity. The first generations of Christians were fired by hopes for the kingdom; the second wave of Christianity built the church as an interim device while waiting for the kingdom; later generations identified the two. Today the task is to reactivate the Christian hope by pointing to the kingdom of God whose biblical images have been blurred in the history of Christianity.

III

In the dialogue with Bloch there is no question of taking over modern secular forms of hope as such; the task is rather to rediscover the "logos of hope"[17] inherent in Christian eschatology. Moltmann begins his *Theologie der Hoffnung* with this question. He calls eschatology "the medium of Christian faith."[18] What is needed is not so much "a new version of the *articulus de novissimis*, but rather a 'thermal current' of hope in all articles of the Christian faith."[19] Since Christian faith lives absolutely from the resurrection of the crucified Christ, it is directed as hope toward the universal future of this Christ. The future is the real problem of Christian the-

---

[16] Cf. W. Pannenberg's essay, "Der Gott der Hoffnung," in which he speaks of God as "the power of the future."

[17] J. Moltmann, "Hope Without Faith," *op. cit.*, p. 28.

[18] J. Moltmann, *Theologie der Hoffnung* (München: Chr. Kaiser Verlag, 1965), p. 12.

[19] J. Moltmann, "Hope Without Faith," *op. cit.*, p. 39.

ology, not just any future, but the future of Jesus Christ. But how is it possible to speak of the future when it has not yet happened? In a certain sense there can be no "eschato-*logie*," for the Greek *logos* concept presupposes that language can grasp the truth about reality that is always and already there. In Greek ontology reality is not open-ended; it has no real future; there is no need for hope; and there is no problem of history. Thus, if we operate with a Greek *logos* concept, we can have no eschatology, for the future of Christian hope is not an extension of the past, or recurrence of the present. Reality as nature is circular; reality as history is always unfinished, opening forwards toward a real future of new events that have never happened before.

Christian eschatology speaks of the future in utterances of hope based on the history of promise. These utterances do not conform to reality experienced in the present; they do not correspond to empirically verifiable reality. In fact, it is their very nature to contradict reality as it is experienced at the present. They are a "negation of the negative," which Tillich calls the principle which guides hope in the formation of its language and pictures.[20] These statements of hope do not express our experiences of reality; they stand over against that experience and provide "the condition for the possibility of new experiences."[21] They do not mirror reality as it now stands; they look for a *change* in reality. Hope lives from the promises that reality can and will be changed. How? And in what manner? That is what the dialogue is all about with Ernst Bloch and with every other form of humanism that is seriously concerned about the future of mankind.

The element of contradiction is essential in the language of hope. Hope contradicts experience; the future will contradict the present—so we hope. There can be no empirical verification of hope, for it is of the nature of hope to press toward that which cannot yet be seen. "Now hope that is seen is not hope. For who hopes for what he sees?" (Rom. 8:24). Christian hope itself, Moltmann says, is born from contradic-

[20] Paul Tillich, "Die politische Bedeutung der Utopie im Leben der Völker," *Der Widerstreit von Raum und Zeit*, Gesammelte Werke, VI (Stuttgart: Evangelisches Verlagswerk, 1963), p. 186.
[21] J. Moltmann, *Theologie der Hoffnung*, p. 13.

tion, from the contradiction of the resurrection to the cross.[22]
The mission of hope is to radicalize the existing discrepancy
between righteousness and sin, joy and suffering, peace
and war, good and evil, life and death, and to look to the
absolute future of Christ for a universal and transcendent
resolution of this discrepancy. Faith acknowledges that this future has already erupted in history in the Christ event. Without this knowledge of Christ hope would become merely
utopian, that is, a leap forward into the empty air.[23] Because the limits of finitude, sin, and death have been trans-
gressed by the resurrection of Christ, hope becomes a confidence that all the promises of God for humanity and the
world will reach an ultimate fulfillment. This hope is not
utopian; utopia comes from *u-topos*, that which has "no place."
Hope, on the contrary, looks to the future for that which only
as yet has no place, but which might have place—if the God
of hope is faithful to his promises. Hope does not allow man
to resign himself to despair in the face of unchangeable situations and brute facts. It points man ahead to the horizons
of really new possibilities. It presupposes what Bloch calls
an "ontology of not-yet-being," a dynamic ontology with a
really new future as an open possibility of reality historically
understood. In an ontology of history that includes futurity,
the statement of faith that "with God all things are possible" makes more sense. As Moltmann argues, the "God
of Parmenides" is the basis of an ontology of static being
which makes a meaningful experience of history impossible,
and undercuts hope by collapsing the future into the present.
If the Eternal makes its epiphany in the present, if the "moment" is an atom of eternity, what is there left to hope for
from a new future?[24]

IV

Both Pannenberg and Moltmann see the resurrection of Jesus
as the anchor of hope in history, and as the bridge between
the universal expectations in late Jewish apocalypticism and

[22] *Ibid.*, p. 14.
[23] *Ibid.*, p. 16.
[24] *Ibid.*, pp. 24–25.

the eschatological mission of the church in world history. The "theology of hope" is both a "theology of the resurrection" and a "theology of universal history." This comes out with special force and frequency in Pannenberg's writings.

In post-exilic apocalypticism the idea of the resurrection of all the dead is an element in its theology of universal history. Pannenberg observes, "Jewish apocalypticism completed the extension of history so that it covered the whole course of the world from Creation to the end."[25] When the early Christians spoke of the resurrection of Jesus of Nazareth, as those who shared the apocalyptic expectations of a general resurrection of all the dead at the end of the world, they knew they were speaking eschatologically. It is not the case that they first encountered the risen Christ, and then generalized from that particular instance of resurrection to all others. The question they would ask is not whether the resurrection *could* happen, but whether it already *has* happened. If it has happened, it is a world-historical event of eschatological significance.

For Pannenberg the apocalyptic expectation of resurrection as an end-event is an abiding presupposition of Jesus' significance for all later times. The basis of primitive Christian faith in Jesus as the Christ of God was so closely bound up with basic features of the apocalyptic hope that Pannenberg concludes, "If the apocalyptic expectation should be entirely untenable to us, then the primitive Christian faith in Christ is also untenable to us; then the continuity of that which would remain of Christianity after discounting such [apocalyptic] features would be broken with Jesus and primitive Christian proclamation, including Paul. We must be clear on what is at stake when we discuss the truth of the apocalyptic expectation of a future judgment and the resurrection of the dead: we are dealing directly with the foundation of the Christian faith. Without the horizon of the apocalyptic expectation we could not grasp just why the man Jesus should

25 W. Pannenberg, "Redemptive Event and History," *Essays on Old Testament Hermeneutics*, ed. by Claus Westermann (Richmond, Virginia: John Knox Press, 1964), p. 319.

be the finally valid revelation of God, why in him and only in him God himself should have appeared. . . . If this horizon should disappear, then the foundation of faith is lost, then Christology becomes mythology, and it no longer has any continuity with Jesus and the witness of the apostles."[26] That is rather strong endorsement of apocalypticism, especially at a time when major schools of biblical interpretation have tried to teach us that neither modern man nor the real message of the Bible has any permanent stake in apocalypticism.

The apocalyptic hope for resurrection that early Christianity declared had reached its preliminary fulfillment (its first fruits) in the Easter event is still relevant for man today if he looks for a fulfillment of his essential being as man. If man is to hope for individual personal fulfillment, in some sense he must hope for life beyond death, for he knows that such fulfillment cannot occur within the finite limits of his earthly existence. The question whether hope can survive cannot ultimately disregard whether there is something to hope for that transcends death, the last hindrance to hope. By way of a "phenomenology of hope" Pannenberg states that "it belongs to the nature of man's being to hope beyond death."[27] In modern anthropology this specific element of man's nature is expressed in the concept of "openness to the world." This is an openness beyond every finite situation.[28] Man seeks to go beyond every limit, even that final limit which he can anticipate as his own death. He expresses his infinite striving to cross over even the boundary line of death in his images of hope. A classical image of this quest for self-fulfillment is the idea of the immortality of the soul; the biblical expression is the resurrection of the dead. Pannenberg's point is that these expressions are not imposed upon men through a revelation from the outside, but are rooted in the nature of man's very being to push back all frontiers which obstruct a total fulfillment of hope. In a sense, then, hope is the voice of man's "essential" (Tillich) or "authentic" (Bult-

---

[26] W. Pannenberg, *Grundzüge der Christologie* (Gütersloher Verlagshaus Gerd Mohn, 1964), p. 79.
[27] *Ibid.*, p. 81.
[28] *Ibid.*

mann) being. Wherever man does not raise the question about life beyond death, there man's being as man has not yet come to full expression.

Pannenberg sees a structural correspondence between man as a hoping creature, phenomenologically ascertained, and the resurrection of Jesus proclaimed by the apostles against the background of apocalyptic expectations. The end of history has been preactualized in his resurrection. The Christian looks forward to that which has already occurred at Easter. The presence of the eschaton in Jesus Christ has far-reaching significance for the interpretation of all history as God's history. This eschaton casts a light on the entirety of world history and its destiny, and not only on my personal existence and its meaning, as Bultmann interprets the resurrection. For Bultmann the resurrection has nothing to do with world history, only with personal existence here and now, because he thinks it possible to separate Jesus and the kerygma from the universal historical framework of apocalypticism. Pannenberg concludes that what Bultmann means by calling Jesus the eschatological event is something other than what it means within the apocalyptic concept of history.[29]

Pannenberg adduces testimonies from recent philosophers of history to substantiate his notion that the understanding of history as a whole and as a unity is possible only from the standpoint of the end of history. The same philosophers, however (Dilthey, Heidegger, Gadamer, Löwith), have no confidence in the possibility of universal history because in the nature of things history runs on without yielding an overarching perspective from which to view all particulars. One would have to stand outside of history or at the end of history in order to grasp the totality of history. As long as history has a future which has not yet happened, we are limited to only partial glimpses; perhaps at best we can deal with meaning *in* history,[30] but not the meaning *of* history. Ever since Hegel tried to sketch out a universal history, philosophers and his-

---

[29] See Pannenberg's discussion with Bultmann's eschatology in "Redemptive Event and History," *op. cit.*, pp. 320 ff.
[30] This is the argument of Karl Löwith's *Meaning in History* (Chicago: The University of Chicago Press, 1949).

torians have shuddered before the very prospect. It was the *hybris* of Hegel to imagine that he possessed the key for a philosophy of universal history as the self-unfolding of the absolute spirit. Pannenberg's concern is to recover the concept of universal history that actually roots in apocalypticism, and to free it from its particular liabilities in Hegel's system.

If the end of history alone can provide us with the perspective from which to understand the total course of history, then Christian theology cannot eschew the concept of universal history so long as it claims that Jesus is the eschatological event. The end of history is present proleptically in Jesus of Nazareth. In his resurrection the final end of universal history has been anticipated; it has occurred beforehand. Among other things, Pannenberg differs from Hegel's concept of universal history because of this insistence on the eschatologically differentiated structure of the resurrection of Jesus. Therefore, history is not abolished,[31] as in Hegel. Nor is it abolished as in the realized eschatologies of such different thinkers as C. H. Dodd, on the one hand, and Bultmann, on the other.[32]

Pannenberg places the notion of universal history under careful restrictions. He is aware of its pitfalls, and notes: "The anticipated coming of the end of history in the midst of history, far from doing away with history, actually forms the basis from which history as a whole becomes understandable. This does not make possible, however, an oversight over the drama of world history as from a stage box. . . . Jesus Christ, the end of history, is not available to us as the principle of a 'Christologically' grounded total view of world history. Christ's Resurrection, the daybreak of the eschaton, is for our understanding a light which blinds as Paul was blinded on the Damascus road. . . . Also our participation in this event, the hope of our own resurrection, is still hidden under the experience of the cross. No one can make the eschaton into a key to calculate the course of history, because it is present to us in such a mysterious, overpowering, incomprehensible way."[33]

[31] W. Pannenberg, "Redemptive Event and History," *op. cit.*, p. 334.
[32] *Ibid.*, p. 333.
[33] *Ibid.*, p. 334.

V

Lest it appear that I have unduly homogenized the thought of Pannenberg and Moltmann, it may be worth mentioning that Moltmann holds some reservations on Pannenberg's idea that the resurrection of Jesus is the anticipated end of all history. If that is the case, he says, then the risen Jesus himself as such has already attained the end and himself no longer has any future.[34] Also this would mean that believers do not look forward in hope toward the future of the risen Christ, but instead only for that to happen to them that has already happened to him. The resurrection of Jesus is not only the first instance of the final resurrection of the dead, but is also the source of the resurrection life of believers. This means that believers will find their future *in* him and his future, and not only in a final event which was like his. Moltmann thinks that what is at stake is the meaning and purpose of the future in history between the resurrection of Jesus and the final resurrection of all the dead. The purpose of the church during this interim is not merely to interpret the world or history or humanity differently, but in the expectation of the divine transformation to be busy changing it.

I have not seen anywhere a direct reply from Pannenberg to Moltmann's criticism; yet it is most clear from his latest writings that for him as for Moltmann the category of the future provides the basic perspective for all theological and ethical reflection. The resurrection of Jesus breaks history open for real changes to occur as the life of hope not only anticipates a transformation by God in the ultimate future, but shares in the processes of change in the present time. The standard Marxist criticism of Christian hope is that its hope of heaven deadens the nerve to work step by step in history toward the future total transformation of the world. If heaven is a guaranteed gift to us, all our efforts to change this world may even be accused of "works righteousness"; therefore it's better that we don't do anything at all. In the ethic that fol-

---

[34] J. Moltmann, *Theologie der Hoffnung*, p. 73.

lows from this "theology of hope," the Marxist criticism is taken seriously. Moltmann states, "This humanism [of esoteric Marxism] reduces the transcendent hopes of Christianity in order to bring them into life and an active alteration of the world; it is able to stimulate that aspect of hope in Christ which is concerned with the changing of this world."[35] The Christian hope for the kingdom and justice of God in Christ must enter into partnership with those who work for the economic relief of the "heavy laden," and who work politically for the freedom and dignity of man. An ethic of "faith active in love" has easily managed to fit into the prevailing structures of society, however unjust, with its work of private charity for the relief of individual victims; an ethic driven by "hope for the future" can stimulate the courage to alter the world, to change the course of history, and to seek the future of the kingdom of freedom and justice. For this hope for the future is a hope and trust in God as the power of the future who says, "Behold, I make all things new." "God appears as the power of the future to contradict the negative moments of existence that we now experience and to set free the forces through which victory is achieved. Only in the real transformation of an individual life and of the conditions of life, by breaking the bonds of the present, and in essential change, does this freedom penetrate the history that its future lays open for it."[36]

The traditional ethic of orthodox Christianity has been most concerned to make room for the church in society, to fit in, or to find a means of co-existence alongside of the state. But it is doubtful that an ethic that is eschatologically motivated can receive its due in such a framework of concern. Moltmann states, "Although it is clear that faith in God and expectation of the future are indissoluble in the Old and New Testaments, Christian theology pays far too little attention to the future as a divine mode of being. The exegetical discoveries of the eschatological nature of the original message, as seen by the early Christians, have not received enough weight; they have

[35] J. Moltmann, "Hope Without Faith," op. cit., pp. 35–36.
[36] Ibid., pp. 38–39.

been outbalanced by the pressures of theological tradition and the social position of Christianity."[37]

The deepest ontological basis of this "theology of hope" is the idea which both Pannenberg and Moltmann develop, namely, the future as a divine mode of being. The biblical God is the God of promises who leads history onward toward the future; he is the God of the coming kingdom; biblical thought is filled with passion for the future. The future is not only to be thought of subjectively as the referent of man's hope to transcend the given in his present, but as ontologically grounded in God's own mode of being. The traditional concept of God as *summum ens* or as *ens perfectissimum* is hardly reconcilable with the notion of the future as a divine mode of being. Pannenberg asks, "Is the future of God's lordship, of his kingdom, something unessential to his divinity, only something that is supplementary to it?"[38] "As the power of the future God is no thing, no extant object . . . He appears neither as a being among others nor as the quiet background of all beings."[39]

Only if we think of God as the power of the future can hope be directed toward him, for it is the power of the future that can contradict the negativities of the present and free man to overcome them. God as the power of the future is not only the power to determine the future of our present, but he has determined the future of all past times on their way to becoming present. A thought difficult enough to grasp, this reflection, says Pannenberg, "on the power of the future over the present leads therefore to a new concept of creation, which is oriented not to a primeval event in the past, but to the eschatological future."[40] The traditional doctrine of creation has been enveloped by an "Urzeit-Mythologie," without ever being converted in the light of the eschatological message and history of Jesus. "In the message of Jesus creation and the eschatological future are most closely connected."[41]

[37] *Ibid.*, p. 39.
[38] W. Pannenberg, "Der Gott der Hoffnung," *op. cit.*, p. 217.
[39] *Ibid.*
[40] *Ibid.*, p. 218.
[41] *Ibid.*, p. 219.

The futurity of God does not altogether exclude the notion of his eternity; but it transforms it. For God is to be thought of as the future of every past, the future of every present, as ontologically prior in his futurity to every event and epoch at the remotest distance from us. "But there is a difference whether eternity is thought of as timelessness or as an endless continuation of something in existence from primeval time, or in terms of the power of the future over every present."[42] Eternity is thus not an attribute of an absolutely immutable being, but expresses the primacy of the future of the God of the kingdom, the future for which man as man hopes.

VI

Because this essay is getting too long for the occasion of its writing, and at the same time is too brief to deal adequately with the scope and complexity of the subject, I must refrain from attempting a lengthy critical assessment of this new theology. It should be plain enough, however, that I think it is on the right track. Whatever its eventual liabilities may prove to be as the guns of criticism are turned upon it, it has some immediately recognizable assets.

(1) First of all, its very conception is an attempt to bring to fruition at last the exegetical findings on the thoroughgoing eschatological nature of the biblical message, all along the line from the prophetic and apocalyptic eschatologies of the Old Testament to the New Testament message of Jesus and the early church. What has been largely confined to biblical monographs, written in the key of historical research, is now the point of departure and "thermal current" of all dogmatic and ethical reflections, of all hermeneutical and methodological procedures.

(2) It seems to me to have touched the nerve endings of that "modern man" who has become, for good or ill, an invisible partner in contemporary theology without whom we cannot get along. The secular translation of the religious ques-

[42] *Ibid.*

tion today is: what about our hope for the future?[43] Modern man is not interested in the past, certainly not for its own sake. Only as it has any bearing on his future will he bother with his past. Modern man is also restless and dissatisfied with his present; he has become *homo viator*; the world for him is *mundus viator*. He is tired of theories about the world. He intends to change the world. If there is one word which is constantly appearing in the titles of major addresses and conferences around the world, under religious and secular auspices, it is the word "change." Here is a theology which takes change seriously, and lays bare the foundations and aims of the Christian vision of change. It is a vision guided by hopes suspended between the historical promises of God and his coming kingdom.

(3) I think this theology offers a new angle of approach to the doctrine of God, which seems to have become encased in a conceptual system of propositions that resulted from the encounter of the gospel with Hellenistic metaphysics. Much rearguard action has been devoted to updating this metaphysic, to bring it in line with a modern sense of reality and consciousness of history. The zeal for this attempt is rapidly flagging, even in Roman Catholic theology, which has had so many of its treasures stored away in the Thomistic synthesis. Leslie Dewart's revolutionary book *The Future of Belief*, which speaks for a growing edge in Roman Catholic thought, has numerous affinities with this German theology of hope, and seems to me to be a symptom of a trend that is only barely beginning. There is a parallel also in that the thought of the French Marxist, Garaudy, serves as a stimulus to Dewart's theology similar to Bloch's influence on Moltmann and Pannenberg.

(4) Finally, this theology, in making contact with modern

---

[43] I agree with Karl Rahner's picture of the modern man in "Christianity and the 'New Man'," *The Christian and the World* (New York: P. J. Kenedy & Sons, 1965). "It cannot be doubted . . . that the spiritual situation of man today is essentially determined by the blueprint of the new man of the future. The man of today feels himself to a larger extent to be someone who must overcome himself in order to prepare himself for a new and quite different future. He feels himself to be someone whose present can be justified only as the condition of his future" (p. 207).

man in a way that is deeply grounded in what is biblically central, can help the church to escape its ghettos in two directions. It places before the church its divine appointment as mission in world history. At a time when there are so many signs that the church doesn't know what its mission is in the world, whether it be conversion of individuals, dialogue with other cultures or religions, or simply Christian presence in showing a vague concern for others, this theology is a "hermeneutic of Christian mission" in the world.[44] Secondly, its eschatological centeredness provides a needed dynamic and direction for the social ethical involvement of the church in the penultimate questions of modern society. There is no question that the church is becoming involved in the public and political issues of modern society, willing to cooperate with humanists and all so-called "men of good will." The church needs a "practical eschatology or eschatological praxis."[45] What is the relation between church and society, between eschatology and ethics, between the kingdom of God and history? Moltmann lays down a challenge: "A dialogue with these humanists who are seeking a 'future without God' can become a suasion to Christians to cease seeking 'God without his future.' In such a meeting of ideologies, the aspect of Christian eschatology which is concerned with this world must be emphasized, for the very purpose of showing the significance of that aspect of Christian hope that transcends this world."[46]

[44] J. Moltmann, *Theologie der Hoffnung*, pp. 250 ff.
[45] J. Moltmann, "Die Kategorie *Novum* in der christlichen Theologie," *op. cit.*, p. 256.
[46] J. Moltmann, "Hope Without Faith," *op. cit.*, p. 28.

Appearance as the Arrival of the Future

Wolfhart Pannenberg

"A New Trio Arises in Europe," an article by John B. Cobb, Jr., which appears in *New Theology No. 2* (1965), discusses the work of theologians Gerhard Ebeling, Heinrich Ott, and Wolfhart Pannenberg. According to Cobb, Pannenberg is the most "radically original" of the three: "He finds himself free to set aside principles that have been commonly assumed by all schools of German theology since Ritschl. His attitude toward theological problems shares the freedom of the Anglo-American scene to reconsider all assumptions and always be ready to start over again." A prominent voice in the new future-oriented theology, Pannenberg in the following essay argues against the traditional philosophical view "which sees what appears in the appearance only as a timeless universal." In opting for a view that takes adequate account of contingent events and "the arrival of what is future," he employs as a paradigm the ministry of Jesus, in which "the futurity of the Reign of God became a power determining the present." The essay, based on a presentation before the Philosophical Society in Basel in 1965, was published in the June 1967 *Journal of the American Academy of Religion.**** Dr. Pannenberg is Professor of Systematic Theology at the University of Mainz. The most recent of his numerous writings is *Grundzuge der Christologie.*

AMBIGUITIES OF LANGUAGE often indicate a problematic subject matter. That is the case with the word "appear" (*erscheinen*). When I say that an acquaintance (or someone with whom I was previously unacquainted) "appeared" to me, in order to speak with me, the meaning is: he came to me, he showed up in my habitat, perhaps at my home. He did not only seem (*scheinen*) to be there; he

* 1010 Arch Street, Philadelphia, Pa. 19107.

really was there. When something appears to us, it does not only seem to be with us, it actually is present. Appearance and existence are here very closely connected. But on the other hand, my acquaintance still exists even when he does not appear to me. Whether that would still be true if he appeared nowhere—whether my acquaintance would then still exist—that is, of course, questionable. But that question I will set aside. In any case, the existence of my acquaintance is not the same as his appearing to *me*. Thus, we differentiate between what something is in and for itself (or also for others) and the way it appears to and for us. This distinction is already present in the word "appear." What appears to me is precisely that which is, in and for itself, something more than it is as it presently appears to me. In this sense, according to Kant, the idea of appearance points back to a being-in-itself which is different from the appearance, since it would be nonsense to say that there is appearance without there being something to appear.[1] What is meant is not only that appearance has a concrete form. Rather, the concept of appearance implies that in it something manifests itself which is something more than that part of it which appears. The ambiguity of the word appearance is thus based on the relation of appearance to being. On the one hand, appearing and existence mean the same thing. But on the other hand, appearance, taken literally, points to a being transcending it. How are these two sides of the word's meaning to be united? Or do they fall totally asunder, so that the unity of the word connecting the two is only an insignificant coincidence?

I

With this question we turn to the history of thought about appearance. Since Parmenides at the latest, and especially under the powerful influence of Plato, the tendency to separate appearance and being has been dominant. The world of appearance, of *doxa*, is considered a mixture of being and nonbeing, of a lesser order than the being which exists in itself.

[1] Kant, *Critique of Pure Reason*, Preface to Second Edition.

In Platonism this latter being is depicted as the being of the ideas, which is reflected only imperfectly in the appearances and which remains inaccessible to sense perception, although the understanding grasps it. This being is held to exist in itself, eternally and unchangeably; the appearances in which it is reflected add nothing to it. Of course, it must be mentioned that this interpretation, which was expressed most decisively by Plato himself in the *Phaedo* and the *Republic*, does not exhaust the full profundity of his thought about the idea. Originally, the appearance was included in the idea as the perceived form, as especially Julius Stenzel has shown; the idea is precisely the form shining through *in* the appearance, so that, for example, the idea of beauty is experienced in what is beautifully shaped. From such a point of departure the complete separation of the idea from its appearance could only be a fringe possibility for Plato. And he himself showed it to be untenable in his *Parmenides*: If idea and appearance are separated from each other, then another idea is needed to account for the relatedness of the first two. But if this new idea as such is again separated from those things (idea and appearance) for whose similarity it is supposed to account, then a further idea is required, etc.[2] The separation between idea and appearance, the divorce so strongly attacked by Aristotle, was recognized by Plato himself to be untenable. Of course, that Plato overcame it can hardly be asserted. The influence upon him of the Eleatic understanding of being seems to have been too strong for that, especially the notion that true being, in its immutability, *needs* nothing beyond itself for its being.[3] Thus, for the idea, understood as true being, the relation to the appearance must be a matter of indifference, and in this self-sufficiency of the idea the separation from its appearances continues to exist. Even Aristotle, as his notion of substance shows, was not able completely to escape the suggestion of the Eleatic understanding of being. So it becomes understandable that the separation of true being from its appearance, the precedence of self-sufficient ideas or substances reposing in them-

2 *Parmenides*, 132 (the idea of greatness and of great things), 133.
3 Diels, *Fragment*, 8, 33.

selves over the phenomenal reality of sense experience, remained a dominant motif in the history of thought whenever the notion of appearance became thematic.

Against this background it was of great significance when the relation between essence and appearance came to be recognized as reciprocal. In order to find the reciprocity of this relationship explicitly formulated, we must take a broad leap over the whole history of the relation of essence and appearance. We find it so formulated by Hegel. According to him, the relation is such that the appearance not only points back to the essence appearing in it as to its truth. The reverse is also true: "Essence *must* appear. Seeming (*Das Scheinen*) is the definiteness, through which essence is not mere being, but essence, and fully developed seeming is appearance. Essence is thus not behind or beyond appearance, but existence is appearance by virtue of the fact that it is essence which exists."[4] To understand fully Hegel's statement here we would have to go into the changes that the concept of essence had undergone from Plato's notion of true being and Aristotle's category of *ousia* down to Hegel. Only out of the dissolution of the Aristotelian concept of substance could the strange situation become more understandable, that in Hegel's statement essence is set over against being, rather than itself being directly depicted as true being. Be that as it may, the statement that essence must appear is still intended by Hegel in the sense of an ontological precedence of essence over its appearance, even if the essence first comes into view by going behind the world of being into its ground, since being is now characterized as appearance of a ground that differs from it, i.e., the essence. Appearance thereby presents itself as mere reflection, as self-alienation of the essence, which, in the process of Hegel's logic, is to be more precisely defined as concept and idea. Since the Hegelian idea is thought of as timeless, logical structure—being therein similar to the timeless being of Parmenides—appearance in Hegel's philosophy (contrary to his insight into the reciprocity of the relation of essence and appearance) is again reduced to the

[4] Hegel, *Enzyklopädie*, 131.

status of the nonessential. Instead of—as Hegel asserted—the idea existing only in the appearances, it in fact finds in the appearances of religion or history merely subsequent illustrations of its fixed, logical structure.

The separation of being (or essence) and appearance can then evidently be avoided only if one approaches being and essence by beginning with appearance even more decisively than Hegel himself did. Kant offers a beginning in this direction with his thesis that all functioning of the understanding is related to appearance. However, since he presupposed the traditional opposition of the thing in itself and the appearance, Kant meant to express with this thesis the fundamental limitation of all human knowing. Nevertheless, his thesis could lead to thinking of appearanceness as the fundamental characteristic of being itself. To my knowledge, Heinrich Barth has taken this course more consistently than anyone else. Barth allows being in the sense of subsistence only to appearance[5] and rejects every "reduction of the appearance to non-appearing being-in-itself."[6] Finally, he understands the "something" that appears, and apart from which (according to Kant) appearance cannot be thought, as the eidetic content in the act of appearing itself, which forms the theme of the *interpretation* of the appearance. The statement that the meaning of the appearance (which is, in its actuality and contingency, already presupposed) is expressed in the *eidos*,[7] reverses the traditional interpretation of the relation of *eidos* and appearance. The appearing as existence takes priority over all notions of essence. Barth's understanding of appearance accordingly reveals itself as bound up with the post-Hegelian situation, in which the priority of "being-there," of existence, over against all "whatness," all eidetic structures, has been repeatedly affirmed. When it is not limited to anthropology, this priority agrees, albeit remotely, with the Anglo-Saxon tradition of empiricism. Over against modes of thought that take what

[5] Heinrich Barth, *Philosophie der Erscheinung*, II, p. 617.
[6] *Ibid.*, p. 437 (against Kant).
[7] *Ibid.*, p. 617.

exists in its pure facticity as the point of departure, Barth's orientation in terms of phenomena, his view of existence as what appears,[8] proves itself superior by the fact that the notion of appearing simultaneously comprehends both the act of coming-into-appearance and the "something" that appears, thus the eidetic or essential element.

Heinrich Barth's new interpretation of the notion of appearance opens the way for the contingency of events, for the historicity of all experience, in so far as its occurrence is always presupposed in the interpretation of its content. Nevertheless, the interpretation of the contingent appearances is not limited to the sphere of events, but goes beyond it. Interpretation can take place only by going beyond the event that gives rise to the interpretation. In so far as this is true, the "something" that appears cannot be thought of as totally exhausted in the act of appearing. It is precisely and only for this reason that the characterization of the existing as *appearance* can be justified. In going beyond the event in the process of its interpretation, a difference arises anew (and in a new sense) between appearance and being, between appearance and essence.

This going beyond the appearance in its interpretation can be clarified by reference to very old themes, which are, not accidentally of course, also Socratic themes: In saying *what* appears in the individual appearance, a something is always named that appears not only here, but elsewhere as well. By virtue of this generality (however it is to be interpreted), the *eidos* transcends the individual appearance in which it is encountered.

Connected with the possibility of manifold appearances of one and the same *eidos* is the fact that it exhausts itself in none of its appearances. There always remain other ways in which "the same" *eidos* could appear. One could draw from this the completely unplatonic consequence that the *eidos* contains in itself an element of indeterminacy beyond what can be known of it from its appearance or from a plurality of such appearances. Yet, in any case (and this is only the other side of the

[8] Or "emerges" (*ibid.*, p. 633 f.).

same thing), the individual appearance always presents itself as only a partial realization of the possibilities of the
eidos appearing in it. The work of art seems to be an exception to this rule. In the harmony of part and whole that
exists in the work of art, the difference between essence and
appearance is, in a certain sense, overcome. This is the basis
of the perfection of the work of art. But in everyday reality
such harmony is not found. Here the multiplicity of appearances is the sign of the imperfection of each individual one.

So far we have seen that neither the separation of true
being and appearance nor the thesis of their identity can be
maintained without turning into the respective opposite.
From the *separation* of idea and appearance, or essence and
appearance, we are directed to the fact that they belong together. But with the assertion of the identity of the appearance and the existence of the appearing something, the difference between appearance and essence breaks out anew,
because the interpretation of that something which appears
unavoidably goes beyond the event of its isolated appearance.
Now that the theses of the separation and of the identity of
appearance and true being have both been shown to be one-
sided, the question is raised of whether the unity of the
identity and non-identity of appearance and being is acces-
sible to a more penetrating description.

II

The theologian may be excused for introducing a theological example at this place in the train of thought. This is not
done to silence the intellectual question with an authoritative
answer. Rather, the example may directly contribute to a
better understanding of the difference and the unity of appearance and that which appears.

The well-known and controversial problem of the relation
of the futurity and presence of the Reign of God in the
ministry of Jesus seems to me to be relevant for illuminating
the unity and difference of appearance and that which appears. In the oldest layers of the New Testament traditions
of Jesus are sayings that speak of the presence of the Reign

of God in the ministry of Jesus. These stand alongside sayings that differentiate the Reign of God as something future from the present ministry of Jesus. Whether and how both groups of sayings are to be reconciled is today a major exegetical question. I myself find most convincing the arguments of those exegetes who do not opt in favor of one of the two sides, and do not unravel the difficulties by eliminating one group of opposing sayings as unauthentic, but rather seek the uniqueness of the message of Jesus precisely in this juxtaposition of seemingly opposing sayings. But how is such juxtaposition to be understood? In the sense of a future extension and completion of that which has broken in in the present? I prefer the opposite view: that in the ministry of Jesus the futurity of the Reign of God became a power determining the present. For Jesus, the traditional Jewish expectation of the coming Reign of God on earth became the decisive and all-encompassing content of one's relation to God, since the coming Reign of God had to do with the coming of God himself. Thus, obedience to God, with the complete exclusiveness of the Jewish understanding of God, became turning to the future of the Reign of God. But wherever that occurs, there God already reigns unconditionally in the present, and such presence of the Reign of God does not conflict with its futurity but is derived from it and is itself only the anticipatory glimmer of its coming. Accordingly, in Jesus' ministry, in his call to seek the Kingdom of God, the coming Reign of God has already appeared, without ceasing to be differentiated from the presentness of such an appearance. The divine confirmation of this matter, which came to Jesus' disciples through the Easter appearances, was the basis for the later Christian mode of expression, that God himself had uniquely and definitively appeared in Jesus without the difference between Jesus and God himself being thereby dissolved. The later christological doctrine speaks appropriately of the deity of Jesus, which nevertheless, as that of the "Son," remains different from that of the Father. This, in the final analysis, is still a matter of the interpretation of the "appearance" of God, of the presence of his Reign, in the ministry of Jesus. The difference of the Son from the Father, to which the christological doctrine holds fast, corresponds to the continuing difference in the message of Jesus between the futurity of the Reign of God and its presence in Jesus' ministry. And just as the future, precisely in its abiding difference from the present, is the basis for the present efficacy of God's Reign (and thus for its entrance into the present), so is the deity of Jesus himself, as that of the "Son," based precisely on Jesus' holding fast to the difference between God the Father and himself. Jesus did not raise the claim of divine authority for his own person—as his opponents evidently misunderstood him. Rather, he subjected himself totally to something different from himself, which he called "the Father," to God's coming Reign; only so was the coming Reign of God—God himself—already present in him. The difference between Jesus' present and the Father's future was ever again actualized in the surrender of the man Jesus to the coming Reign of God that he proclaimed, in so far as it was the future of another. Jesus pointed away from himself; therefore, the interpretation of that which appeared in him must go beyond the appearance of Jesus, to God, whom his message concerned. For this reason any mixing of the divine and human in the event of the appearance of God in this man is in error. And yet, precisely in Jesus' *pointing away* from himself to God's future did this future as such become present in and through him. The appearance of God in this man, which transcends his finite existence, means, just because of this, an existence of God in him, a oneness of God with him. The coming-to-appearance of God in Jesus has thereby a different meaning from the epiphanies of gods in human or animal form, of which we hear, e.g., in the history of Greek religion. There, any particular form of the appearance, being replaceable, remains external to the essence of the deity, just as in Plato or Parmenides, its appearance remains non-essential to true being.[9] In the ministry of Jesus, on the contrary, the God of Israel, the future of his

[9] Is there perhaps expressed in this a devaluation, which is quite widespread in mythical thinking, of the profane, everyday reality, as opposed to that primordial reality, which is spoken of in myth and carried out in the cult in order to draw profane existence, which is unholy in itself, into it?

Reign, comes definitively to appearance once. He manifested himself in this single event conclusively and for all time, and just for this reason only once. This is how the later ecclesiastical doctrine of the Incarnation expressed the matter, over against all Hellenistic notions of an epiphany. The finality of Jesus' ministry is based on its eschatological character, on the fact that through it the ultimate future of God's Reign becomes determinative of the present and therefore becomes present. Appearance and essential presence are here one. Is not this character of the appearance of God in Jesus—as opposed to the different religio-historical background of the Platonic-Parmenidean relation between appearance and true being—also relevant for considering the problem of appearance in general?

Of course, little would be gained if without further ado we tried to abstract a general concept of appearance from the way in which God came to appearance in Jesus of Nazareth. In so proceeding one would merely arrive at theological postulates for which he could, at most, try to claim general validity. We would rather ask whether our theological example throws light on certain, perhaps otherwise hidden, sides of the general philosophical problem of appearance. The pursuit of this question can be sufficiently motivated by the fact that in Christian reflection on the appearance of God in Jesus of Nazareth the two elements are united which have again and again broken apart in philosophical reflection, although they are both suggested when appearance is discussed, i.e., the effective presence of what appears in the appearance, and its transcendence of the individual appearance. In the idea of the revelation of God in Jesus of Nazareth both are combined: God is completely and conclusively present in this individual man, and yet he remains different from him; in fact, it is just as the One who is different from Jesus that God is in him. We have seen that this unity of the seemingly mutually exclusive elements is understandable (and grounded) in the way that God's Reign is still future in relation to the ministry and message of Jesus and yet, as future, is present in it. Does the connection of identity and difference in the relation of being (or essence) and appearance have something to do with the temporality of this relation? And does that which appears in the appearance thereby present itself in the mode of futurity?

III

If we look at the beginnings of Greek philosophizing, it can well be said that Heinrich Barth has rightly described the theme of appearance as already the theme of the Ionian philosophers of nature. This judgment seems to me to be confirmed precisely through the structure of the quest for the *archē*, in which Heinrich Barth found the point of departure for the ontological "reduction" of appearance to semblance (*Schein*).[10] In going beyond the immediately experienced multiplicity in the quest for its common ground, all that is achieved at first is that the element of difference between appearance and appearing essence, which is constitutive for the appearance as such, receives its due. That things "are" different "fundamentally" (i.e., in their ground) in contrast to what they "seem" to be—is this not the basic conviction of every view that experiences reality as appearance, as opposed to a superficial empiricism content with what is immediately observable? But this conviction of fundamental difference is not enough to distinguish the Ionian thinkers from the experience of existence that found its expression in myth. For the mythical intuition also saw something deeper in that which is immediately visible. The intuitive certainty of this vision, which grasps precisely in the phenomenon what the things "fundamentally" are, did not, of course, seem to the Ionian philosophers of nature to be a possibility. What the true nature of the "ground" is had become questionable. Different answers were given. By becoming questionable the phenomena had already lost their transparency to their deeper ground. In so far as the philosophical answers now named the one ground, to which, however, the phenomena are not transparent, the "possibility of a devaluation of the

10 Heinrich Barth, *Philosophie der Erscheinung*, I, p. 10.

appearance" arose.[11] It is thus implicitly presupposed that the ground has always been there, so that the phenomena really—if they were not deceptive semblance—would have to set the viewer free to see through them to the ground present in them. Parmenides is the first to affirm the present givenness of the ground in a reflective way, in that the "is," being absolutely self-identical and unconditionally present, is accorded the function of the *archē*, as the common and unifying element of everything that is.[12] Since the "is" is absolutely self-identical and one, and as such is present, everything manifold and changeable becomes deceptive semblance. This devaluation of the phenomena into mere semblance does not yet follow from the difference of the ground from the phenomena in which it appears, but only from the situation where the phenomena no longer show what they already are "fundamentally." When "in ground" the only true being is already present, then the phenomena, in their difference from the ground, can only be considered deceptive concealment.

In Parmenides, therefore, the future has no place in the understanding of appearance. It is different with the second root of the classical philosophy of appearance, which confronts us in Plato. The Platonic idea points, on the one hand, back to the Parmenidean understanding of being, but its other and original root lies in the Socratic quest for the good in the life of the *polis*, and thus for ἀρετή, the true virtue, which knows the good and the useful, and acts accordingly. An element of futurity is contained in the notion of the good. In so far as everyone strives for the good and the useful, as is said in the *Gorgias*, it is clear that no one already finds himself in its possession; rather, he hopes to attain unto it. Thus, in the essence of the good, as that which is striven for, there is something future. This is confirmed by the famous Platonic expression in the *Republic* that the good is to be thought of as transcending what exists (ἐπέκεινα τῆς οὐσίας). Of course, the transcendence of the good is

---

[11] *Ibid.*, p. 11.
[12] Whatever else the *archē* may be, it must in any case be *being*, in order to be the origin and the unity of all things (ὄντα).

not there based on the fact that striving is a going beyond that which is presently given, but on the transcendence of the cause (the ideas as true being) over that which is caused by it. But causality itself (αἰτία) is, for Plato, connected with striving.

Now if we, with Julius Stenzel, understand the Platonic idea as the full form of the goodness and virtue of the things in question, which it "imitatively" strives to attain, then it is clear that the Platonic understanding of the relation of idea and appearance includes, from its Socratic background, a relation to the future. And this is not a relation of visible things to just any sort of future, but to their essential future, to their "good." The idea of the good might then perhaps be understood in a precise sense as the "idea of the ideas," that is, it in sum has as its content that which constitutes every idea as idea. Already the Socrates of the Platonic *Phaedo* could say, not only of the society, but also of the whole cosmos, that "the good and useful is that which connects and holds together" and thus fulfills the *archē*'s function of unifying the many.

In Plato's conception of the idea, of course, the Socratic motif of the good clashes with the Parmenidean conception of true being. Since the ideas are understood in the Eleatic sense as true being, the motif of futurity, which is present in the Socratic striving for the good, cannot lead to a new understanding of being. It is only as presently at hand that the Platonic ideas form that world of true being behind the real world which has so often been a source of reproach against Platonism. And it is with this world behind the real world that the notorious difficulties are introduced into the question of how the appearances can then participate in the ideas. For the original "ethical" question concerning the good there were no such difficulties: the good as the sought after, essential future was just as much connected to present things as it was different from them. In so far as the good as idea could be viewed in what was present, the arrival of its essential future was therein experienced.

To a certain extent the thought of Aristotle seems in our

questions, as in so many others, to be a renaissance of the Socratic mode of thought. In the Aristotelian connection of *eidos* and *telos*, the Socratic striving for the good (and the futuristic element implied therein) finds a new ontological formulation. The essence of a thing, its *eidos*, is the goal of its movement—at least of its natural, unforced movement. Thus, the yet unattained goal is present in an anticipatory way in the moved as entelechy, and this indwelling of the goal effects the movement toward the goal. For Aristotle, this was explicitly connected with the Socratic question about the good: "According to our doctrine, then," he says in the first book of the *Physics*, "there is, on the one side, something divine, good, desirable; on the other side, the opposite (privation, formlessness); and in between, something which by nature strives for the good."

The futurism of this Aristotelian analysis of movement is neutralized, however, by two notions. The first is the notion of self-movement, already conceived of by the later Plato. According to this doctrine the entelechy is not the anticipation of the *not yet* attained goal, but is the already present (*vorhanden*) germ, out of which the goal unfolds itself. This inner teleology, which reverses the relation of present and future, has robbed evolutionary thought until our day of the possibility of seeing what is new in each event as something really new. Even more decisive for Aristotle himself is the notion expressed in his *Metaphysics* that the goal of the movement, in order to be able to cause the movement, must already be somewhere. But if the movement brings forth nothing except what is already actual somewhere else, then nothing new can arise. Also, for Aristotle the realm of forms is timeless, i.e., unlimited presence. Thus, in Aristotle the Eleatic understanding of being prevailed once again. From this followed the Aristotelian downgrading of individual and contingent entities, which were not seen as coming from the future, but only negatively as non-essential. The Christian Aristotelianism of the Middle Ages saw itself driven to a re-evaluation here, since the Christian doctrine of creation ascribes to God the bringing forth of something new.

Here the contingency of the occurrence was positively understood as expressive of the freedom of the Creator. But the
coherence of contingency with an ontological priority of
the future was not reflected upon even here, so that in the
Christian scholastics the Aristotelian metaphysics of form
remained as an unrecognized and unconquered alien element.

Modern philosophy has dissolved the Aristotelian metaphysics of substantial forms, and dissolved it, indeed, into
appearance. However, since the primary qualities (the spatial
body) as well as the secondary qualities of sense perception,
and finally (in Kant) the substance itself, disappeared into a
general relativity, that which appears "receded" from the horizon of modern philosophy. Philosophy no longer succeeded
in thinking of what appears independently of the way in
which it appears. So only human experience, as the place of
the appearing itself, remained to determine the content of
what appears. When this is rightly reflected upon, the origin
of appearance can no longer be specified as a presently
existing being. But this did not lead to thinking of appearance
in its contingency as the happening of that which is future
(*des Zukünftigen*). Instead, Kant construed the appearing
content to be conditioned through the forms of our faculty
of knowledge. In their synthetic nature, these forms portray
constructions of the productive power of imagination, which
finds in experience what is not really present to be perceived
in the sensibly given, yet characterizes what appears in the
sensibly given. Thus, the productive imagination goes beyond what is primarily given in experience. But in thus going
beyond, where does it go? If we raise this question in view
of the way that modern subjectivity is related to its world
in general, which is, among other things, represented by
Kant's productive imagination, is it not then to be said that
the subjectivity goes beyond the given and alters it, in that it
makes *itself* into the future of its world, be it through technology or by the constructions of the imagination? Do we not
then have to understand the synthetic constructions of the
productive imagination (if we set aside Kant's hypothesis of
an unchanging structure of human experience) as *anticipa-*

tions of the essential future of what is given in appearance? Is it not only with this presupposition that we can possibly understand the miracle of the correspondence to objective reality and of the realizability of spontaneous human constructions? Inversely, if appearance were to be understood as something that happens out of the essential future of that which appears, then its interpretation with reference to *that which appears* would only be possible by an anticipation of the future, as this anticipation characterizes the creative subjectivity of the imagination. (It may be mentioned in passing that such anticipation remains in itself ambiguous, because it can misrepresent the essential future of the appearing reality as well as grasp it.)

IV

I must now interrupt this line of thought in the midst of such open questions and summarize. In the section above we have dealt with the question of whether the appearing reality is to be understood more as the appearance of something that always is or as the arrival of what is future. Both ways have their religio-historical backgrounds: the one coming from myth's orientation to primal time and the archetypical, the other from being grasped by an eschatological future. The first way is a well-beaten path and has been impressed on all our familiar habits of thought. The second way has until now been hardly considered. And yet, the beginnings of it are shown even in classical statements of the traditional understanding of being. There is much to be said in favor of orienting philosophical thinking to that which always is. Above all, one may point to the possibility of forming general concepts and of making general structural statements that can be applied to the most diverse individuals and to changing situations. And yet, against this view is the truth that such a position, which sees what appears in the appearance only as a timeless universal, will inevitably underestimate or totally fail to recognize the importance for our experience of reality of the contingently new, of the individual, and of time.

Accordingly, it seems more appropriate to consider the universal as a human construction, which indeed proves itself useful by its ability to grasp a reality that is probably of quite another character, since it is conditioned by contingency and time.

The real basis of the universality of the abstractions we construct is perhaps to be sought in *repetition*, which plays such a large role in all events. Innumerable new events "repeat" earlier ones, although they always bring forth something new. The element of change remains unobservable in the overwhelming majority of events; thus, from a sufficiently broad perspective, one can speak of a repetition of *the same* structures in an indefinite multiplicity of events. And from this can arise the conception of that which is ever the same, of the eternal presence of the *eidos*. This interpretation is particularly suggestive because man, by means of such constructions, asserts himself over against the unfathomable number of contingent events. Is not man seeking an absolute confirmation of himself in the apotheosis of what always is? But, in reality, do not men succeed in producing such constructions, which must be made ever anew, only by exposing themselves to the uncertainty that lies in the contingent experience of reality and in the contingency even of one's own constructing? Must not man endure this lack of security, since he himself does not yet live in the final future, but rather is ever again surprised by what comes upon him from the future? Eternal presence could be the experience only of what is itself the final future.

Perhaps even the phenomenon of repetition can be approached in terms of the arrival of what is future: The contingently new becomes present event by taking up into itself, or by repeating, the existing situation, in so far as it is not able to transform it into a new synthesis. This is the basic idea of Alfred North Whitehead's philosophy of nature. The contingency of the event apparently includes an element of faithfulness. As is well known, the first discussion of repetition in connection with the idea of faithfulness was Kierkegaard's treatment of it in the human realm. But perhaps this notion has a wider significance. The arrival of what is future may be thought through to its conclusion only with the idea of repetition (which does not exclude the new), in the sense that in it the future *has* arrived in a *permanent* present.

If we reflect once more upon our theological example, upon the *definitive meaning* of the *appearance* of God's future in Jesus of Nazareth, in which God's *love* is revealed, then perhaps this can be said: The future *wills* to become present; it tends toward its arrival in a permanent present.

Creative Hope

Johannes B. Metz

Writing with compelling cogency about "productive and militant" Christian eschatology is Johannes B. Metz, who, though turning forty just this year, is already recognized as a highly original thinker and one of the outstanding exponents of the theology of hope. One of Metz's primary emphases is that Christian theology as guided by creative hope must be political theology, in the sense that it must be related to the forces in society which seek to transform it. "Eschatological faith and temporal commitment do not exclude each other, but rather imply each other. . . . For the salvation to which Christian hope is related is not simply or primarily the salvation of the individual . . . but salvation of the covenant, of the people, of the many." Father Metz, Professor of Fundamental Theology at the University of Münster, is a contributor to a variety of periodicals and encyclopaedias and is one of the editorial directors of the *Concilium* series of volumes in theology. First appearing in the April 1966 issue of the British publication *The Month** and then in the Spring 1967 issue of *Cross Currents*,** Father Metz's article is a somewhat shortened version of a lecture he gave at the 1965 Paulusgesellschaft meeting with Marxists.

CHRISTIAN FAITH HAS TO ANSWER FOR ITS HOPE TO CONTEMPORARY MAN WHOSE SENSIBILITY IS CHARACTERIZED BY BEING DIRECTED TO THE FUTURE; HE IS MORE CONCERNED WITH EFFECTIVE ACTION THAN WITH CONTEMPLATION.

A feature of the contemporary world is its concern for what is "new." This drive to the "new" has its effect in the contemporary revolution in the social, political and technical

* 114 Mount Street, London W. 1, England.
** 103 Van Houten Fields, West Nyack, N.Y. 10994.

fields. Modern humanity knows only one *fascinosum*: the future as the what-has-not-yet-been.

This new sensibility is, in other words, determined by what Kierkegaard called the "passion for the possible." Meanwhile, the force of tradition grows weak; the old quickly becomes out-of-date; the "golden age" is not behind us, but ahead of us; it is not remembered in dreams but rather creatively awaited from the future. The relationship to the past takes on more and more a purely aesthetic, romantic or archaic character or it depends on a purely historical interest which simply confirms that the past is over and done with. This modern consciousness has a purely historical relationship to the past, but an existential relation to the future. It frees man from the tyranny of a history concerned only with origins, and turns him towards a history conceived with ends.

The future is essentially a reality which does not yet exist, which has never been: the "new" in the proper sense of this word. The relationship to such a future cannot be purely contemplative and cannot remain in the order of representations, since representations and pure contemplation both refer to what has already come into existence or what still is. Rather, the relationship to the future is an operative one and the theory of this relationship is directed to effective action. In this approach to the future, man no longer experiences his world as a destiny imposed on him, as inviolable nature surrounding him, but rather as a "stone quarry" out of which he must build his own "new world." He transforms the world and fashions it into the setting of his own historical activity. The world depends on man and his technical activity and so it is a secularized world. The process called "secularization" and the contemporary primacy of the future are intimately connected with each other.

This primacy of the future in modern consciousness and modern understanding of the world has caused a growing crisis in the familiar religious concepts of Christian faith. The "world beyond" and "heaven above us" seem not only to be hidden but to have disappeared. (What is hidden can be powerful and close to us.) Slowly but surely the world "above us" has been brought within reach. It seems to have fallen into our hands and be at our disposition. It can no longer be thought of as "the lowest circle" in which we recognize the "numinous forecourt" of God. No longer do we directly discover in the world "traces of God," but rather the "traces of man" and his transforming activity. We seem to encounter in the world only ourselves and our own possibilities. The glow of the "world above" seems to have faded. What moves contemporary man most deeply is not any commitment to the "world above" but a commitment to the future. Modern man who seems so a-religious and disenchanted is open to the future as the one challenge to reach beyond himself.

All effective world views and humanisms in the East and the West are today directed to the future: We only have to think of Marxism and its theory of the classless society in a future which is to be brought about by the activity of man. The salvation sought—the successful and fulfilled humanity —is to be found not "above us" but "ahead of us." The modern critiques of religion, and especially that of the Marxists, can be reduced to one common factor; Christianity as well as religion in general is powerless when faced by the primacy of the future in modern sensibility. That is why this new sensibility often claims to be an instrument for the elimination of religious consciousness altogether and the inauguration of a post-religious age in which any concern for transcendence is dismissed as purely speculative and replaced by a practical attitude to the future.

What account does Christian faith give of itself in this situation? How does it answer for its hope (cf. 1 Pet. 3, 15)? Can it understand this situation in a way which does not exclude completely theological consciousness or reduce it to empty and formal paradoxes? Yes, it can—but under *one* condition: if faith is appalled at the unimportance of eschatology in its theology, if it is disturbed by the way the future has been forgotten in theology, which in the end goes so far that all modern theological discourse on the historicity of faith stresses only the relationship of the past to the present. Bultmann is an example of this along with all existential theology dependent on Heidegger. The so-called "existential interpretation of the New Testament" is understood as a representation of this historical message in the ever-present moment of decision.

What is our relation to the future? What theology has for so long unhealthily kept apart must be brought together again; are not future and transcendency linked in the biblical message of the Christian faith? Only then can faith be brought into dialogue with this new consciousness. Only then can it also ask critically: What is the origin of this primacy of the future which determines modern consciousness and to which the political, social and technical revolutions of our time bear witness? What is it based on?

CONTEMPORARY MAN'S ORIENTATION TO THE FUTURE AND HIS UNDERSTANDING OF THE WORLD AS HISTORY ARE THEMSELVES GROUNDED IN THE BIBLICAL FAITH IN GOD'S PROMISES.

On this position we can give here only a few hints. This direct reference to statements of Scripture is not arbitrarily made: it is based on the findings of recent exegesis. This, in its post-Bultmann phase, has brought out the inner unity and relationship between the Old and New Testaments, and has likewise stressed the fact that the Old Testament provides the background and the setting for the thought and expression of the New Testament.

Most recent research has shown that the word of revelation in the Old Testament is not primarily a word of information or even a word of address, nor is it a word expressing the personal self-communication of God, but is rather a *word of promise*. Its statements are announcements, its preaching is the proclamation of what is to come and therefore an abrogation of what is. The principal word of promise points to the future; it founds the covenant as the solidarity of those who look forward in hope, those for whom the world for the first time has a history ordained to the future—in contrast to the Greeks for whom the world appears as a consistent and closed cosmos.[1]

Central passages of the Old Testament reveal this touching sense of the "new," of the "not-yet"—again in contrast to the Greeks for whom the "not-yet" is the impossible, since there is for them "nothing new under the sun"; all that is to come is simply a variation on what has been, a renewal and consolidation of memories. History is for the Greeks only the indifferent return of the same thing within the fixed frame of the cosmos. The essence of history is the cycle, and history can be said in a sense to devour again and again its own children; nothing really new happens and the essence of history is basically nihilistic.

I stress this contrast between biblical and Greek ways of thinking, so as to bring out sharply the specific quality of the biblical understanding of the world and existence: as an historical process directed to God's promise, for whose fulfillment those who look forward to it in hope are responsible. Even the creation stories of the Old Testament are originally stories of promise, and faith in creation is faith in the promise. This eschatological horizon appears most clearly as the central point of God's self-revelation in Exodus 3, 14, which a modern exegete has taught us to translate: "I will be who I will be." The divinity of God reveals itself here as the dynamism of our future and not primarily as a being "above us" in the sense of an unhistorical transcendence. God is a "God before us." His transcendence is revealed as the power of our future.[2]

He is revealed as a future which is grounded in itself and belongs to itself—as a future which does not come into being out of the possibilities of our human freedom, but which calls our freedom to its historical possibilities. For only a future which is more than a correlative and a projection of our own possibilities can free us for something truly "new," for new possibilities, for that which has never been. Insofar

[1] Cf. the article, *"Welt,"* by J. B. Metz in Lexicon für Theologie und Kirche, X, 1023–1026.
[2] W. Pannenberg, "Der Gott der Hoffnung," in *Ernst Bloch zu ehren* (Frankfurt, 1965), *passim.*

as it relates human existence to the "new," biblical faith contains a revolutionary dimension.

In the message of the New Testament the forward-looking quality of biblical faith is in no way diminished. On the contrary, "belief in the nearness of the kingdom preached and inaugurated by Jesus produces such a concentration and stress on the future promised by God, that in contrast everything which was simply handed on or simply present lost its intrinsic meaning, and the future of God determined the present."[3]

It would be a mistake to think that after the Christ-event our future already is over and done with, as if after the birth of Christ there is no future to be realized but only one to be unfolded. On the contrary, the Christ-event gives added stimulus to attempts to shape the future. The preaching of the resurrection, which can never be separated from the preaching of the cross, is essentially a missionary preaching of promise. In obedience to it the Christian attempts to transform the world in the direction of that new world which is promised to him once and for all in Christ Jesus.[4] Creative expectation is the secret essence of Christian existence in the New Testament.

All this demands the development of theology as eschatology. Paul defines Christians simply as "those who have hope" (cf. Eph. 2, 22; 1 Thess. 4, 13). Christians must therefore develop eschatology in all parts of their understanding of faith. It must not be reduced to a *part* of Christian theology but must be understood radically: as the determining factor in all theological statements. The attempt to understand theology as anthropology is an important achievement of contemporary theology. Yet this anthropological theology, so long as it is not understood as eschatology, runs the risk of becoming unhistorical and out of this world. For it is only in the eschatological horizon that the world appears as a becoming reality whose development is entrusted to the freedom of men. Christology and ecclesiology must also be

[3] *Ibid.*, p. 212.
[4] J. Moltmann, *Theologie der Hoffnung* (Munich, 2nd edition, 1964), p. 173.

developed in the context of eschatology, or they run the risk of being reduced to a purely existential or purely cosmological system.

It would be tempting and important to show that the development of the so-called "secularization of the world" was only possible because the world was experienced and interpreted in the eschatological context of promise. In this context the world appears not as a complete and inviolable pre-established harmony, but rather as a becoming reality, which can be transformed through the free historical activity of men into a yet greater future. The universal transformation of the world through an offensive of human freedom upon it characterizes that process which we call secularization. But we must leave this question here and move on to our next thesis.

THE RESPONSIBILITY OF CHRISTIAN HOPE TOWARDS THE WORLD OF HISTORY CAN BE THEOLOGICALLY DETERMINED THROUGH THE IDEA OF "CREATIVE ESCHATOLOGY." THIS IMPLIES INTRINSICALLY A KIND OF "POLITICAL THEOLOGY."

The discussion and founding of this position can best begin with a reference to a thought-provoking opinion of St. Thomas Aquinas. He says in his scholastic language: Man has not an ultimate natural end *and* an ultimate supernatural end, he has only one single ultimate end, namely the future promised by God. In relation therefore to mankind's future one distinction disappears, which theology uses, and all too readily uses: the distinction between the natural and the supernatural. In relation to the future and the end to which history is moving, theology cannot be content with this distinction and cannot separate the natural future of the world and the supernatural future of faith and of the Church. The two dimensions converge in relation to the future. The hope which relates Christians to the future cannot ignore the world and its future.

The Christian hope should therefore be committed and be responsible for the one promised future, and therefore also for the future of the world. Faith does not hope for its own sake and the Church does not hope only for her own sake, but for the world.

The Church is not the goal of her own movement; this goal is the Kingdom of God. "The Church, if we rightly understand it, lives always from the proclamation of her own provisional character and her progressive historical surrender to the coming Kingdom of God towards which she moves like a pilgrim."[5] The hope to which the Church bears witness is not a hope which bears upon the Church herself, but upon the Kingdom of God as the future of the world. *Ecclesia est universale sacramentum spei pro totius mundi salute.* Thus the relationship of the Church to the world is not chiefly one of place but of time. The Church is not simply the not-world, she is that world of men who draw their stimulus and inspiration from the future promised by God and who call into question the world which is emerging from the present and human possibilities. She offers to the self-confident world with its hopes and dreams a liberation and a positive critique. For the Church looks towards that "new world," whose "newness" is not simply the planned product of our own potentialities which in the end would only lead to "the melancholy of fulfillment." The "newness" here rather corresponds to a promise which originally set in motion our search and our creative and active drive to the future.

How does the Church realize this mission for the future of the world? It cannot be achieved through pure contemplation, since contemplation by definition is related to what has become and what is now. The future for which the Church hopes for the world is rather something which is being formed and to be formed. And so the hope to which the Church commits herself for herself and for the world must be essentially creative and militant, and must be realized in a creative-militant eschatology. The goal of our eschatological hope, the heavenly-earthly Jerusalem, the promised city of God, is not simply ready-made ahead of us like a distant goal which would be already there, and simply hidden

[5] K. Rahner "Kirche und Parousie Christi," in Schriften zur Theologie VI (Einsiedeln, 1965), p. 351.

for the time being and for which we yearn in imagination. The eschatological city of God is still coming into being. And as we move forward to it in hope, we build it up, as collaborators in and not simply interpreters of a future whose driving force is God himself.

The constitution *On the Church* says: "The renovation of the world . . . is in a sense really anticipated in this world." The Christian is a collaborator in this promised kingdom of universal peace and justice. The orthodoxy of his faith must constantly be confirmed through the orthodoxy of his practice, his activity ordered to the last end; for the promised truth is a truth which must be "done" as St. John makes clear (cf. 3, 21). Christian eschatology is not simply an eschatology of the present, in which all passion for the future would be set aside in the making-present of eternity in the individual moment, however much this eschatology may have been developed in the theology of today, and however right it is in understanding the present as the permanent starting-point of eternity.

But neither is Christian eschatology an eschatology of passive expectation, for which the world and the present age would be like a kind of waiting room, in which man would have to sit around bored and uncommitted—the more bored, the more hopeful—until the door to God's audience room is opened. Christian eschatology must be seen rather as a productive and militant eschatology. Christian hope is a home in which we—as Ernst Bloch has already remarked—"have not only something to drink but also something to cook." Eschatological faith and temporal commitment do not exclude each other, but rather imply each other.

The theology of the world which is guided by this creative militant eschatology cannot be developed in the style and with the categories of the older theological cosmology. Nor can the task be done in the style and with the categories of a purely transcendental personalistic or existentialist theology, which as far as this task goes remains too private.

The theology of the world is neither a purely objective theology of the cosmos nor a purely transcendental theology of personal existence, but rather and above all *political theology*—I grant that this expression could be misunderstood. The creative militant hope which commands such theology is essentially related to the world as society and to the forces in society which transform it. Such a theology must be concerned with the great political, social and technical utopias, with the modern promises of universal peace, universal justice and the universal liberation of man for which our society longs. For the salvation to which Christian hope is related is not simply or primarily the salvation of the individual—whether this is understood as the salvation of one's soul or as individual resurrection of the body—but salvation of the covenant, of the people, of the many: in a word salvation as "resurrection of the flesh," where "flesh" in contradistinction to "body" indicates, according to biblical usage, interpersonal and social existence and characterizes the existence of man in the covenant. This "salvation of all flesh" is found originally and not subsequently in the concrete social dimension of human existence, and it aims at a universal peace and final justice (cf. II Pet. 3, 13), so that "tears are dried and there shall be an end to death and to mourning and crying and pain" (Apoc. 21, 4). This dimension of the creative hope of salvation in Christianity seems to have been overlooked in recent times. The importance and the insistent emphasis of modern theology on the subjectivity of the believer, on his need to say a personal "Yes" to salvation, brought with it at the same time a dangerous tendency to turn salvation into a private reality, and this affected the understanding of salvation in general. This transformation of salvation into a private matter through transcendental, personalistic or existential factors, must be overcome through the working out of a theology which we have characterized with the phrase "political" theology.

THE CREATIVE MILITANT ESCHATOLOGY IS NOT AN IDEOLOGY OF THE FUTURE.

This creative eschatology is essentially distinct from any militant optimism. It does not canonize the progress we are bringing about. It is and remains the expression of a hope—

against all hope—which we set among the self-erected idols of our secularized society. Three remarks on this point:

1. Christian hope is not the attempt of reason to pierce through the future and so to rob it of mystery. The man who hopes is not making the irritating claim to know more about the future than others. Christian eschatology therefore is not an ideology of the future. It values precisely the poverty of its knowledge about the future. What distinguishes it from the ideas of the future both in East and West is not that it knows more but rather that it knows less about the hoped-for future of mankind, and that it stands by the poverty of this knowledge. "By faith Abraham obeyed the call to go out to a land destined for himself and his heirs and left home without knowing where he was to go" (Heb. 11, 8).

2. The creative hope of the Christian does not seek to outbid by its optimism all forms of human alienation or the "pain of finiteness," nor to unmask them as provisional. It concentrates rather on those forms of human alienation which can in no way be removed through any economic and social transformation of situations and destiny, however perfect they may be. For example: the experience of guilt and of evil, or the experience which theology describes with the word "concupiscence."

Here we have an experience of self-alienation which plainly cannot be overcome simply by social and economic means. For man always feels the discrepancy between the level on which he projects to live and that on which he in fact lives, between idea and existence. He constantly falls below the great experiences of his life and does not allow himself to be changed by them, but rather transforms them and levels them down to everyday banalities. As Camus put it: "It seems that great men are less disturbed by pain than by the thought that it does not last." It does not last because we are not equal to its claims and do not remain equal to its claims. In such and similar experiences we become aware of a situation of human self-alienation which cannot be removed or nullified by social, economic or technical progress. Christian hope strives to remain faithful to such experiences and precisely through them to realize all the painful breadth and depth of its hope against hope.

3. Finally Christian hope is aware of the greatest risk of all: It is aware of death, before which all glittering promises are threatened and grow dim. Christian hope has been called an anticipated practice for death, practice, that is, in a hope against all hope.

But even this movement of hope should not be narrowed down to an individualistic hope which forgets the world; it has lost its private character or should lose it. This too must take place with a glance on the world, on the world of our brothers, in the self-forgetting oblation of love for others, for the "least of the brethren," in selfless commitment for *their* hope.

For through our love of the community we overcome death in anticipation: "we know that we have passed over from death to life because we love the brethren" (1 Jn. 3, 14). Only one who loses his soul in this way will gain it. Christian hope draws to itself and overcomes the passion of death, which threatens our promises, as it accepts the adventure of brotherly love of the least—in imitation of Christ, whose being is not originally self-perfection, not a *reditio subjecti in se ipsum* but a "being for others" (Bonhoeffer).

Christian hope is creative imitation of this "being for others"; and so it is at the service of creative responsibility for the world.

God and the Supernatural

Leslie Dewart

Convinced that the classical understanding of God—dependent as it is on abstract, static Greek concepts of nature and being—has in our time ceased to be tenable, Leslie Dewart has sought to achieve a revolutionary reconstruction of the doctrine of God, a reconstruction which in effect "desupernaturalizes" the deity. The fruits of his effort are available in *The Future of Belief*, a work both widely acclaimed and widely controverted. But fortunately for those who like their theology in brief compass, that book's essence—if its author will pardon our using such a metaphysical term—is contained in an article which Dr. Dewart wrote for the February 10, 1967, issue of *The Commonweal*,* a special issue devoted to the "God" question. Dr. Dewart, whose other writings include a study of Cuba titled *Christianity and Revolution*, is Professor of Philosophy at St. Michael's College, University of Toronto.

THE CLASSICAL Christian concept of God has endowed him with transcendence of, and at the same time immanence in, creation. In part this has reflected an essential truth of Christian religious experience. But the specific meaning given to it by classical Christian speculation—transcendence and immanence being so understood that they were conceptually opposed to each other, yet mysteriously reconcilable in God himself—has reflected only a specific, contingent conceptualization of the Christian faith in the cultural forms of a specific, contingent historical situation.

In St. Thomas' metaphysical (hence, hellenistic) philosophy, for instance, this opposition was implicit in the twofold doc-

* 232 Madison Avenue, New York, N.Y. 10016.

trine that although "what the intellect first conceives is being and being-ness (*essentia*)," Being, He Who is, "is the most proper" name of God. God is so truly being that he is Being Itself—and yet, we learn the "name" being not in any way from God but from creatures. The doctrine of analogy tries to rationalize this with the assertion that, in effect, "names" learnt only from creatures are truly applicable to God if only we confess, as we apply them to God, that they are not actually applicable to God. But the attempt scarcely succeeds: we know that God is Being—yet we do not know what God is. This ancient contradiction has not been resolved by the claim of some neo-Thomists (both absurd and quite un-Thomistic, as Maritain has shown), that God has no whatness—that is, no essence, no being-ness—though he truly *is* Being.

But the real difficulty with this doctrine is hardly that it has created insoluble academic problems; it has rather to do with the growing inadequacies of the classical concept of God for the real-life needs of the Church. For despite original advantages this understanding of God has shared the fate of all conceptualizations of the Christian faith: its deficiencies have become increasingly apparent and, in the end, intolerable. Western Christendom's division against itself, its schizophrenic apostasy (so well described by Toynbee) from its own religion, the paradox that Western Christendom no longer professes as a whole the belief that even today continues to animate it culturally and to describe it historically—this is the best illustration of how the mere inadequacies of an originally adequate concept of God have been allowed, through lack of suitable redevelopment, to degenerate to a scandalous point.

Apologists may suggest, of course, that the unbelief of the modern Christian world has to do not with the inadequacies of Christian concepts but with the world's moral degeneration. There may well be some truth in the second part of the claim. But to suppose that modern unbelief is wholly attributable to moral failure is not self-evident—and we must be careful not to argue circularly that the modern world's unbelief proves its immoral character. Nor does this opinion take account of the increased moral sensibility of man as he has developed culturally—whether or not he has actually abided by the morality of which he has become increasingly conscious as he has become more civilized. Nor is this view easily reconciled with the largely intellectual character of some of the causes of unbelief—for instance, the typical scientific attitudes. Nor does this apology recognize that *some* of the world's moral reasons for disbelief in the Christian God are at least partly valid in concrete cases—for instance, among those of rebellion against inhumanities perpetrated, with utter sincerity, in behalf of God.

In any event, the inadequacies of the classical concept of God are borne out not so much by that part of Christendom that has ceased to believe, as by that which continues to do so. For the believing remnant of Christendom too, has schizophrenically divided itself against itself. It has managed to preserve orthodoxy, but only at the cost of severing faith from ordinary, everyday life. Thus, we *confess* the true God, both immanent and transcendent. But in real life we find it very difficult—often impossible—to *live* the contradiction, to "hold on to both ends of the chain, confident that the two are joined, out of our sight, in God himself." Impaled on a dilemma whose nature and reality we do not always recognize, we instinctively opt for the "safer" extreme. And so, our contemporary belief typically bears, in effect, only upon a transcendent God. We continue to believe in an immanent God, to be sure, and to do so sincerely—but only ineffectively. We confess it, but we do not *mean* what we confess.

This does *not* mean that by sin we deny practically our belief in God, or that we fail to live up to the moral requirements of what we actually believe. It means that there is a gap between what we simply *admit* to be true, and the truth we spontaneously *engraft* into our experience, our creativity and our collective life. The existence of this gap, I believe, is the only possible conclusion to be drawn from the history of the Church since the beginning of the modern world—and particularly from the Church's abdication of its responsibility to provide *effective* leadership to a mankind but recently embarked upon the task of consciously creating its own history (an abdication, I happily add, in some indeterminate measure withdrawn since Vatican II). For each different way—and there have been many—in which Christians have held the world in contempt, distinctively constitutes a living rejection of the immanence of God. Not only our readiness to convict the world of sin, sometimes prematurely and usually with indecent haste, but also our consignment of the world to perdition on account of whatever true, real and unrepented sin it may bear: what does this amount to, but to a living act of faith in the absolute absence of God from the world? What does it mean but that Christians have, in effect, believed that when man kills God, God does not rise again?

The classical concept of God has become *unviable*. It can no longer enter fully and integrally into the life of believers themselves. It is cold comfort to warm ourselves with the thought that we have avoided every naturalism, every scientism, rationalism and pantheism, if we have not effectively avoided every supernaturalism. Indeed, we have not even feared it as a grave danger: we have tended to assume that it is impossible to err in this direction. But the contemporary difficulties of the Christian faith suggest otherwise. Let us attempt to trace the difficulty to its root.

A Spiritual Kingship

The heart of the Christian Gospel was Jesus' proclamation that Israel's messianic hope had been realized in him: He, Jesus, was the Christ. But Jesus maintained that his advent had not merely realized the Jewish hope; it had in a sense also transcended it. He was indeed the expected King. But his kingship was not quite of the sort that had been expected: it was "not of this world," or of Israel alone. It was a spiritual and catholic kingship. Therefore, the *Christian* Kingdom of God had a distinctive character: it was not merely the morally ideal way of life anticipated by Judaism, but a new way of life not previously available to man. It was not simply a *better* way in which ordinary human existence could be exercised: it was a *new* way to be. This is why the Gospel proclaimed a New Covenant, a new age in man's relations with God. In this new age God offered to man the possibility of existing at a level of existence other (and indeed nobler and more perfect) than that which man *already* had. Hence, the "spiritual" Kingdom of God was no mere continuation of "fleshly" human life with but its evils and imperfections removed. It was literally a "new life." To have entered into it was truly to have been "born again." By baptism into the new Israel the Christian became a "new man," one who had "died" to the "flesh" and "risen with Christ" to the "spiritual life." Like St. Paul, every Christian could say: "with Christ I am nailed to the cross. And I live, now not I; but Christ liveth in me."

But it must be remarked that the "new life" was offered to man only through the saving events, the "mysteries" of the Incarnation and Redemption. The Christian Gospel of the "new life" supposed, in the first place, that the Kingdom instituted by the Christ Jesus differed from that expected by Israel only because the Christ of the Gospel was *not merely* a Christ. Jesus was no mere champion sent by God; he was the epiphany of God himself. Clearly, then, the Gospel implied a new self-revelation of God. In the New Testament God was not only the creator and protector of man but, more fundamentally, self-gift or self-communication: *Deus caritas est.* The Incarnation and the Redemption meant that God had *literally* given himself to man.

This affirmation had a twofold weight. In the first place, it is literally true that God *gives* himself to us. But it is also literally true that he gives *himself* to us. If so, when God, by manifesting himself to us in Jesus, reveals himself to us as self-communication, he reveals not simply what he is *for us*, but also what he is *for himself*. (Thus, the doctrine of the Incarnation and Redemption implied the doctrine of the Trinity: the different ways or "modes" in which God relates himself *to us* are the truly distinct—and even, in hellenic terms, separately "subsistent"—ways in which he is related *to himself*. This must be true if the God who comes to man in the Incarnation is "true God," with no part of his divinity held back from man—i.e., there are *only* three "persons" in the one divine nature of God). In brief, God's gift of himself to us is identical with his offer of the possibility of a "*new* life" over and beyond the life we *already* had. But why is it the possibility of a "new *life?*"

The existence every man *already* has when he is called by the Gospel is in a very real sense a gift *from* God. In fact, for the Christian, existence *means* most fundamentally this: God's original and gratuitous gift of being to being, God's uncaused gift to being of *itself.* But this gift from God is not God himself: it is being, existence. It is God's gift of being, not God's gift of himself. The difference between the "new life" and the "old" is not that only the first is a gift from God: existence means gift from God, and gift from God means existence. On the other hand, there is a difference between the "new life" and the "old": the "old" life is *already* had when the "new" is given. This is precisely what opens up the possibility that the "new life" be not merely a gift from God, but God's yet more gratuitous gift of himself. In other words, God's gift of himself and his offer of a "new life," are identical because his gift of himself to man is of the order of existence: it means that henceforth God lives within man. Therefore, when man *receives* God within himself he accepts God's offer to participate in the life of God himself.

Evidently, God cannot create a being without giving it being. Nothing forbids it: it is simply that to create being and to *give* being are the same. Thus, God need not create being—but if he does create being, *ipso facto* he gives it being. For instance, if man is a being, he *already* exists. But to be already existing is to *have* existence—which is not the same as to *have received*, that is, *accepted*, existence. The gift of that sort of existence which man already has when he is called by the Gospel, is a gift from God that can only be given: it cannot be received. This means that God can create man without giving him more than being: God need not give himself to man, even after man already exists. But if, on the other hand, God *does* give himself to man, then the gift is, in a true sense, the gift of a new mode of existence —but because man already exists, this mode of existence must be received, accepted, or else God cannot give himself to man.

In the idea that the root meaning of all existence is that of a gift from God, that there is no meaning to existence except that of being a gift from God, but that the existence man already has when called by the Gospel is (though truly given) a gift that cannot be actually received, for being does not already exist before it is given existence—in this idea we find the reason why, to the Christian faith, being as such does not acquire a necessary relation to God through creation, but remains always, even after it exists, totally contingent and historically factual. And even man, who is conscious of existence, who is existence aware of itself, cannot, simply as conscious being, *receive* existence from God unless God gives himself to him. But because he is present to himself man can *recognize* that existence is a gift he holds from God: this recognition is, by another name, the experience of the contingency of being *as such*. It is man's recognition that he holds existence gratuitously, without reason—"superfluously," if you wish—and that he truly holds it having never had the opportunity to turn it down before it was given.

To sum up: if *existence* is essentially the same as *gift from God*, the gift offered by God to a conscious being which already exists, is literally, not metaphorically, the offer of a new, additional level of existence. Conversely, this new mode of existence is, precisely as "new," as obtaining over and beyond the mode of existence already held by man, definable as participation in the life of God himself. This is possible only because God gives himself to us in his true reality: the "new man" lives, as such, by the life of God himself, a life gratuitously communicated to him by God himself. And since the "new man" lives, as such by the life of *Another* living in him, his "new life" is *not a substitute* for the "old" life—except in one most important respect. For it is clear that as to moral effects, the "new life" must indeed replace the old. Hence, the Christian loves—or should love—his neighbor for the love of God. This does not mean that he must love his neighbor in order to deserve God's love. It means that God's self-gift to man creates the *obligation*, and confers the efficient *power*, for man to rise to the historical occasion created by the events of the Incarnation and Redemption: the vocation to imitate God through his free decision to define himself, to reveal himself to himself in actual, conscious existence as self-communication, self-gift.

Needless to say, the Christian faith I have rendered above, as I hope, in fidelity to the spirit of the Gospel but in concepts which reflect contemporary experience, could have been rendered during the formative centuries of Christian dogma, or even during the Scholastic period, only in a hellenic conceptual form. This was, of course, not only legitimate (and, in any event, unavoidable) but also most advantageous for the Christian faith. (For instance, the Trinitarian formulation of the novel Christian belief in God was made possible by the adoption—and, to be sure, the adaptation—of hellenic philosophical categories.) But this historical development also contained potential difficulties which, as they appeared, should have been disarmed. Unfortunately, circumstances conspired. In the end, they were compounded instead.

As has been implied above, every conceptualization of the Christian belief in the "new life" must be relative to a prior conceptualization of the "old." Gentile Christianity, which as a whole was culturally hellenistic, could not have conceived the "old" existence, the life that man already has when he is called to "conversion" and "rebirth," except as a *natural* one. And this, of course, had corresponding consequences for its understanding of the nature of the "new life."

To the Greek mind nature accounted intelligibly for the actions of a natural being only in terms of an inner necessitation. For every being acts strictly in accordance with what it is—and a being is what its essence determines it to be. But what a being is essentially, is that which it is necessarily in order to be intelligible—on the assumption, following Parmenides, that intelligibility was the condition of the possibility of existence. (Indeed, it was identical with that possibility: "that which can be and that which can be thought are the same.") Nature, therefore, accounted *exhaustively* for a being's operations, since a being's essence accounted for what it was necessarily as intelligible and, therefore, as being. Free human actions, for instance, were both intelligible and possible only because they were *natural* operations. They were free not because they were unnecessitated (which would have made them unintelligible and hence impossible), but because they were *self*-necessitated. But this implied that free human actions could proceed *only* from human nature: they could be attributed only to that which (by definition) could be the only intrinsic principle of human operations—namely, human nature. Conversely, any principle other than nature could be the source of human operations only as an extrinsic principle of necessitation—and this was (by definition) a source of *violence*. In short, human behavior was either necessitated naturally—in which case it was free—or else it was necessitated from without—in which case it was coerced.

Grace and Freedom

It is instructive to note that the problem of grace and freedom was preceded by a period during which Christian speculation was bent upon maintaining a truer and more radical idea of human freedom than that of contemporary philosophy—and that this was conceptualized, however, in terms of maintaining the autonomy of nature. Christian thought easily apprehended its fundamental opposition to the Greek philosophical attitude towards the human situation, particularly that of the Stoics and Epicureans. Hence, it was bound to emphasize the utter reality and puissance of man's freedom, and the benevolence of a God who did not subject man to Fate. Christians admitted that there was a Providence, quite as the Stoics said. But Pro-vidence was not the fore-seeing power that frustrated man's freedom; it was not the supreme principle of natural necessitation, indifferent to man and human striving, to which man must, however unhappily, intelligently submit under pain of greater unhappiness still. Providence was rather God's wise, benevolent, loving and helpful guidance of creation towards its final achievement. But when this doctrine, not illogically, issued in the conclusions of Pelagius, it was necessary on the contrary to emphasize that the life of grace (implying, for instance, a call to an end that man could not merit or achieve by nature) could not be brought about by the efficiency of the operations posited by human nature as such. Otherwise the life of grace would have been indistinguishable from the state of human perfection to which Stoic and Epicurean philosophy naturally led through intellectual and moral *askesis*. But to emphasize this, once the Greek conception of nature was assumed, was in effect to emphasize that in a very real sense Providence *was* a sort of Fate. Man, therefore, was in a sense truly fated or predestined. Having accepted the terms in which the problem naturally posed itself to Christianity's hellenic mind, Christian thought doomed itself to assert thereafter that *somehow* man was both free and predestined, that God was *somehow* the cause of Fate and nevertheless the friend of man.

The *somehow* has never been satisfactorily explained. This would not have been too unfortunate if it had been actually possible for Christian thought to "hold on with equal firmness to both ends of the chain." And the process was far from complete when St. Augustine wrote his last anti-Pelagian word. If, to repeat, one can understand the "new life" of Christian belief only in relation to one's prior understanding of the "old," then the assumption that the "old" life was a "natural" one potentially contained more than the foregoing problem of the opposition between grace and freedom. It also implied that any reconciliation of the two should be based upon an understanding of the "new life" as functioning in essentially the same way as nature did, albeit without actually being an integral part of nature. The "new life" was not a substitute for nature—on the other hand, it was not unnatural. Conversely, it was non-natural—but nonetheless it was somewhat like nature. Its nature, as it were, was that of a nature which was not natural. Hence, it was a sort of second nature, a nature over and above human nature. It was, in the Scholastic expression devised *ad hoc*, man's *super-nature*. The "new life" communicated by God was a *super-natural* life.

The supernatural life of grace was, therefore, truly a sort of nature. It was, to be sure, a *super*-nature. It was, nonetheless, a (super) *nature*. Therefore, to the extent that the life of grace became a super-*natural* life, it was no longer identical with man's participation in the life of God living within him. It would have been unthinkable, of course, actually to deny that man did so participate. But the "new life" was not itself such participation: it was the *means* whereby such participation could obtain. Thus, a distinction obviously suggested itself: on the one hand, uncreated Grace, which was the life of God himself insofar as it included the act by which he gave himself to man; on the other, created grace, which was a created reality, a second nature (both in the sense that it presupposed nature, and in the sense that it was a "habit" rather than a substantial nature), a super-nature which so modified man's substantial nature that he could achieve, through its efficiency, what he could not achieve by nature alone.

The traditional belief that by grace man participated in the divine nature was thus retained, but considerably weakened. In his meaningful religious experience the Christian no longer sought God himself—at least not in this life. He sought grace, an insubstantial ectoplasm flowing from above, a spiritual coin issued by God *ex opere operato* and certified as legal moral tender by the decrees of Providence. Man's acceptance of supernatural life no longer meant literally that "I live, no not I; but Christ liveth in me." It did not convey that man had risen to a new level of *existence*. It simply meant that a certain quality—given from God, but not itself God— now qualified inwardly (but proceeding from without) the powers of nature with a perfection which was not due to nature but which enabled nature, precisely as supernaturally perfected, to attain a supernatural end.

Moreover, since it occurred only through the *means* of grace, participation in the life of God now referred to a God who was not immediately present to man. (It was also thought that an immediate participation would be dangerously near to Pantheism—as it would indeed be, on the continued assumption of the hellenic concepts of nature and being.) In fact, God was not *effectively* present to man, immediately or otherwise: the presence of God was still affirmed, but it did not necessarily have a meaningful role in Christian religious experience. The operative note became God's transcendence. But, of course, transcendence was no longer understood as an attribute of God's immanence, his incommensurability with the being in which he lives and to which he is present. It was rather the incommensurability of creator and creature, the infinite distance between created being and uncreated Being. God's immanence was confessed, but no longer effectively believed in.

As Christianity's sense of God's immanence became dulled, as the Christian God receded into the infinity beyond, and as the experience of his presence was no longer facilitated by the immediately meaningful teaching of the Church or by the everyday institutions and practices of believers—and it should be noted that even the sacrament most directly concerned with the Real Presence tended to give less emphasis to the presence itself than to the metaphysical mechanism whereby that presence could be harmonized with a *hellenic* understanding of nature—as these things came to pass the Christian God became increasingly unbelievable. For, at the limiting case, a strictly transcendent God is both utterly unreasonable and thoroughly immoral; whereas, at the other extreme, a strictly immanent God may amount to no Christian God at all, but is not positively absurd and is at least superficially moral. In this way, to most science and philosophy, belief in the Christian God became synonymous with superstitious credulity; and to many of the dispossessed, institutional religion became the opium of the people. No doubt, these and like judgments of the modern world have been precipitate and undiscriminating. But it may be equally precipitate and undiscriminating to suppose that they have been altogether wrong.

Yet, if nature is not that which determines a being to act in accordance with its inner, immutable, constitutive principle of intelligibility but, on the contrary, that which emerges from the contingent history it undergoes (or the contingent history it creates, in the case of man), the level of existence to which man is called by the Gospel need no longer be super-natural. If so, the Christian God need not have a super-natural character which alienates him from man, and the Christian faith may again become directly relevant to real, everyday, present life.

God Enters History

The level of existence of fellowship with God to which the Gospel calls is not superimposed upon an independently evolving history of creation: it is the same level of existence as that in which as a matter of fact creation evolves historically, but under the concrete, contingent, historical condition brought about by God's free decision to be present to creation and to take part in its history by making its history his home. Grace is, then, a historical fact: the irruption of God into man's history, a definitive and actual event within a merely possible event.

But this means that God does not reconcile in his private life the opposed transcendence and immanence of his cryptic public announcements. Therefore, he must be conceived as that which, though other than being, is revealed by and within being only because he is present to being. For the historicity of grace means that the "natural" order does not, as such, actually exist. But if, having reached this point by transcending the hellenic idea of nature, we were to proceed without transcending the hellenic idea of being, the conclusion would be inevitably reached that nothing which exists in reality is other than God.

Being exists—but God is present to it. God creates being—but he creates it in his presence. And, moreover, within the totality of being he brings forth the being to which he gives the power effectively to define itself, the power indeed truly to create itself—for this being is no longer simply being in relation to another, whether God or man, but being which is present to itself and, hence, being which exists in and for itself. To this being, God is freely present in a correlative way, namely, by giving himself, in his very reality, to it—hence, by offering himself to man so utterly gratuitously that he actually creates the possibility of being unaccepted, positively rejected by man.

Correspondingly, then, God is found *in* being, but only as that which is *other than* being. And it is indeed his presence *in* being that leads us *beyond* being. There is, thus, no infinite gap separating God from man—but there is an openness to being, and in this opening God stands. There is no distance between God and man: on the contrary, the God of the Gospel has come into the world in his true and utter reality, leaving nothing behind and, evidently, planning to stay. The Christian God is not elsewhere: he is always *here* and, therefore, he is always faithful, always he who abides, always *Yahweh*, he who remains present here and now with us. To sum up, the transcendence of the genuinely immanent God means this: if the God whom we find always *here* is not to vanish into thin air, if he is not to become an idol, if he is not to be reduced to the totality of being, and if he is not to be explained away as the becoming of the world or the projection of man—in a word, if the God who is actually *here* within being is the God of Christian tradition, it follows that he is not to be conceived as being.

To be sure, a whole *problematik* issues from this. But if the foregoing observations are correct this affirmation is not itself problematic; it is an empirically derived principle of investigation. This means: the history of Christian speculation about God suggests that henceforth the starting point of its quest should be, not the idea that although we do not experience God he must be nonetheless Being, but the observation that we do experience God, although evidently we do not experience him as being.

The Dehellenization of Dogma

Bernard J. F. Lonergan, S.J.

While acknowledging the limitations of hellenistic philosophical categories as vehicles for the conceptualization of
Christian faith, Bernard J. F. Lonergan, S.J., finds Leslie
Dewart guilty of a kind of critical "overkill" in his all-out
assault on those categories: "He fails to discern the elements
of Hellenism that still survive in the cultural vanguard."
Lonergan is particularly perturbed by Dewart's theory of
knowledge, which, with its hostility to propositional truths,
he sees as excluding the correspondence view of truth—the
relation between meaning and what is meant. "Such an exclusion is as destructive of the dogmas as it is of Dewart's
own statements." Justly termed "one of the most original and
synthetic minds within contemporary Catholicism" by the
editors of *Theological Studies**—from whose June 1967
number his review is taken—Father Lonergan is perhaps
best known for his work titled *Insight*: *A Study of Human
Understanding*. At present he teaches dogmatic theology at
Regis College in Toronto.

       WITH CONSIDERABLE warmth Prof. Leslie
Dewart, in his book *The Future of Belief: Theism in a World
Come of Age*, appeals to Pope John's decision "to adopt a
historical perspective: to 'look to the present, to new conditions and new forms of life . . . to dedicate ourselves with an
earnest will and without fear to that work which our era demands of us'" (p. 172). This decision, he feels, and the un-
hesitating acclamation that greeted it reversed a policy that
had been gaining strength for centuries. "This policy was, for
the sake of protecting the truth and purity of the Christian
faith, to resist the factual reality, and to deny the moral

* Woodstock, Md. 21163.

validity, of the development of man's self-consciousness, especially as revealed in cultural evolution" (p. 172).

His purpose, then, is "to sketch an approach to . . . the problem of integrating Christian theistic belief with the everyday experience of contemporary man" (p. 7). He aims at "the integration of Christian belief with the post-medieval stage of human development" (p. 15). He understands contemporary experience "as the mode of consciousness which mankind, if not as a whole at least in respect of our own civilization constituting man's cultural vanguard, has reached as a result of its historical and evolutionary development. And the integration in question must be a true organic process of co-ordination, interrelation and unification" (p. 9). What is at stake is the unity and coherence of Christian and, in particular, Catholic consciousness: ". . . the problem is, at its most basic level, whether one can, while complying with the demand that human personality, character and experience be inwardly integrated, at one and the same time profess the Christian religion *and* perceive human nature and everyday reality as contemporary man typically does" (p. 19).

So much for the problem. The suggested solution is "that the integration of theism with today's everyday experience requires not merely the *demythologization of Scripture* but the more comprehensive *dehellenization of dogma*, and specifically that of the Christian doctrine of God" (p. 49). Demythologization integrates no more than the Christian's *reading of Scripture* with his contemporary everyday experience; and it creates several dogmatic problems for each scriptural one it solves (p. 47). To go to the root of the matter, to become both coherent and contemporary, we have to transcend our Hellenic past and consciously to fashion the cultural form which Christianity requires now for the sake of its future. So "dehellenization means, in positive terms, the conscious creation of the future of belief" (p. 50). This future, he feels, is likely to depend on whether Christian theism "chooses to contribute to the heightening of man's self-understanding and to the perfection of his 'education to reality.' This would in turn imply that Christian theism should first become conscious that its traditional form has necessarily and logically been childish and infantile to the very degree that it corresponded to an earlier, relatively childish, infantile stage of human evolution. Theism in a world come of age must itself be a theism come of age" (p. 51).

I

The principal means for dehellenizing dogma and obtaining a mature theism seems to be "the theory of knowledge assumed here" (p. 168n.). While its precise nature is not disclosed in any detail, apparently it involves a rather strong repugnance to propositional truth in some at least of its aspects.

In the theory of knowledge suggested here human knowledge is not the bridging of an original isolation but, on the contrary, the self-differentiation of consciousness in and through its objectification (of the world and of itself); and conceptualization is the socio-historical mechanism through which the self-differentiation can take place. Concepts are not the *subjective* expression of an *objective* reality (nor, therefore, a means whereby we become reflectively conscious of a self which already existed prior to reflection). Concepts are the self-expression of consciousness and, therefore, the means by which we objectify (the world and the self), and the means by which we self-communicate with another self (*including God*), that is, the means by which we objectify ourselves for another self, and by which we objectify ourselves for ourselves (p. 116 n.; here and elsewhere italics in text).

Hence we are repeatedly warned against the view that truth involves an *adaequatio intellectus et rei.*

Truth is not the adequacy of our representative operations, but the adequacy of our conscious existence. More precisely, it is the fidelity of consciousness to being (p. 92).

It is the result of the mind coming-into-being through the self-differentiation of that-which-is into self and world (p. 93).

Now we have seen that . . . truth can be understood as an existential relation of self to being which must by definition develop in order to realize itself—and not as the relation of conformity to an objective thing which must by definition be stable in order to be at all (p. 97).

Although truth is not the adequation of the *intellect* to *being* . . . truth might nevertheless be called an adequation of *man* to *reality*, in the sense that it is *man's self-achievement* within the requirements of *a given situation.* . . . In this context *adequation* would not connote *conformity, correspondence, likeness* or *similarity*. It would connote *adjustment, usefulness, expediency, proficiency, sufficiency* and *adaptation* (p. 110).

The truth of human experience is the result of consciousness' incessant tending towards being—a tendency which, far from satisfied by the achievement of its goal, is further intensified by whatever success it may meet. Hence, the only valid "criterion" of truth is that it create the possibility of more truth (p. 111).

. . . the concept is true *to the degree* that by its elevation of experience to consciousness it permits the truth of human experience to come into being (p. 113).

. . . the concepts in which Christian belief are cast are true, not in virtue of their representative adequacy, but in virtue of their efficacious adequacy as generative forms of the truth of religious experience (p. 113).

To conclude with a citation from Maurice Blondel's *Carnets intimes*: ". . . truth is no longer the *adaequatio rei et intellectus.* . . . But truth remains, and this truth that remains is living and active. It is the *adaequatio mentis et vitae*" (p. 118).

Prof. Dewart's grounds for his view on truth seem to be partly the flood of light he has derived from phenomenological and existential thought and partly the inadequacy of his interpretation of Scholasticism.

To the light I have no objection. I would not deny that the authenticity of one's living, the probity of one's intellectual endeavors, the strategy of one's priorities are highly relevant for the truth by which one is truly a man. I have no doubt that concepts and judgments (on judgments I find Dewart strangely silent) are the expression of one's accumulated experience, developed understanding, acquired wisdom; and I quite agree that such expression is an objectification of one's self and of one's world.

I would urge, however, that this objectification is intentional. It consists in acts of meaning. We objectify the self by meaning the self, and we objectify the world by meaning the world. Such meaning of its nature is related to a meant, and what is meant may or may not correspond to what in fact is so. If it corresponds, the meaning is true. If it does not correspond, the meaning is false. Such is the correspondence view of truth, and Dewart has managed to reject it without apparently adverting to it. So eager has he been to impugn what he considered the Thomist theory of knowledge that he overlooked the fact that he needed a correspondence view of truth to mean what he said.

Let me stress the point. Dewart has written a book on the future of belief. Does he mean the future of belief, or something else, or nothing at all? At least, when he asserts that God is not a being, he assures us that what his statement "means is literally what it says, that God is not a being at all" (p. 175). Again, he wants his proposals tried by the touchstone of public examination (p. 50). But what is that examination to be? What can the public do but consider what he means and try to ascertain how much of what he says is certainly or probably true or false?

Dewart urges that the correspondence view of truth supposes what is contrary to both logic and observation, "as if we could witness from a third, 'higher' viewpoint, the union of two lower things, object and subject" (p. 95). But such a statement is involved in a grave confusion. The witnessing from a higher viewpoint is the nonsense of naive realism, of the super-look that looks at both the looking and the looked-at. On the other hand, the union of object and subject is a metaphysical deduction from the fact of knowledge, and its premise is the possibility of consciousness objectifying not only itself but also its world.

Again, Dewart urges that a correspondence view of truth implies an immobility that precludes development (p. 95) and, in particular, the development of dogma (p. 109). Now I would not dispute that a woodenheaded interpretation of the correspondence view of truth can exclude and has excluded the possibility of development. But that is no reason for rejecting the correspondence view along with its mis-interpretation. Least of all is that so at present, when "her-meneutics" has become a watchword and the existence of literary forms is generally acknowledged. For the root of hermeneutics and the significance of literary forms lie pre-cisely in the fact that the correspondence between meaning and meant is itself part of the meaning and so will vary with variations in the meaning.

Just as he discusses truth without adverting to herme-neutics, so Dewart discusses the development of dogma with-out adverting to the history of dogma. But the development of dogma is a historical entity. Its existence and its nature are determined by research and interpretation. Moreover, on this approach there are found to be almost as many modes of development, almost as many varieties of implicit revela-tion, as there are different dogmas, so that a general dis-cussion of the possibility of cultural development, such as Dewart offers, can provide no more than philosophic prole-gomena.

Unfortunately, it seems of the essence of Dewart's pro-legomena to exclude the correspondence view of truth. Such an exclusion is as destructive of the dogmas as it is of Dewart's own statements. To deny correspondence is to deny a relation between meaning and meant. To deny the corres-pondence view of truth is to deny that, when the meaning is true, the meant is what is so. Either denial is destructive of the dogmas.

If there is no correspondence between meaning and meant, then, in Prof. McLuhan's phrase, it would be a great mis-take to read the dogmas as if they were saying something. If that is a great mistake, it would be another to investigate their historical origins, and a third to talk about their develop-ment.

If one denies that, when the meaning is true, then the meant is what is so, one rejects propositional truth. If the rejection is universal, then it is the self-destructive prop-osition that there are no true propositions. If the rejection is limited to the dogmas, then it is just a roundabout way of saying that all the dogmas are false.

II

The same view of truth is applied not only to the dogmas but also to faith and revelation. We are told that "belief must bear directly upon the reality of God, not upon words or concepts" (p. 167). In a footnote we are warned against the doctrine of St. Thomas which has faith terminating at God Himself through the mediation of the propositions of the Creed. Dewart holds that to believe in God by believing a proposition about God is to believe in a proposition and not to believe in God. But this follows only Dewart's assumption that truth is not correspondence. On the contrary assumption, to assent to the truth of the proposition does not differ from assenting to what the proposition means. *Verum est medium in quo ens cognoscitur.*

With faith detached from assent to propositions (p. 167), it has to be ontic rather than ontological (p. 136 n.).

Faith is the existential response of the self to the openness of the transcendence disclosed by conscious experience. It is our decision to respect, to let be, the contingency of our being, and, therefore, to admit into our calculations a reality beyond the totality of being. It is a lived response, identical with our freely willing to exist in a certain self-conception and self-resolution. . . . It is no less a coming-into-being than the "act" of existence which is, likewise, a perpetual achieving of the unachieved. In real life we find not the act but the life of faith (pp. 64 f.).

Such faith seems to coincide with religious experience. This differs from ordinary knowledge inasmuch as it is an experience of a transcendent reality first adumbrated negatively in the empirical apprehension of the contingency of our own being. So it is a conscious experience of something inevident, something which unlike this desk and this chair is not seen to be there, even if it enters into the fabric of our personal relations to reality with at least as much force, relevance, and moment as things which are seen to be there. Further, in the traditional phrase, faith is due to God's initiative. Again, faith as Christian is faith as conceptualized under some or other cultural form of the Christian tradition. Its continuity in truth requires the continuity of God's self-communication to man, and the continuity of man's correlative religious experience in response to God's initiative. But this is not the continuity of sameness or the continuity of that which remains (substantially) unchanged in the midst of accidental change. Truth cannot remain the same. It would make as little sense as to say that existence remains the same, that one moment of consciousness is the same as another, or that life is the same thing over and over again (pp. 113–16).

Correlative to faith is revelation:

. . . although God does not reveal propositions or formulae or concepts about himself, he truly reveals himself. . . . He does it personally, by his own agency, through his personal presence to human history, in which he freely chooses to appear and to take part. . . . His revelation to man in the Judaeo-Christian tradition is unique and extraordinary: the Christian religion and the Catholic Church are, in this extraordinary and unique sense, the true religion and the true Church to which all men are called (p. 115 n.).

Dewart, however, does not seem to consider that the call to the true Church calls for some attention to the pronouncements of Vatican I and II on revelation and faith. Instead we have the caricature of a "popular faith" in which "revelation has indeed tended to become God's transmission of cryptic messages. Correlatively, the magisterium of the Church has tended to become the decoding of these messages, and faith the Christian's assent to the accuracy of the translation . . ." (p. 165 n.).

No doubt, Dewart's esotericism is inevitable, once the mediating role of propositions has been eliminated both from God's revelation to man and from man's faith in God. But if one is inclined to doubt the soundness of the "theory of knowledge assumed here" (p. 168 n.), if one's modernity includes a greater interest in exegesis and history than is exhibited in the opinion that "Christianity has a mission not a message" (p. 8), then one will find abundant evidence from New Testament times right up to the present day that the Church has been explicitly aware not only of a mission but also of a message. Moreover, while it is true that the message can be and has been abused to the detriment both of living faith and of the transcendent Revealer, such an abuse does not show that a rejection of the message is not also a rejection of the mission.

III

Prof. Dewart dislikes the Greeks. He deplores the "inability of hellenic metaphysical thinking to discern *reality* except in *ens*, that-which-is" (p. 180). He places at the sad root of both Greek and Scholastic thought Parmenides' postulate that "that which can be thought is identical with that which can be" (p. 153). He would get beyond "speculative-ideological metaphysics" (p. 163) and establish a metaphysics of presence (p. 169). Then we could get along without the training and education that only relatively few can afford. "Christian theology and philosophy would then cease to be 'academic' subjects, and theo-logical enquiry would once again take place predominantly within the public, everyday, real life of the whole Church" (p. 145 n.). In anticipation of this imminent utopia, he notes that "there is no need, if we discard Parmenides, to make God fit in the mould of being" (p. 176). Hence, he desires a philosophy concerned with the presence and reality of God, a God that is not even partially the God of Greek metaphysics (p. 170). Similarly, he suggests that Christian theology is not to assume any fundamental principle or essential part of that very mode of philosophizing on which was erected the concept of God which can no longer be integrated with contemporary experience (p. 41).

This hostility to Hellenism is of a piece with the already

noted hostility to propositional truth; for not only do propositions mediate reality, but also the first-level propositions that do so may be themselves mediated by second-level propositions. So dictionaries speak of words, grammars of languages, logics of the clarity, coherence, and rigor of discourse, hermeneutics of the relation between meaning and meant, and, to come to the villain, metaphysics of what is meant. Such second-level mediation of the first-level mediator was the secret of the Greek miracle that effected the triumph of *logos* over *mythos*.

Obviously, then, if one does not want a first-level mediation of reality by propositions, much less will one tolerate the second-level mediation associated with Greek metaphysics. Moreover, if one does not care to be entirely cut off from reality, one will have to turn to some nonpropositional mode of access such as presence. So Dewart praises a metaphysics of presence but blames a Hellenic metaphysics.

Again, the Greek miracle had its price. It demanded a second differentiation of consciousness, a second withdrawal from the world of immediacy. In that world of immediacy the infant lives, but when the child learns to talk, he also learns to inhabit the far larger world mediated by meaning. For the student, however, there is the further learning that mediates the mediator, that reflects on articulate sounds to correlate them with an alphabet, that uses dictionaries, that studies grammars and logics, that introduces hermeneutics and even perhaps metaphysics. The basic purpose of this further learning is to control the mediation of reality by meaning, to hold in check the affect-laden images that even in the twentieth century have the power to make myth seem convincing and magic seem efficacious.

But however beneficial, the second differentiation of consciousness is onerous. It is all the more onerous, all the more resented, when compulsory, universal education attempts to extend to all what once had to be endured by but few. So the word "academic" acquires a pejorative sense that expresses disapproval of any cultural superstructure. Despite his devotion to the mode of consciousness reached by man's cultural vanguard (p. 9), Dewart feels free to appeal to that disapproval and to look forward to the day when Christian philosophy and theology will no longer be "academic" subjects (p. 145 n.).

A similar ambiguity appears in Dewart's attitude to science. On the one hand, he assures us that "modern man creates himself by means of science, that is, by means of his scientific mode of consciousness," and "it is *scientific culture* that defines *contemporary man*" (p. 18). On the other hand, he is all for discarding Parmenides' identification of the possible object of thought with possible being (pp. 153, 165, 168, 174, 176, 181, 184). But to attack this identification is also to attack a cardinal point in contemporary science; for what is defined by a hypothesis is a possible object of thought, and what is to be ascertained by verification is a real state of affairs. But modern science demands that every hypothesis be verifiable, and so it demands that its hypothetical objects of thought be possible beings. Not only is it thoroughly committed to the Parmenidean identity, but also it has so extended and developed the second differentiation of consciousness as to erect a cultural superstructure far more elaborate and far more abstruse than anything attempted by the Greeks or the Scholastics.

One begins to suspect that Dewart is not a reformer but just a revolutionary. He is dealing with a very real and very grave problem. He would have written an extremely important book, if he had distinguished between the achievements and the limitations of Hellenism, if he had listed the ways in which modern culture has corrected the errors and so transcended the limitations of its ancient heritage, if he had pointed out the precise bearing of each of these advances on each of the many levels on which Christians live and Christianity functions. He has not done so. He fails to discern the elements of Hellenism that still survive in the cultural vanguard, and so he plumps for vigor. Let's liquidate Hellenism. He does not distinguish between integrated consciousness and undifferentiated consciousness, and so he thinks and talks and prescribes his remedies as if prayer, dogma, systematic theology, philosophy, and contemporary common sense were or should be a single homogeneous unity.

IV

Prof. Dewart conceives the development of the Trinitarian and Christological dogmas to have been a matter of taking over Hellenic concepts for the expression of Christian doctrine; for he feels "it would be unhistorical to suppose that at the first moment of the development of Christian consciousness this consciousness could have created the concepts whereby to elaborate itself—it is not until our own day that such a possibility has begun to emerge" (p. 136). Further, he laments that the Church still retains such outworn tools, for today this results in a crypto-tritheism (p. 147) and in a crypto-docetism (p. 152).

It is, I should say, quite unhistorical to suppose that the development of Catholic dogma was an effort of Christian consciousness to elaborate, not the Christian message, but Christian consciousness. Further, it is unhistorical to suppose that Greek philosophy supplied all the principal elements in which we have for centuries conceptualized the basic Christian beliefs of the Trinity and the Incarnation (cf. *America*, Dec. 17, 1966, p. 801). My first contention needs no elaboration, and so I turn to the second.

It is true, then, that profound affinities may be discerned between Hellenic thinkers and some ecclesiastical writers. The Stoic notion that only bodies are real seems intrinsic to Tertullian's account of the divinity of the Son in his *Adversus Praxean*. Middle Platonism is prominent in Origen's account of the Son in his *De principiis* and *In Ioannem*. But the subordinationism of these two writers, along with Arianism, was rejected at Nicaea. Moreover, the term enshrining that rejection was *homoousios*, and while one might speculate that here if anywhere one has a concept forged by deep Hellenic thought and simply taken over by the bishops at Nicaea (see p. 136), it happens that historical research does not justify such a view. According to G. Prestige (*God in*

Patristic Thought [London, 1936], p. 209; cf. p. 197), down to the Council of Nicaea *homoousios* was understood in one sense and in one sense only: it meant "of one stuff"; and as applied to the Divine Persons, it conveyed a metaphor drawn from material objects. The Fathers at Nicaea, then, did not find ready to hand a sharply defined, immutable concept which they made into a vehicle for the Christian message; on the contrary, they found a word which they employed in a metaphorical sense.

It may be urged, however, that the metaphor meant something and that meaning must be some other Hellenic concept. It happens, however, that while the metaphor had a meaning, still the meaning was determined not by some Hellenic concept but by a Hellenic technique. What *homoousios* meant exactly, was formulated by Athanasius thus: *eadem de Filio quae de Patre dicuntur, excepto Patris nomine.* The same meaning has been expressed in the Trinitarian Preface: *Quod enim de tua gloria, revelante te, credimus, hoc de Filio tuo, hoc de Spiritu sancto, sine differentia discretionis sentimus.* Now such a determination of meaning is characteristically Hellenic. It is a matter of reflecting on propositions. It explains the word "consubstantial" by a second-level proposition to the effect that the Son is consubstantial with the Father, if and only if what is true of the Father also is true of the Son, except that only the Father is Father.

Let me add five observations on this typically Hellenic technique. The first is that it offers an open structure: it does not determine what attributes are to be assigned to the Father and so must be assigned to the Son as well; it leaves the believer free to conceive the Father in scriptural, patristic, medieval, or modern terms; and of course contemporary consciousness, which is historically minded, will be at home in all four.

The second is that, when reality and being are contrasted, the technique decides for being; for being is that which is; it is that which is to be known through the true proposition; and the technique operates on true propositions. On the other hand, reality, when contrasted with being, denotes the evident or present that provides the remote grounds for rationally affirming being, but, unlike being, is in constant flux.

The third is that specifically Christian thought on being came into prominent existence in Athanasius' struggle against Arianism and, in particular, in his elucidation of *natum non factum*, of the difference between the Son *born* of the Father and the creature *created* by Father and Son. No doubt, such an explanation presupposes a Hellenic background for its possibility. But the problem and the content are specifically Christian. A divine Son was simply a scandal to the Hellenist Celsus; and the Christian notion of creation is not to be found in Plato or Aristotle, the Stoics or the Gnostics. When Dewart talks about the God of Greek metaphysics (p. 170), one wonders what Greek metaphysician he is talking about.

My fourth observation is that the Hellenic technique of second-level propositions is not outworn. The modern mathematician reflects on his axioms and pronounces them to be the implicit definitions of his basic terms. This technique, then, pertains not to the limitations of Hellenism antiquated by modern culture but to the achievements of Hellenism that still survive in modern culture and, indeed, form part of it.

My fifth and last observation is that the technique is not within everyone's competence. The matter seems to have been settled with some accuracy; for, in his celebrated studies of educational psychology, Jean Piaget has concluded that only about the age of twelve (if my memory is correct) do boys become able to operate on propositions. It follows that other means have to be found to communicate the doctrine of Nicaea to less-developed minds. So much for my five observations.

For Dewart, "person" is a concept taken over from Hellenic thought and, though we have not managed to improve on it, we must do so (pp. 143 f.). I find this a rather inadequate account of the matter.

For Augustine, *persona* or *substantia* was an undefined, heuristic concept. He pointed out that Father, Son, and

Spirit are three. He asked, three what? He remarked that there are not three Gods, three Fathers, three Sons, three Spirits. He answered that there are three persons or substances, where "person" or "substance" just means what there are three of in the Trinity (*De trin.* 7, 4, 7 [*PL* 42, 939]). Obviously, such an account of the notion of "person" does no more than indicate, so to speak, the area to be investigated. It directs future development but it cannot be said to impede it. The only manner in which it could become outworn would be the rejection of the Trinity; for as long as the Trinity is acknowledged, there are acknowledged three of something.

Moreover, the original heuristic structure, while it has remained, has not remained indeterminate. It has been developed in different ways at different times. There was the stage of definitions, indeed, of the three main definitions contributed by Boethius, Richard of St. Victor, and Thomas Aquinas. There was the Trinitarian systematization that conceived the three Persons as subsistent relations and based the relations upon psychologically conceived processions. If I may cite my own views, I have maintained not only in my classes but also in a textbook that the three Persons are the perfect community, not two in one flesh, but three subjects of a single, dynamic, existential consciousness. On the other hand, I am of the opinion that the Christological systematization, from Scotus to de la Taille, had bogged down in a precritical morass. For the past thirty years, however, attention has increasingly turned to the consciousness of Christ, and my own position has been that the doctrine of one person with two natures transposes quite neatly into a recognition of a single subject of both a divine and a human consciousness.

I may be more brief on such terms as *substantia, hypostasis, natura*. All three were ambiguous. We have just seen Augustine use *substantia* in the same sense as *persona*, a usage that had vanished by the time the *Quicumque vult* was composed. Next, in the *Tomus ad Antiochenos* there is the account of Athanasius reconciling those that argued for one hypostasis with those that argued for three; he asked the former if they agreed with Sabellius, and the latter if they were tritheists; both groups were astounded by the question put them, promptly disclaimed respectively Sabellianism and tritheism, and dropped their now obviously verbal dispute. "Nature," finally, which for Aristotle meant either the form or the matter, and the form rather than the matter, meant neither of these to Christians some eight centuries later. They, however, had their own ambiguous usage, and it was recognized solemnly and explicitly in the sixth and seventh centuries. In successive canons Constantinople II explained the correct meaning both of Chalcedon's two natures and of Cyril's one nature (*DS* 428 f.). More abruptly, Lateran I imposed both the Cyrillian and the Chalcedonian formulas (*DS* 505 f.).

So much for the process of Hellenizing Christian doctrine. Let us add a few words on the meaning of the technical terms; for Dewart roundly asserts that no Christian believer today (unless he can abstract himself from contemporary experience) can intelligently believe that in the one hypostasis of Jesus *two* real natures are united (p. 150). Let me put the prior question. Does Dewart's Christian believer today accept the positive part of the Nicene decree, in which neither the term "hypostasis" nor the term "nature" occurs? If so, in the part about Jesus Christ, does he observe two sections, a first containing divine predicates, and a second containing human predicates? Next, to put the question put by Cyril to Nestorius, does he accept the two series of predicates as attributes of *one and the same* Jesus Christ? If he does, he acknowledges what is meant by one hypostasis. If he does not, he does not accept the Nicene Creed. Again, does he acknowledge in the one and the same Jesus Christ both divine attributes and human attributes? If he acknowledges both, he accepts what is meant by two natures. If he does not, he does not accept the Nicene Creed.

What is true is that Catholic theology today has a tremendous task before it, for there are real limitations to Hellenism that have been transcended by modern culture and have yet to be successfully surmounted by Catholic theology. But that task is not helped, rather it is gravely impeded, by wild statements based on misconceptions or suggesting unbelief.

V

Prof. Dewart has treated many other topics besides those I have been able to mention, but his principal concern, no doubt, is "theism in a world come of age," for that is the subtitle of his book. The substance of his proposal here seems to come in two parts. Positively, it is that God is to be thought of, not as being or as existing, but as a reality that at times is present and at times is absent (pp. 173 ff.). Negatively, it is that atheism is fostered by unsuccessful efforts to prove God's existence, and such failures are due to the real distinction between essence and existence (pp. 156–58).

He contends, then, that one need not conceive God as being, once one gets beyond the metaphysical method grounded on Parmenides' identity. Remove that method, and "being" need no longer be identified with that-which-is. So the way is opened to giving to "being" a new meaning, and this new meaning is to be found in man. It is because he is present to himself as object that man is most truly a being; for through that presence man may transcend the subjectivity of mere objects and the objectivity of mere subjects to reach an understanding of himself as being. But to associate being with man is to disassociate being from God. As God is simply beyond man, so He is simply beyond being (pp. 173–75). By the same token, God cannot be said to exist (p. 176). He cannot because to exist is proper to being (p. 180).

We are reassured immediately, however, that the denial of being and existence to God takes away nothing of His reality and presence. To exist and to be present are quite different things. A man could be in the same room sitting beside me without being present to me, without making his presence felt. Conversely, God's real presence to us (and, therefore, His reality "in Himself") does not depend upon

His being a being or an object. On the contrary, to post-primitives a reality beyond the totality of being reveals itself by its presence (pp. 176 f.).

I do not find this very satisfactory. First of all, Dewart's views on truth are not defensible. Moreover, the cultural vanguard has not yet surmounted the requirement that hypotheses be verifiable, and so Parmenides' identity still stands. It follows that "being" still is that-which-is, that intelligence still is related to reality, that "is" and "is not" are not open to reinterpretation, and that there do not exist the premises for the conclusion that "being" and "existing" are appropriate only to creatures.

Secondly, it is obvious that a person can exist without making his presence felt and that he cannot make his presence felt without existing and being present. But it is also obvious that one can have the feeling that someone is present when no one is there. Especially in a world come of age such feelings should be examined, scrutinized, investigated. The investigation may result in the judgment that someone really is there. It may result in the judgment that really no one is there. It may result only in an unresolved state of doubt. But in any case, what is decisive is not the felt presence but the rational judgment that follows upon an investigation of the felt presence.

My point here is that man's coming to know is a process, that the earlier stages of the process pertain to knowing without constituting it completely, that in each instance of coming to know it is only with the rational act of judgment that the process reaches its term. Dewart does not want propositional truth and so he does not want "being" or "existing" or "that-which-is" or assent to propositions or judgments issuing in propositions. He does very much want the reassuring sense of present reality that can be savored in the earlier phases of cognitional process and, I have no doubt, is to be savored all the more fully if the unpleasant and tiring business of questions, investigations, and possible doubts is quietly forgotten. But this seems to be less "coming of age" than infantile regression.

Thirdly, maturity is comprehensive. It does not refuse to

acknowledge any part of man but embraces all from the entities of Freud's psychic embryology to the immanent norms of man's intellectual, rational, existential consciousness. As it does not deny propositional truth, so it does not disregard or belittle religious experience. On the contrary, it is quite ready to claim with Karl Rahner that a mystagogy will play a far more conspicuous role in the spirituality of the future (*Geist und Leben* 39 [1966] 335), and it is fully aware that spiritual advance brings about in prayer the diminution and at times the disappearance of symbols and concepts of God. Still, this differentiation and specialization of consciousness does not abolish other, complementary differentiations and specializations, whether social, sexual, practical, aesthetic, scientific, philosophic, historical, or theological. Nor is this multiplicity in any way opposed to integration. For in each of such diverse patterns of conscious operation one is oneself in accord with some facet of one's being and some part of one's universe; and while one lives in only one pattern at a time in some cycle of recurrence, still the subject is over time, each pattern complements, reinforces, liberates the others, and there can develop a differentiation of consciousness to deal explicitly with differentiations of consciousness. That pattern is, of course, reflective subjectivity in philosophy and in theology. It follows the Hellenic precept "Know thyself." It follows the example of Augustinian recall, scrutiny, penetration, judgment, evaluation, decision. It realizes the modern concern for the authenticity of one's existing without amputating one's own rational objectivity expressed in propositional truth.

Fourthly, maturity understands the immature. It has been through that, and it knows what it itself has been. It is aware that in childhood, before reaching the age of reason, one perforce works out one's quite pragmatic criteria for distinguishing between the "really real" and the merely imagined, desired, feared, dreamt, the sibling's trick, joke, fib. Still more clearly is it aware of the upset of crisis and conversion that is needed to purge oneself of one's childish realism and swing round completely and coherently to a critical realism. So it understands just how it is that some cling to a naive realism all their lives, that others move on to some type of idealism, that others feel some liberation from idealism in a phenomenology or an existentialism while, at the opposite extreme, there is a conceptualist extrinsicism for which concepts have neither dates nor developments and truth is so objective that it gets along without minds.

Such is the disorientation of contemporary experience, its inability to know itself and its own resources, the root of not a little of its insecurity and anxiety. Theology has to take this fact into consideration. The popular theology devised in the past for the *simplices fideles* has to be replaced. Nor will some single replacement do; for theology has to learn to speak in many modes and on many levels and even to minister to the needs of those afflicted with philosophic problems they are not likely to solve.

There remains, finally, the contention that "the ultimate epistemological consequence of the real distinction between essence and existence in creatures is to render the *intellect* incompetent for knowing the actual existence of *any* essence, be it created or uncreated, necessary or contingent" (p. 158). In this statement the emphasis seems to lie not on the reality of the distinction but on the mere existence of any, even a notional, distinction. For the author has just argued:

. . . the doctrine that there is in God *no real* distinction between essence and existence implies that nonetheless there is a *conceptual* distinction between them. We *cannot* empirically intuit the real indistinction of essence and existence in God. We *must* nonetheless conceive the two as distinct. There is, therefore, an unbridgeable difference between the way in which God is *in himself* and the way in which he is *in our knowledge*. Therefore, unless God were the object of empirical intuition, our concepts are *in principle* unable to make known to us the actual existence of God. For, as Kant was to conclude. . . . (p. 158)

Now this argument has a certain validity if in fact human knowing consists in concepts and empirical intuitions. But empirical intuition is just a misleading name for the givenness of the data of sense and of consciousness. In linking data to conception, there are inquiry and gradually developing understanding. The result of all these together is not knowledge but just thinking. To reach knowledge, to discern between astronomy and astrology, chemistry and alchemy, history and legend, philosophy and myth, there are needed the further activities of reflection, doubting, marshaling and weighing the evidence, and judging. Finally, this process of judging, in an important because clear instance, is like scientific verification, not as verification is imagined by the naive to be a matter of looking, peering, intuiting, but as verification in fact is found to be, namely, a cumulative convergence of direct and indirect confirmations any one of which by itself settles just nothing.

I quite agree, then, that our concepts are in principle unable to make known to us the actual existence of God. I would add that they are in principle unable to make known to us the actual existence of anything. For concepts are just thinking; thinking is not knowing; it is only when we reach judgment that we attain human knowledge of anything whatever, whether of essence or existence, whether of creature or Creator.

There is, however, a further point; for Dewart asserts an unbridgeable difference between the way in which God is in Himself and the way in which He is in our knowledge. This, of course, while absolutely possible, is not possibly known within our knowledge, and so the reader may wonder how Dewart got it into his knowledge. The fallacy seems to be Dewart's confusion of thinking and knowing. In our thinking we may distinguish a concept of divine existence from a concept of divine essence. In our knowing we may affirm (1) that we think in the above manner and (2) that there is no distinction between the reality of the divine essence and the reality of the divine existence. The contrast is, then, not between God in Himself and in our knowledge, but between God in our knowledge and God in our thinking. Nor is there anything unbridgeable about this contrast or difference; for the thinking and judging occur within one and the same mind, and the whole function of our judging may be described as determining how much of our thinking is correct.

But let me conclude. On the dust cover of *The Future of Belief* Harvey Cox is credited with the opinion: "A mature, highly erudite, and utterly radical book. It could be epoch-making." If for my part I have made certain reservations about the first two epithets, I must express the hope that the book will be epoch-making in the sense that it will contribute forcefully to the removal from theology of the many limitations of Hellenism. To that topic I shall in due time return.

The Future of Belief Debate

Justus George Lawler

Generally sympathetic to the anti-metaphysical, history-centered approach of Leslie Dewart's "watershed" book *The Future of Belief*, Justus George Lawler, editor of the Roman Catholic quarterly *Continuum* and editor-in-chief of the publishing house Herder & Herder, examines and replies to some of the criticisms of that book. Singled out for especial scrutiny is the stance of the neo-Thomists, which is characterized by "continuity, order and great breadth of learning," in contrast to Dewart's "radical penetration into the concrete, the empiric, and profound insight into the actuality of the immediate present." Despite his affinity for Dewart's approach, Lawler finds intelligence and sophistication on both sides of the division and feels that they share a sufficiently large patrimony to be able to engage in conversation free of acrimony. Among Dr. Lawler's books: *The Christian Imagination*; *Nuclear War: The Ethic, the Rhetoric, the Reality*; and *The Christian Image: Studies in Religious Art and Poetry*. His article is from the June–July 1967 issue of *The Critic*,* a publication of the Thomas More Association.

FORTY YEARS ago when Karl Rahner was a student, the writings of one of his confreres of the preceding generation, Joseph Maréchal, were scorned and proscribed in almost all Catholic seminaries, particularly those of the Jesuits. Rahner, who was forced to read Maréchal secretly after hours when his fellow-seminarians as well as his superiors were asleep, has referred to himself as "the Nicodemus of Maréchal," that is, as one who, like Nicodemus in the gospel, came to know the truth "by night," who derived the basic insight animating all his subsequent works from these noctur-

* 180 North Wabash Avenue, Chicago, Ill. 60601.

nal forays into Maréchal's famous fifth cahier where Kant is put into the service of Aquinas. Now Maréchallian Thomism, where there is any functionally relevant Thomism at all, holds the field, and a new philosophy, which according to its critics puts all things in doubt, is the current candidate for condemnation and censuring, and unquestionably somewhere is being conned by flashlight in seminary garret or basement by the Nicodemuses of a new generation. With the usual ironies of history, the most effective assaults upon this new object of banning and burning—Leslie Dewart's *The Future of Belief*—are coming from that same Maréchallian Thomism which four decades ago was itself the butt of the interdictions of officialdom.

However, we have more to do with here than merely a matter of current philosophical vogues. For the author of *The Future of Belief* is not simply challenging a rival school of thought, he is calling into question a whole tradition's way of grappling with the concept of God. This is a revolutionary enterprise, and Dewart is both philosophically and politically conscious of his revolutionary heritage. Born in Spain during a decade of bloody anti-monarchist uprisings, a bomber pilot on submarine patrol in World War II, and an ardent defender in the world press of the Castro rebellion against Batista, Dewart does not view the dislocation engendered by radical changes, whether religious or social, as a necessary evil.

But the revolutionary label may be misleading; for Dewart would contend that his is not some kind of subversive mission aimed at overthrowing the beliefs of modern Christians. On the contrary, he suggests, those beliefs have been bankrupted by the pressures and forces released in the last century of intellectual history, by the new insights born of Marx, Darwin, and Freud, and represented in orthodox Christianity by the achievement of Teilhard. The real subversives, then, would be those fundamentalists—Blondel's "veterists"—who in the name of an ossified tradition refuse to recognize this bankruptcy and continue to preach a God and church that have no bearing on twentieth-century man. Unfortunately, as soon as one says "twentieth-century man" a formidable problem arises, because both veterists and modernists, conservatives and liberals, contend they have nothing else but his good at heart, and that they alone know best what his real feelings and needs are.

Thus the initial premise, on which everything subsequent hinges, borders on the sociological: who truly speaks for that "contemporary experience" on which both Dewart and his severest qualified critics—Michael Novak, David Burrell, H. de Lavalette: Maréchallians all—peg their antagonist views? Michael Novak, in a needlessly shrill *Commonweal* review, insisted relentlessly that Dewart simply was not familiar with the secular mind of today, that he was merely a kind of academic bystander. And combining high dudgeon with low blows, Novak went on to oblate his personal anguish over napalm bombs, bloodshed in Cicero, etc., in order to evidence his own superior qualifications as trustee and legatee of the common man's "contemporary experience." Whom one ought to believe probably won't be known until we hear from the people at NORC; but on a priori grounds—and notwithstanding the introduction of shudders over war and racism—there is no more reason for thinking that Mr. Novak, only a few years out of seminary and graduate school, has any tighter a grasp on the hard realities of secularity than does Mr. Dewart, who in his late teens fled alone from tyranny in Cuba, flew with the RAF, charted the rationale of the Castro revolution, and has agitated repeatedly for US disengagement in Vietnam: the latter during a period, one is embarrassed to recall, when Mr. Novak with neo-Niebuhrian punctilio was defending the American role in that mad conflict. If the discernment of the signs of the times requires some empathy with the spirit of the times, one imagines that Dewart's credentials are at least as much to be honored as those of any of his critics who have thus far spoken up. But of course, ultimately if one is going to judge which of the two opposing views is the more accurate, he will just have to look carefully at both of them and see which of the two better jibes with his own "contemporary experience."

One thing is certain. Dewart seems to have exposed the

distortions that are latent in the beliefs of great numbers of restless Christians. Nothing else can explain the extraordinary impact of his book which is at once abstruse, obscure, here rigorously argued and there lyrically elliptic, highly sophisticated throughout, fascinating in what it offers and infuriating in what it portends but does not explicitate. For a book as difficult as Dewart's to enjoy such immediate fame and to be so quickly translated into other tongues (French, German, Spanish, Catalan, Portuguese, and Polish translations are in preparation) one cannot invoke the conventional public-relations formula in explanation—though the phenomenal acclaim for the book has been ascribed to the fact that (1) Roman Catholics are awed by celebrated Protestant thinkers; (2) Harvey Cox, celebrated . . . etc., has praised Dewart's work in glowing terms; (3) therefore: instant popularity. The reason Cox liked the book, it is further alleged, is that Protestants will applaud any attack on scholasticism. But the truth is, as every publisher and every author knows, no endorsements from however high up can galvanize a book into a vitality it doesn't natively possess. As for Cox's praise, it was based explicitly on Dewart's "doctrine of God," and not on any anti-scholastic leanings. Moreover, it is growing clearer day after day that the attractiveness of Dewart's premises, if not of his entire program, to such distinguished non-Catholics as the Calvinist Vahanian, the Baptist Cox, the Anglican Macquarrie, and the Marxist Garaudy is due to the realization that all institutionalized dogmatisms are trammeled by the same or similar cultural growths as those encrusting Roman Catholicism. The ecumenical import of Dewart's work is the result of its addressing itself to the common problems of atheists and believers, Catholics and non-Catholics. The demand for answers to such problems is very deeply and very widely felt.

The Dewart project, then, is not just some spasmodic reaction within the Catholic camp to such extramural fads as secularization or the death of God; though both of those, even when marketed by the media like hoola hoops and miniskirts, have been important in articulating the two central themes in modern religious culture: the act-centeredness, that is, the radical historicity of religion, and the cleavage between real belief and official theologies. ("God is dead" was really a Protestant rune for "theology as traditionally undertaken is dead.") Dewart's book, as an embodiment of these two themes, is utterly open to history, and therefore is in the best sense of the word, "Teilhardian."

That is why "dehellenization" looms so large in his program—though that is not the aptest description of what Dewart wants. The word is too negative, like the English "demythologize"; what is needed is a more affirmative concept, like "Entmythologisierung," a concept that might then be translated "the personalizing of history." As everyone knows, for sixty years or so biblical students have been pointing up the disparity between the scriptural understanding of man and the notion of man embodied in what may loosely be termed the hellenic tradition. All that, as Michael Novak has correctly noted, is a commonplace. It is also *not* what Dewart is primarily concerned about. His preoccupation is with the more fundamental fact that because the hellenic understanding of man negated his reality as a being in history, there was no possibility of relating the experience of selfconsciously evolutionary man, of modern man, to a religious doctrine inextricably bound to ahistorical categories. All churchmen could offer, up till now, was the option of bending the will, that is, of distorting lived experience, in order to conform it to a static conception of reality.

Dewart would be the last to suggest that the hellenization of Christianity has been simply catastrophic; rather what he is objecting to is the perpetuation of the hellenic mindset in an evolutionary age, in an age of technology, in an age when man is knowingly shaping his own culture. The hellenization of dogma could hardly be regarded as an unmixed evil: Dewart is very explicit on that point. Hellenization was an imperative in its own time; it was the necessary response of churchmen in a given age to their own history. But blind fidelity to this legacy now would be to live an institutionalized lie, for in the present age history demands a different response.

But an adequate response is not merely inhibited by the fact that one cultural pattern from the past is stifling the emerging pattern of the present; even more, it is inhibited by the fact that it is intrinsic to that earlier pattern that the very possibility of *any* other cultural pattern be denied. Those who would argue against dehellenization as implying a rupture in the continuity of humanity's spiritual achievement fail to recognize that the hellenic *Denkform* (i.e., mindset) is by definition inimical to the only continuity modern man knows: the continuity of discontinuity. As Bernard Lonergan has noted in "Dimensions of Meaning," "Classical culture cannot be jettisoned without being replaced; and what replaces it, cannot but run counter to classical expectations."

The traditional identification of God as "being," as supreme Being, is regarded by Dewart as typical of the hellenic hang-up. Once God is so denominated, it is suggested, there is no way that he can be immanent to man and his history except by a quasi-pantheist confusion with whatever else that is: in fact, nothing else truly is. If Being is being, God is creation. To avoid such patent heresy, as Dewart sees it Catholicism has tended to pay lip service to an immanent God while in practice worshipping one who was entirely and only transcendent. It is true that both traditional philosophy and theology have a devisal for apparently obviating Dewart's difficulty: the theologians call it the distinction between created and uncreated grace, and the philosophers call it the analogy of being. In either case one is faced with the construction of a tautology to explain the radical paradox of a God at once immanent and transcendent. Dewart would not fault the tradition at that point: all speculative thought is ultimately the tautologizing of paradox. His criticism would be that the analogical character of the being-Being polarity is true neither to God's immanence nor to his transcendence, and that it is therefore equally untrue to man's historicity and his destiny. In the practical order, as a result of the failure of Christianity to maintain a hold on one of the poles of the paradox (the divine immanence), not merely was God conceived to be *really* only "out there," but the Christian's existence in history was effectively undercut, his commitment to the temporal order, to "this world," was dissolved in favor of his service of the "other world" where his God *really* dwelt. The task of building the earth was seen as a mere sideline, when it was not entirely condemned—as by nineteenth-century Catholicism—as "anthropocentric humanism."

For speculative and practical reasons, therefore, Dewart would wish to conceive God as something other than "being," even though it is only *in* being that we discover a reality that is *beyond* being. This reality "beyond being" is the God that Dewart is somehow seeking to limn. For Dewart there is no opposition between God's immanence and his transcendence because it is God's experienced presence in being that leads man beyond being. As he remarked in his *Commonweal* "God" paper: "The transcendence of the genuinely immanent God means this: if the God whom we find always here is not to vanish into thin air, if he is not to become an idol, if he is not to be reduced to the totality of being, and if he is not to be explained away as the becoming of the world or the projection of man—in a word, if the God who is actually *here* within being is the God of Christian tradition, it follows that he is not to be conceived as being."

In sum there are two reasons for abandoning the concept of God as subsistent Being: the first—which sociologists will have to debate—is that it does not answer to the spiritual longings of contemporary man; the second—which historically would seem not to be debatable, though difficult of explicitation theoretically—is that it effectively negates God's immanence, and in practice leads to the traditional "Christian" attitudes of contempt for the world, disdain for the concrete and the temporal. The positive explicitation of what is thus far in Dewart a negative critique will therefore be crucial to the success of his project, and must necessarily be the theme of his future work. If God is not to be conceived as being, yet somehow must be conceptualized, how is he to be conceived? What would seem to be called for immediately is a phenomenology of "presence" which will ultimately sketch out what the something *is* that is present.

The present writer is convinced that in pursuit of this goal

Dewart will enrich our understanding of the God-concept immeasurably; this writer is less convinced that Dewart may not end up, if not a Maréchallian Thomist, then a kind of Maréchallian existentialist. The Blondel-Maréchal-late Lonergan axis would seem then to be strengthened rather than cracked by the following from the Introduction to the forthcoming French edition of *The Future of Belief*:

Yet, this view need not imply that faith (that is, religious experience) is *reducible* to non-religious, secular or "natural" experience. Quite the contrary, the point is that *ordinary* human experience is *insufficient* unless it extends itself into a new extra-ordinary dimension. When it so extends itself, experience becomes *religious* experience or faith. Thus, the apparent opposition between faith and experience simply means this: precisely insofar as experience is *immanent* to the being of man, experience has a *transcendent* dimension, namely faith. But faith *transcends* experience only because faith is the transcendence *of experience*. Faith *transcends* experience by *ceasing* to be experience. Faith is, as it were, the *ultimate* meaning of that which *already* exists, namely, human experience.

Furthermore, with regard to the future of *The Future of Belief*, Dewart would probably say that the goal of reconceptualization cannot be realized here and now—and of course never realized fully: that just as the notion of God as subsistent being represented the climax of centuries of speculation which were nurtured as much by non-Christian insights as by biblical data, so too the formulation of the non-hellenic concept of God is yet to come. But as Teilhard would say it is as much *en avant* as *en haut*: the two in fact are one.

If one truly believes in salvation history (and that is the key to Dewart's doctrine) then the reconceptualization will be the product of another marriage of biblical revelation with philosophical insights that are not formally Christian. But one should not overemphasize "philosophical" insights since it is a question, in moving towards more significant formulae of belief, of travelling *a via practica*; the meaning of the experience of God's presence to men in this world will be elaborated through the interplay of a host of historical and social factors (including necessarily those of the past that can survive) with a concomitant new and deeper understanding of the gospels and of the mission of the Church. Since we are talking about a truly existential understanding of man, about an understanding which is empirically based and socially committed, one would expect to see all the resources of all the humane sciences drawn upon, and most particularly those which are specifically concerned with the personal and concrete, that is with the "esthetic." Purely by way of casual examples from the present of the kinds of insights this radically future-oriented religious philosophy will have to depend upon, one might think of those flowing from Hugo Rahner's theology of play and dance, from Joseph Powers' use of communication theory in a theology of the Real Presence, from William Lynch's grasp of the function of the dramatic for a, perhaps unformulated, theology of death; and perhaps somewhere in that future Dewart is tentatively charting, a yet unborn thinker may even construct a theology of Rilke's aphorism, *Gesang ist Dasein.*

The watchword of the entire program will be the recently coined phrase, *"doing* philosophy." "Speculation," "theorizing" —etymology notwithstanding—can no longer mean as they did for the ancients and for the scholastics a mere "seeing," any more than faith can be conceived as merely intellectual assent, or the bliss of the blessed as a beatific vision. The phrase, "to do" philosophy or theology is, first, more nearly true to the experience of our encounter with the world and others as entailing not so much a looking at as an action and transaction; and second, is more closely akin to the injunction of St. Paul that we should "do the truth." It is this act-centered, historical dimension that is at the bottom of Dewart's dehellenization project and also of his solution to the dilemma that, on the one hand, "although we do not experience God he must be nonetheless Being," and on the other, "that we do experience God, although evidently we do not experience him as being."

Without entirely endorsing either of those propositions, one must still maintain, as does the present writer, that Dewart has undeniably addressed himself to a major aspect, if not *the* major aspect, of the malaise of that contemporary man who is, in Pascal's words, "wounded by mystery." And one would hope that rather than the acrimonious and cavilling criticism to which his work has too often being subjected, thinkers of differing religious and philosophical perspectives might try to grapple with the issues on his terms, even as he has so obviously grappled with them on theirs. It is no contribution whatever to decry his entire effort on the grounds that the brand of scholasticism he is indicting is not quite as pure as some others he allegedly skirted because they were less vulnerable. The fundamental presupposition of Dewart and of his writings has been that we must take our point of departure from present existent realities; and while the scholasticism he is opposing may not be, in this or that partisan's view, the most orthodox or creative or rigorous or up-to-date, it is undeniably the most influential on historical Christian belief. That Maréchal may be a more formidable Thomist than Maritain—who is to say?—is largely irrelevant. Maréchal has been a considerably less influential Thomist than Maritain, and most emphatically so in the English-speaking world for which Dewart is writing.

What one would prefer to the present lamentations on the part of Maréchallian Thomists that Dewart has ignored them would be an effort to engage him in close debate on specific topics. Obviously neither Dewart nor any brand of Thomist can afford to simply affirm that experience implies this or that. Any such affirmation must be correlated with large areas of history and sociology, must be supported by analogous evidence from individual psychology and political life, and must be integrated with other broad-gauge theories of scientific and philosophic understanding. Thus far it is clear that Dewart has bolstered his general contention—God cannot now be conceived as subsistent being—by a brilliant critique of Gilson's epistemology, by a global synthesis of some prevalent currents in non-scholastic religious philosophy (notably Tillich and Marcel), by an assessment of the phenomenon of Marxist socialism and of the unifying of humanity. The convergence of all these elements on one focus makes his a very strong point, and if it is going to be blunted, his critics will have to answer him patiently, not denounce him shrilly. One of Dewart's own favorite quotes is from Heidegger: "Zealous attempts at refutation never get us on a thinker's path."

It is true Dewart himself has not always appeared to make his critics' task an easy one. He has not of course demeaned his cause by descending to personal polemic with some of his opponents who have brashly called into question his academic competence, his moral judgment, his mere understanding of the world. But he has left himself a kind of moving target—which, however, is exactly what one would expect of a consistent "projective" and non-retrospective philosopher. The book, after all, is called *The Future of Belief*. Nor is this a particularly novel style of religious speculation in our time: it is characteristic of Schillebeeckx's unfinished sacramental theory, of Rahner's "investigations," and von Balthasar's "sketches." That it is the only possible style or the best possible style in an age of transition, the existence of so masterly a work as Lonergan's *Insight* would seem to deny. But it is without question a style which has been sanctioned by the creative thought it has generated.

What the controversy over Dewart's book fines itself down to, then, is not, certainly, an academic debate over the real distinction of essence and existence (a highly serviceable formula), nor even over the more weighty question of how we denominate "God"—more weighty because even the cleanest ascriptions, once fabricated, crystallize our thinking. What the debate is really over is the very nature of man's understanding of his world. For Dewart, history is not just the setting, is not just the background, is not just the framework of man's knowledge; it is the very "principle" that "structures" it. There can be therefore no eternal verities, or at least no eternal verities understandable as such. The only absolute truth discernible is that there is no absolute truth discernible. This is frightening: one had not known the wound in nature went so deep. It is frightening, and precisely because it is, salvation is revealed through this very wound, in history. As corollary, there can be no universal synthesis of knowledge, but only variant clusters coherent within themselves and, hopefully, not too at odds with one another taken individually. The Age of Aquinas and Spinoza is over; dead as well is *The Degrees of Knowledge* and even *The Unity of Philosophical Experience*. This, with all it implies, is what is at issue.

One should hardly be surprised that the severest responsible criticism of Dewart has been made by the disciples of the most challenging and stimulating systematic thinker within the Christian community, Bernard Lonergan. On both sides of the division are intelligence and sophistication, complete fidelity to the living Church and total commitment to the Christian message. On the one hand are continuity, order, and great breadth of learning; on the other are radical penetration into the concrete, the empiric, and profound insight into the actuality of the immediate present. *The Future of Belief* is the testing ground on which will be determined what accommodations can be tolerated by the two different approaches without destroying the essential orientation of either. A genuinely irenic spirit will be required of the participants on both sides. But this is hardly unattainable, both because we have reached a stage in philosophical discussion where a healthy strain of ambiguity necessarily prevails, and because there remain, notwithstanding many differences, intersecting vectors marking off a large patrimony which both viewpoints must share. Apart from a common reliance on revelation there is the kind of mutually acceptable ground which the following from Dewart exemplifies:

Every man sooner or later in his life confronts himself as a being, grasps the awful reality of the fact that he really exists. When we so meet existence, I think we come in contact with a reality which points to something beyond all that it itself is—despite the fact that it itself is *all* that we experience.

Of course, no one would imply that the differences will be resolved merely by translating from one idiom to another; but it is obvious that at least there is enough by way of shared premises for genuine dialogue to begin.

I close with some words from Lonergan on the transitional period from a classical to a non-classical culture:

There is bound to be formed a solid right that is determined to live in a world that no longer exists. There is bound to be formed a scattered left, captivated by now this, now that new development, exploring now this and now that new possibility. But what will count is a perhaps not numerous center, big enough to be at home in both the old and the new, painstaking enough to work out one by one the transitions to be made, strong enough to refuse half-measures and insist on complete solutions even though it has to wait.

But a center can only exist in terms of its boundaries, one component of which is by definition that left which *The Future of Belief* now holds.

Ernst Bloch and "The Pull of the Future"

Harvey Cox

How can Christianity regain its original posture of radical hope and transmute the content of that hope so that it becomes available to contemporary man? This, in the opinion of Harvey Cox, is the crucial question for the church. In endeavoring to aid such recovery, Christian theologians would do well, he says, to attend to the thought of one who might at first seem an unlikely ally: the German Marxist-humanist Ernest Bloch. Cox does not do Bloch the injustice of making him out to be a kind of crypto-Christian; he grants that Christians will differ with the Marxist as to the content of hope. But he finds in Bloch's vision of the "not-yet" and in his understanding of man as he-who-hopes, as having a basic stance of "creative expectancy," much that is akin to the biblical understanding and much that Christians can profitably appropriate. Communist-Christian exchange is a subject treated at greater length in Cox's newest book, *On Not Leaving It to the Snake*. Dr. Cox—also the author of the phenomenally influential *The Secular City*—is Associate Professor of Church and Society at Harvard Divinity School. His essay on Bloch was commissioned by Herder and Herder* to introduce a selection of Bloch's writings that firm is to publish; rather than tamper with it, we have decided to present it intact as the book introduction it obviously is.

AFTER YEARS of hearing about him indirectly, American readers will now be able to taste some of the fruits of Ernst Bloch's long and productive career for themselves. These essays, drawn from Bloch's more recent writing, will hopefully whet so many appetites that the translation of his major works will occur before too long. Ranging over an incredibly wide variety of subjects, from musicology to epis-

* 232 Madison Avenue, New York, N.Y. 10016.

temology, from social and literary criticism to political theory, Bloch's books will eventually delight and stimulate many different people. Why, then, it might reasonably be asked, should this first book-length collection of his ideas be introduced by a theologian, and a so-called "young theologian" at that? Whatever else Ernst Bloch may be he is not a "young theologian." He misses that condition on two counts. First, he is an octogenarian, an alert and hard working one but nevertheless a man born in 1885 (of Jewish extraction in Ludwigshafen am Rhein). Also, Bloch is not a theologian—even though some of his critics have occasionally hurled that epithet at him. Bloch is a philosopher—and an atheist at that, at least in his own terms.

Still there are reasons why a theologian should introduce Bloch to English speaking readers. Bloch's delayed "discovery" has been largely the work of theologians. This became especially clear in 1965 when Bloch reached his eightieth birthday and a group of friends and admirers published a *Festschrift* in his honor (*Ernst Bloch zu Ehren*, Suhrkamp Verlag). To the astonishment of many readers, who knew Bloch as an old Marxist, nearly half the contributors to the volume turned out to be theologians, among them some of the youngest religious thinkers of Europe. Why this interest in Bloch among younger theologians?

Bloch himself might enjoy trying to answer that question. One of the continuing interests of his life has been the riddle of why certain insights emerge at one point in history and not at another, why some men appear "before their time" and others seem to live in an age which has already disappeared. As a theologian it seems to me that while Bloch's work is certainly not of exclusive interest to theologians, there are compelling reasons why he is particularly relevant for us today.

The first reason Bloch fascinates us is that we feel very strongly, and quite correctly I think, that the world today stands "*zwischen die Zeiten*," between two ages. We disagree on how those two ages should be defined. Some see us emerging from Christendom into a "post-Christian era." Others see us moving from the religious to the secular epoch in theology. Still others insist that God is dead, that all forms of theism are passé and that we are already in the period of post-theistic Christianity. Yet, despite the disagreements, most agree that we are now leaving one identifiable period behind but have not yet arrived at the next. We are experiencing what Bloch calls a period of "*Zeitwende.*"

Such periods, claims Bloch, are particularly fruitful to study because during them, if often only very briefly, we catch a glimpse of man as he really is. In such periods we live in radical anticipation, hope and expectation. This is valuable, says Bloch, because existence in hope should not be a periodic episode in man's life; it should be the basic posture of his existence at all times. Man *is*, Bloch contends, that creature who hopes, who phantasizes, who dreams about the future and strives to attain it. These features are not merely accidental to his nature but are utterly constitutive of it. To be human is to be on the way to something else. To be man is to be *unterwegs*. Man's nature eludes definitive description because by the time it is described it has already begun the transmutation into something else. Thus Bloch helps us to seize the day, to enjoy and profit from the discomfort of transition, to see in the dislocations of our own period an epiphany of what is real in history at large. Consequently theologians, for whom the changes of today are especially momentous, see Bloch as especially significant.

But what does Bloch help us to see? How would his thought be capsuled if it had to be described in a few words? Bloch himself, Adolph Lowe reports, was once faced with this challenge. A few years back at a late afternoon tea in the home of a friend, someone challenged the old man to sum up his philosophy in one sentence. "All great philosophers have been able to reduce their thought to one sentence," the friend said. "What would your sentence be?" Bloch puffed on his pipe for a moment and then said, "That's a hard trap to get out of. If I answer, then I'm making myself out to be a great philosopher. But if I'm silent, then it will appear as though I have a great deal in mind but not much I can say. But I'll play the brash one instead of the silent one and give you this sentence: S is not yet P."

"S is not yet P"? Is this a mere evasion? No, in a sense Bloch had succeeded, despite himself, in passing the test of being a great philosopher. His life work has been built on the contention that the dynamic reality always eludes even the most supple agility of language, that it outraces words even while they are being spoken. Thus to say "S=S" is already to falsify the situation since in the time it takes to utter even a short phrase, the inexorable movement of reality toward a still undefined future has relativized the statement.

Does this mean that for Bloch the venerable law of identity in classical logic is passé? Yes it does. For Bloch's ontology, to claim that S must be S and nothing else is to fall into a static view of reality, a condition which can only result in hindering and slowing down the onward march of history, though it can never halt it. In short Bloch is suggesting a logic of change, a new logic appropriate to a time when we have discovered at last that change itself is the only permanent thing we have.

There is another clue in Bloch's one-sentence summary. It is the words "not yet." Just as other philosophers have written at length on the vast worlds that open to our imagination if we examine such tiny words as "love" or "is" or "time," Bloch peers into the creative sources of human existence by examining the words "not yet." Man is not for Bloch principally a product of his past either individually or as a race. Man is not to be described as "thinker" or "symbol maker" or "tool maker" or even as "worker." Man is the "hope-er," he-who-hopes. His essential existence tiptoes along the narrow ridge between the disappearing "now" and the ever newly appearing "not-yet." And his basic stance, when he is true to himself, is that of creative expectation, a hope that engenders action in the present to shape the future.

What is the nature of the "not-yet"? The future that makes man free? Bloch's answers are never fully satisfying. With a trace of teutonic titanism he proclaims himself the discoverer of this new continent. But like Columbus, he admits that the full exploration of the new world must be left to others. He is content to plant his flag in its sand, let his gaze follow its vast horizons and speculate on what may lie behind its towering mountain ranges. Like that great investigator of the unconscious, Sigmund Freud, with whom Bloch likes to compare himself, he can demonstrate how the charting of the new land mass might proceed. But he does not pretend that the rough charts he has made are definitive.

The comparison between Bloch and Freud is an interesting one. Both are secularized Jews. Both thought of themselves as atheists but could not shake off their interests in religious problems. Both offended middle class sensibilities, Freud by meddling with sex and Bloch by becoming a Communist. But both retained in their private lives a conventional bourgeois style. Freud loved to play cards with old cronies in his anti-macassar Vienna home. Bloch thrives on the *Gemütlichkeit* of Tübingen. Freud studied what Bloch has called the *Nicht-mehr-Bewusst*, that which has come to consciousness but has now passed into unconsciousness. Bloch has discovered the *"Noch-nicht Bewusst,"* that which scampers teasingly on the threshold of consciousness, sensed only in anticipation, not yet fully realized. While Freud was interested in night dreams, Bloch is fascinated by daydreams. Fantasy, for Bloch, is not a mere frippery, not a waste of time, but a crucial key to how human beings think. Perhaps the most significant difference between the two is that while Freud did develop a method for examining the no-more-conscious, psychoanalysis, Bloch has not produced its equivalent for the not-yet-conscious. Or perhaps in Bloch's own spirit we should say he has *not yet* produced it.

In theology, the study of the "not-yet," although we do not usually employ Bloch's phrase, is called "eschatology." Although it has usually been the poor step-sister in the household of theology, eschatology, the study of the Christian hope, is today once again claiming a central place. Theologians such as Jürgen Moltmann and Johannes Metz are working today with the assumption that Albert Schweitzer was right when he saw Christianity as essentially eschatological. They see the need not just to recover eschatology but to rethink the whole theological tradition from the perspective of hope. As Moltmann says, eschatology is not just one doctrine among others; it is the *key* in which everything is set, the glow that suffuses everything else. Therefore eschatology cannot be merely part of Christian doctrine; it must be the determining characteristic of all Christian existence and of the whole church.

But how does Christianity recover its lost eschatological stance? Its daring hope for the future which has now been taken over and distorted by revolutionary movements? The trouble is that Christian hope has been either so postponed or so underplayed in the history of Christian thought, that theologians today have an enormous job on their hands. How can we restate that hope, expressed in the New Testament in symbols of the resurrection of the dead and the triumphant return of Christ on the clouds, in images that modern man can understand? For centuries Christianity has persistently minimized any notion that the future would overturn the religious or political institutions of the day. Consequently the church has often become an objectively conservative force in the society. Yet the early Christians hoped for something that *would* transform this world, and today secularized forms of this hope are altering the face of the earth. How does Christianity regain a posture of radical hope, a hope for *this* world? How can the church regain the *stance* that was unswervingly oriented toward the future, but transmute the content of their hope so that it becomes available to contemporary man? With this task set before us it is natural that we should be impressed by a man whose life has been spent examining the "*futurum*," the idea of the new, the "*Impuls der Erwartung*" and the "principle of hope."

The interest in Bloch among theologians is not merely an unrequited love. Like any really significant philosopher, Bloch recognizes that he must deal with religion, so the interest moves both ways. Still Bloch remains, for his Christian suitors, a little hard-to-get and perhaps ultimately even unavailable. But this resistance, in the intellectual as in the romantic, often seems to excite interest rather than to dampen it. How does Bloch deal with religion?

As a Marxist, he knows as Marx did that "all criticism begins with the criticism of religion." Unlike most Marxists, however, Bloch approaches religion neither with distaste nor with condescension, but with genuine sympathy and untiring fascination. He has displayed an interest in religion since his earliest years, and that interest continues to the present day. For Bloch, all religion finds its source in the "dichotomy of man between his present appearance and his non-present essence (*Prinzip Hoffnung*, page 1520)—a statement that calls to mind Marx's own assertion that religious misery is not only the expression of real misery in a distorted and mystified way, but is also a protest against real misery. Marx, however, emphasized the narcotizing effect of religion (the "opiate of the people"), whereas Bloch is more interested in why and how religion functions as an expressive form of protest.

What about Christianity? Unlike some 20th century theologians who insist on a qualitative distinction between "faith in Christ" and religious belief, or between "religion" and "the Gospel," Bloch sees a continuity between religion and Christianity. More in the style of a 19th century theologian, or of recent theologians influenced by contemporary phenomenology of religion, Bloch speaks of Christianity as the purest and most consistent expression of this irreduceable content of all religion. In its universal messianism and its inclusive eschatology Christianity becomes the religious expression par excellence of the hope-laden dissatisfaction which spurs man on toward the future. Bloch also believes, however, that there is a crucial difference between Christianity and many other religions in the way it copes with the present. While some religions stress the mythical and thus tend to become static and to serve as an apology for the status quo, Christianity's messianism gives it a critical perspective on the present and loads it with explosive potential.

Both friends and foes of Christianity may rightly suspect

at this point that Bloch's estimate of its significance seems unduly generous. They should realize at once that Bloch is not talking about Christianity as currently preached and practiced. He has in mind what might be called the "essential meaning" of Christianity, a meaning which for Bloch burned brightly in the early church but emigrated into non-Christian movements when the church surrendered to the wiles of Constantine, sacrificed its eschatological hope and allowed itself to become the sacral ideology of the Empire. He believes that Christianity's great gift was to introduce the "principle of hope" into the world, that is, a way of seeing things from the perspective of the future, what they could become. He says that this essential Christian impulse, although it was throttled by the church, has popped out again here and there in such renegades as Thomas Münzer and Joachim of Fiore, but that its major vehicle in recent years has been movements of revolutionary social change. Christianity kindled a revolution which, instead of devouring its children, disavowed them.

In Bloch's view, not only man but the cosmos itself is an existence moving toward a still unfulfilled essence. Indeed he insists on this point so avidly that one cannot help being reminded of St. Paul's famous assertion in the eighth chapter of Romans that not only man but the creation itself groans and travails waiting for its redemption. But here Bloch adamantly stops short of any agreement with St. Paul. It is not God who is the source of this discontent or the ground of this hope. Drawing on the same "left-wing Aristotelianism" that nourished Marx, Bloch contends that this restlessness of matter, its longing for form, is an inner characteristic of matter itself. Here he seems closer to the vision of Teilhard de Chardin than he does to those theologians who posit a God who beckons to the cosmos from a radically other future. Yet even here his position is not entirely unequivocal.

Bloch is a troubled atheist. He rejects the Christian propensity to hypostasize the future into an existent God. But he is also bothered by the nihilist alternative which sees man's hope merely as wishful projection into the void.

Bloch wants to guard the unconditional openness of this future by arguing that it transcends all images and schemes that seek to give it content, but he refuses to assign it any viable facticity. He attempts to escape from this dilemma by talking about a "vacuum," an unfilled area which exerts a certain magnetic pull on man and on the cosmos. This moving point ahead of human history was once the cinema screen on which religious projections were flashed. Now we must no longer be deceived by the pictures. Still, for Bloch the moving point is no mere oasis, no cruel deception luring man on into destruction and frustration. But at the same time it has no substantial or existent reality. It is the constantly receding threshold over which existence passes in its endless quest for essence, a quest which, for Bloch, is never satisfied as long as man remains man.

Here the point of fruitful encounter between Marx and contemporary theology zooms into focus. Bloch balks at saying this open window to the future "exists." He is understandably afraid that to concede this would drag back into the picture all the static ontologies and superstitious notions of God that Christianity has for centuries erected, thus contributing to the constriction and stupefaction of man. But what Bloch does not realize clearly enough is that many Christian theologians today are equally reticent to claim God "exists" in the sense that makes Bloch so uncomfortable. Tillich, for example, vigorously refuses to allow the verb "exists" to follow the noun "God." For Tillich the phrase "God does not exist" was central to his thought since an existent being could not be the ground of all being and all existence. There is no real difference, therefore, between Tillich and Bloch on the question of the "existence" of God—they both deny it. The point of their essential disagreement is over the question of where the reality Tillich calls "God" and Bloch does not, touches man. For Tillich it was "in the depths," as the source of our being. For Bloch, on the other hand, it is at the "forward edge," where man moves from the present into the future.

The truth is, however, that Tillich's influence in modern

theology is now waning. The dialogue with Bloch is now in the hands of a younger group of theologians with some-what differing emphases and interests. Although it is of course impossible to predict how the conversation between Bloch and these men will unfold, it is tempting to speculate on the contact points at which it will proceed. Naturally this can be done here, however, only with great brevity. Three groups in particular suggest this sort of comment: (1) the so-called "death-of-God" thinkers, (2) the "de-velopment" theologians, and (3) the "secular theologians."

For a death-of-God theologian such as Thomas Altizer, Bloch poses a serious challenge. He appears as a "threat from the left." For Bloch atheism is no issue; he has already accepted it. The death of God cannot become either the con-tent of Christian proclamation nor the determinative condi-tion under which theology must now proceed. It cannot be the proclamation since it is not new and not in itself very interesting. It cannot define theology's task since the mere disappearance of God does not answer what for Bloch re-mains the crucial question, i.e., what holds history open for man and man open for history?

What would Bloch think of Altizer's quasi-pantheistic mysticism? It is safe to guess that the restless old German Marxist would find the young American Christian's work disastrously defective at the very point at which Christianity makes its most telling contribution: eschatology. Altizer's eschatology is in the past. God *has* died in Christ, and his reality now suffuses our whole world in a radically imma-nent way. Any notion of a God who "comes" in judgment, or a Christ who threatens the kingdoms of the earth, is missing from Altizer. Eternity has replaced history. Man, although he should love the world and his neighbor, has no need to open himself to the future since nothing really new is to be expected from there. But eschatology has a way of jarring inert worldliness, sowing seeds of discontent, and launching man into change and history. It would therefore seem reasonable to suppose that an appropriation of certain aspects of Bloch might restore an element of eschatology and therefore of social radicalism to Altizer's theology. Without it his position remains ahistorical with all the dangers of a conservative immanentism.

How would Bloch's thought engage those theologians who are seeking to develop the doctrine of God beyond its present state? Here the best example is the thought of Leslie Dewart. It seems unfortunate to me that in his provocative book *The Future of Belief*, Dewart never once mentions Ernst Bloch. Admittedly, Dewart tries to utilize scholastic thought even as he breaks out of it and shows its insufficiency. Bloch might have been a hindrance to this task. Still, Dewart's effort to push the present forms of Christian theism toward forms that will not elicit immediate atheistic counter-arguments might have benefited from Bloch's ideas on the ontology of the "not-yet."

Dewart, like Bloch, recognizes that the notion of God as a supernatural being, although it may have served a constructive purpose once, now acts as a drag on man's maturation and creativity. When combined with uncritical ideas about divine providence, the conventional doctrine of God saps man's initiative, undercuts his feeling of responsibility for history, and leads to a prolongation of childishness and dependency. Dewart tries to get the discussion on a new course by moving away from arguments about God's "existence" and focusing instead on the question of his "reality." He argues that the reality of God as that which enables man to be aware of and to transcend himself is experientially undeniable, although the word "God" may not be the best way to describe such a reality. He then tries to utilize the category of "presence" derived from Gabriel Marcel to describe the mode of our experience of God. For many readers, however, Dewart's argument, although fascinating, falls short of persuading completely since the crucial question of the ground of this "presence" in reality is left insufficiently developed.

Dewart correctly traces our present myopia about the reality of God to Parmenides and our mistaken insistence on equating being *real* with *existing*. He tries to suggest a possible doctrine of God that would grow out of man's experience of his own questionableness, his capacity for self-transcendence, and his irrefutable awareness of his own freedom. The trouble is that so many writers, Sartre for example, have used just such an approach without feeling any need for a God. Dewart admits that his ideas are provisional and tentative. What his book shows is that when we do leave scholastic categories behind, a new frame of reference will be needed, and that Marcel's somewhat illusive notion of "presence" may not suffice. Dewart's own interest in Marxism suggests that he could profit enormously from Bloch's thought, that the category of "hope" rather than that of "presence" might provide him with a more productive starting point in his exciting effort to facilitate a further stage in the development of theism.

What about that somewhat disparate group of thinkers who have been called "secular theologians" (a group within which I would have to count myself)? Bloch's work provides an insight that will help enormously at just the point where the most vociferous complaints about our position have been lodged. How, we are constantly asked, does one prevent a theology of the *saeculum* from collapsing into a mere theological decoration of the world as it is? What is the source of prophetic criticism? If heaven has faded into oblivion, if the horizon of human history now defines the field of man's existence in faith, where is that Copernican point of perspective from which renewal and insight emerge?

From Bloch we might learn that a horizon is always formed by something, not by nothing. The hidden God, whose very hiddenness is disclosed in Jesus of Nazareth, provides history with its "frame," with what Marshall McLuhan might call its "anti-environment." Bloch helps us to see that this *saeculum*, this world-age, is bounded by the future toward which it hastens every day, a future it never attains but which continually prevents it from accepting itself as finished and final. With Bloch's help, we can be unremittingly concerned with the secular without sacrificing the transcendent. God is not above, or beneath us, or even just "within" us. He is ahead. Christian existence is defined by hope and the church is the community of God's tomorrow, eternally discontent with today.

This tiny volume of essays may begin a new chapter in the career of English language theology. It will certainly bring to many people the voice of a man whom cold war politics and ephemeral intellectual fads have kept from us for far too long. I have often speculated on how different theology would be today if Ernst Bloch, rather than Martin Heidegger, had been our conversation partner for the past twenty years. Would we be as miserably lacking as we are in a theologically grounded social ethic? Would we be as disastrously out of touch with the revolution that is transforming the third world and burning the centers of our American cities? Would we have needed the catharsis of the death-of-God theology? Would we have allowed the ecclesiastical furniture shuffling of recent years to pose as a real renewal of the church? Might we have produced a theology that was truly radical in its impact on the world and not just in its rhetoric?

These questions cannot of course be answered today. Nor can we expect Bloch to do for us the work we must do for ourselves. Bloch is not just a Christian *manqué*. He does not help us much when we seek to spell out the *content* of hope for today's man. For Christians, that must come from a vision of what is possible for a world in which the God of Exodus and Easter is still alive.

The Absolute Future

Michael Novak

Applauding those who reject philosophies that make for stasis and inaction, Michael Novak nonetheless upholds one fundamental function of traditional philosophy—that of raising questions. For "without the drive to ask questions, revolution, reform and progress are inconceivable." Essential though decision-making and responsible action are, it should be recognized that they derive their impetus from the drive to ask questions; indeed, it is this drive which is "at one and the same time the source of man's openness to God and the source of social and political change." Roman Catholic layman Novak is on the faculty of Stanford University's Special Program in Humanities, and is the author of *Belief and Unbelief, The Open Church: Vatican II, Act II,* and, most recently, *A Time to Build.* His article is from the January 13, 1967, *Commonweal,** one of several journals to which he contributes regularly.

AMERICAN CATHOLICS down the years have committed grievous sins of rabid anti-Communism. Consequently, one of the main imperatives of Catholics at present is to puncture the popular myths, biases, and prejudices about Communism that distort American political debate. On the international scene, the time has come for Christians and Marxists no longer merely to ignore or to destroy one another, but to learn from one another and to criticize one another. The shedding of one another's blood is useless, the ignoring of one another is empty.

One of the main points at which the current dialogue between Christians and Marxists converges is the meaning of the future. Contrary to stereotype, Marxist philosophy is not

* 232 Madison Avenue, New York, N.Y. 10016.

materialistic in a Western sense; it hopes for a future in which men's capacities of imagination, decision and creative labor will be completely developed. Such a future may never, in fact, arrive; thus, the Marxist conception of the future might well be open. In that case, the function of the concept of future would be to provide leverage for criticism and reform of the present. *Secularia semper reformanda.*

At a recent conference of Catholics and Marxists in Austria, Karl Rahner defined Christianity in a perspective that might make sense to Marxists: "Christianity is the religion of the absolute future." Rahner's point is familiar to students of Reinhold Niebuhr. Christianity is eschatological: it refuses to call any present social arrangement final; within history, justice is never complete. Christianity refuses to idolize the present or the past, for its Lord is one who is ever to be awaited: "Come, Lord Jesus!" Christians are committed to building up the kingdom of God on earth, a kingdom of truth, liberty, justice and love. Since we do not yet have an international social order characterized by such values, Christians cannot very well rest upon what has so far been achieved; the pilgrimage is not over; there are many painful miles yet to march. *Ecclesia semper reformanda.*

Marxist thinkers have always had a predilection for one of the rather neglected Christian traditions, that of Joachim of Flora, the Anabaptists, and the Free Churches. The more established Christian traditions—Catholic, Lutheran, and Calvinist—have preferred to work in continuity with the institutions of the Holy Roman Empire. They have found it possible to work out various arrangements with emperors, kings, princes, and later with parliaments and economic corporations. They have operated on the assumption that there is a natural, created base for Christianity—a set of pre-Christian or religious or human values on which Christianity can "build." They have been more or less protective of the "moral fiber" of society, of its educational system and its family mores. They are proud of an entity they call "Western civilization," which they think of as "Christian."

206 / Michael Novak

By contrast, Joachim of Flora preached a coming "third age" of the Holy Spirit discontinuous with the pagan institutions, laws, and orders of the past. Anabaptists and Free Churchmen regarded the classical Lutheran and Calvinist reformations as "halfway reformations," much too limited in scope. For under Lutherans and Calvinists, as under Catholics, the establishment of religion remained intact; the social and economic institutions of the pagan past were still being "baptized." Free Churchmen desired a less institutionalized, more voluntary, more demanding church. Their desires were so exigent that the future became a crucial category in their thought. Some of them used the future as escape from the present; but still more of them used it as a weapon of criticism against the present. They demanded an authenticity, an integrity, and a commitment that empowered many poor and simple people to stand firm against feudal and monarchical institutions, and to generate much momentum for change in Western society.

In American theological thought, Harvey Cox stands more nearly than any other in this tradition. It is not surprising, then, that Cox is the Christian theologian most sensitively attuned to the Christian-Marxist dialogue and the importance of the category of the future. In his rejoinder in *The Secular City Debate* (Macmillan, $1.45), in fact, he has promised us an approach to language about God through language about the future. Such an enterprise will be at the heart of the issue between Marxists and Christians. Since the basic notion seems sound, I would like to help the project along by voicing a few critical reflections.

In the first place, Marxist thought regards existentialism as a stage in the progressive decadence of the west. In the Marxist view, existentialism has not healed the split between thought and action which is the disease of Western philosophy. Western philosophy is too "intellectualist"; it does not give sufficient weight to the fact that the role of thought is not merely to reflect the world, but to *change* the world. Again, it does not give sufficient weight to the fact that thinking is highly conditioned by social, economic, and other circumstances. Harvey Cox is not especially interested in epistemological questions, but he has been convinced by the Marxist critique that existentialism is a mere emotional retreat, a philosophy of inaction and Hamlet-like reflection, a disease of inwardness. Moreover, he has joined the Marxist critique of inwardness to Bonhoeffer's complaint about still another kind of inwardness: the concern and anxiety which German and Scandinavian religious thought has cherished as "the religious dimension" of man's subjective life.

Nevertheless, both for Marxist thought and for Cox, the source of thought which changes the world lies in the imagination, the projects, and the decisions of men. The future does not merely happen; men must invent it and take responsibility for it. For both, moreover, responsibility is not merely a factor of social conditioning; first one man must stand firm and then another—decision must well up from the strength of each individual. Otherwise there is no maturity, only docility, passivity, and conformity.

Existentialist emphasis on decision-making often seems to be too emotive and individualistic; even social relations are conceived on the model of eye-to-eye, deeply personal "encounters." With Marxist thinkers, Cox insists on the social dimensions and social realities of responsibility; much less than, say, Camus' Meursault in *The Stranger* will he allow a man to contemplate morosely his own emotional complexities. Does Cox at this point run the risk of evasion, promoting the reform of institutions because the reform of oneself is so difficult? There are some passages in *The Secular City*—particularly those on the "I-you relationship" —which read like the rationalizations of a busy, harried man. But to criticize Cox in this way would be to acquiesce in a dualism that is untenable. The individual and the social are not, in reality, separate; our language and hence even our private thoughts and our personal values are social phenomena. Cox is right to insist that maturity arises through social and political commitment. An accurate criticism, perhaps, is that he has not yet told us very much about how to choose among, or how to criticize, alternative commitments; he has merely announced where he stands.

But even at this point Cox's rejoinder in *The Secular City Debate* offers promise. "In our time the metaphysicians," he writes, "instead of integrating our lives for us, will probably more often challenge the premature integrations and cultural foreclosures that constrict us. . . . Our task today is to transmute the answers of classical metaphysics into questions that will guard the openness of our symbol worlds today." I think Cox is wrong in his historical judgment that such thinkers as Aristotle and St. Thomas thought of their own work as "intellectual systems" which might "integrate whole cultural periods." Neither Aristotle nor Aquinas had much success among their contemporaries, and their work presents to the serious student today a record of tentative, dialectical, constantly changing forays into uncharted areas.) But the main point is that Cox now sees metaphysics as a critical enterprise, as the raising of further questions, as the dialectical exploding of presuppositions. The metaphysical impulse is the question-raising impulse.

Moreover, I would like to point out that the empirical ground which allows men to conceive of the "absolute future" or of an "open future" is precisely the human ability to ask ever future questions. The point of the expression "absolute future" or "open future" is that such a future cannot be conceived merely as a projection from present conditions; for a merely projected future is limited and does not represent the complete realization of historical possibility. Man is gifted with an imagination and a skeptical attitude which makes it possible for him to *alter* the conditions of the future, to *change* the world. Consequently, the human animal "transcends" even his own empirical projections: he calls them into question.

How, then, does a man know *now* that his authentic goal is the absolute future, not merely a projection? He cannot envisage an absolute future; all he can envisage is the projected future. He knows that his goal is the absolute future because he recognizes in himself a capacity to change direction, to shift his presuppositions, to imagine new alternatives: in short, to raise limitless series of questions. Right now, this minute, a man can become aware, at least indirectly, of the profundity and limitless resourcefulness of his drive to ask questions. There is no point in history at which he can imagine himself refusing to ask questions, surrendering his capacity to imagine, project, and break out anew. The ground of the conception of the absolute future is man's unrestricted drive to ask questions, his relentless openness.

This is the point of the question—a traditional one—put to the Marxists at the Salzburg Colloquy by J. B. Metz: "Will the realization of the total man give the final answer to man's questions, or will man, when fully developed, be still more the questioner, more capable still of an ever-expanding future? Will the future be filled with questions which exceed and transcend our projects and our tentative notions of the future? This would in no way contradict the autonomy of the human race since it is this openness to the future which constitutes the very essence of man."

Without the drive to ask questions, revolution, reform and progress are inconceivable. In order for a revolution to be launched, men must question the present and diagnose it; question other possible alternatives and imagine a new world; raise questions in others until a new community takes shape; and question alternative strategies and tactics for realizing the new against the inertia of the old. A theology of revolution depends at each step upon the relentlessness and the skills of the drive to ask questions. Of course, it is not enough to ask questions; one must also make decisions and, above all, act. But it is useful to notice the fundamental role of question-asking in intelligent social and political action.

Moreover, it seems to me that the drive to ask questions is at one and the same time the source of man's openness to God and the source of social and political change. In brief, there is a startling unity between language about God and language about social and political reforms. The human drive to ask questions constitutes the openness which allows men to transcend the present, and gives rise to both languages. To think of the drive to understand as the generator of religious language is, of course, continuous with some strands of tradition; but it is mature to recognize one's continuity with the past.

What is new is the suddenly acquired power of men to change their environment, both natural and institutional. Whereas in earlier days the panorama of human life seemed to confirm that there is nothing new under the sun, nowadays the pace and scope of change are so obvious that someone might plausibly wonder whether there is anything stable. In a world now conceived as a bundle of loose ends, open to the most surprising, contingent, and unpredictable developments—a world of probabilities rather than of certainties—man's sense of responsibility for his values, his actions, and even his survival has become a sign much more cogent as an image of God than the ancient sense of dependence on the God of the ordered cosmos.

In short, theology grows out of reflection upon actual human experience in the world. The experience which captivates the imagination of our age is the experience of change, the move toward further frontiers, the hope of a human brotherly world civilization. In *every* human experience, the language of transcendence is available to men because the human drive to raise questions is present in every experience. It is not necessary to kick the faces of those who preceded us in order to speak of transcendence in our own way. When Heidegger used the language of anxiety and concern, he spoke to the experience of a dying civilization. The God spoken of as *will be* happens to speak more clearly to us, but we are not, except momentarily, at the apex of the human race.

Recognizing that fact, we do not think of God as one on whom we "depend" but rather as one who eludes our attempt to speak adequately of him, even as he eluded the clutches of our ancestors. Taking up our daily, concrete responsibilities, we cannot be sure that we hold God in our hands. Like the atheist, we work in darkness regarding

God. But we accept the symbol of the community of truth, freedom, love and justice bequeathed us in the Gospel of Jesus Christ and interpret our labors in its light. If we are correct, God is the one who is now with us without revealing himself magically, and the one who, in the absolute future, will be all in all.

Communists and Christians in Dialogue

Roger Garaudy

Few Christians will concur with Roger Garaudy's reading of Christianity, and those who are knowledgeable about Marx will know that Garaudy's reading of his mentor is highly selective. Nonetheless it is refreshing to find the French Communist Party's leading theoretician insisting that dialogue between Communists and Christians is not only desirable but necessary: "The future of mankind cannot be built in opposition to those with a religious faith, nor even without them; the future of mankind cannot be built in opposition to the Communists, nor even without them." To be recommended to those who wish to delve deeper into Garaudy's thinking on Communist-Christian dialogue is his important work *From Anathema to Dialogue*. Dr. Garaudy is Director of the Center for Marxist Study and Research in Paris and Professor of Philosophy at the University Institute of Poitiers. Originally an address delivered in December 1966 at Union Theological Seminary in New York City, his article appeared in the March 1967 *Union Seminary Quarterly Review*.*

IN OUR time dialogue is an objective necessity. The absolute necessity of dialogue and cooperation between Christians and Communists proceeds from two incontrovertible facts:

First, in this second half of the twentieth century the presently existing stocks of atomic and thermonuclear bombs have made it technically possible to destroy every trace of life on earth. We have now reached the sublime and tragic moment in human history in which the human epic begun a

* Reprinted with permission from the March 1967 *Union Seminary Quarterly Review*, 3041 Broadway, New York, N.Y. 10027.

million years ago could well come to an end. If mankind is to survive, it will not do so merely through the force of the inertia of biological evolution but rather through a human decision which requires, as Teilhard de Chardin has so admirably said, "the common effort of all those who believe that the universe is still progressing, and that we are in charge of this progress."

The second fact is that on this earth, this vessel floating in space with three billion men aboard, which a dissension in the crew could scuttle at any moment, there are two great conceptions of the world: Hundreds of millions of human beings find in a religious belief the meaning of their life and of their death, the meaning of human history itself; and for hundreds of millions of others it is Communism that shapes the hopes of the world and gives meaning to our history. This, then, is a datum of our time: The future of mankind cannot be built in opposition to those with a religious faith, nor even without them; the future of mankind cannot be built in opposition to the Communists, nor even without them.

It is in the light of these two immense data, which dominate our reflections, that historical problems assume their historical dimension.

What is significant here is that this necessity for dialogue is felt both by Catholics and by Communists.

The Marxist View of Religion

Marxists do not deal with religion in general, in a metaphysical and idealistic way, but as historians and materialists. They seek to discover how under some historical circumstances, which must be scientifically analyzed in each case, faith can play a positive and progressive part. This means simply that if the famous formula, "Religion is the opium of the people," corresponds to an undeniable historical experience, today still very widely verified, the Marxist conception of religion is not to be reduced to this formula. The thesis according to which religion in all times and places diverts man from action, work, and struggle flagrantly contradicts historical reality.

Pointing to what in religion is a reflection of a real distress and what is a protest against this real distress, Marx suggests a method to analyze the real human substance, made mysterious by its religious form: to study at the same time, and in each particular historical case, in what real social relations the fantastic reflection originates, as well as the protest, the active moment of the exigency to go beyond these relations (even if this exigency is led astray and turned away from its social, militant point of application and directed towards the heaven of personal salvation).

The Contribution of Christianity

What has Christianity, whose role was so important in our civilization, contributed to our conception of man?

The basic and constant feature of the ancient wisdom of the Greeks and Romans was to situate and define man in relation to a totality of which he was a moment, or a part, whether a part of the cosmos or the city, of the order of nature or the order of the concepts. From Thales to Democritus the world was conceived as a given fact. Man could know it in its ultimate reality and by this knowledge reach the highest dignity to which a man could attain: the consciousness of his fate and happiness. From Plato to the Stoics it is again knowledge that frees man and leads him to self-control and bliss, even if through diverse conceptions of the ultimate reality, which may be tangible or intelligible, an order of nature or an order of concepts.

At first, Christianity represented a break with this Hellenistic conception of the world. Following Judaism, it substituted a philosophy of act for a philosophy of being. In this philosophy of act the leading notion was not that of *logos* but that of *creation*, and man was worth something inasmuch as he was conscious no longer of what he was but of what he was not, of what he lacked. According to Augustine, man is not to be measured in the dimensions of the earth and the stars, nor according to the rules of the city or of any universality. He exists, not as part of a totality of nature or of concepts, but in his own peculiarity, as subjectivity, as interiority, dependent on the call of the God who lives in him and wrests him from any given "order": "We go beyond the narrow boundaries of our science," Augustine wrote. "We cannot get hold of ourselves and yet we are not beside ourselves."[1]

To this conquest of subjectivity and interiority, by its violent reaction against pagan wisdom, primitive Christianity readily sacrificed the rationality so patiently conquered by the aesthetic and rational humanism of Greek thought. In the fourth century Lactantius, in his *Divine Institution* (ii. 5), set the free divine will against the necessity of the Stoics, against their conception of order and rationality. The world was not the necessary development of a rational law but the bestowal of love.

From this new conception of the world followed a new conception of man: He no longer aimed at being great by equalling himself, through his knowledge, to the supreme law of the city and to the eternal order of the cosmos. He drew his infinite value from being like God, a creator in his own right, capable of giving and loving, on the threshold of an absolute future, which was no logical continuation of the past nor a moment of a given totality but the possibility of starting a new life by answering the call of God. In this new conception God is no longer totality, nor concept, nor harmonious and complete image of the human order, but he is a person, a hidden God, whom no knowledge is able to convey to us and to whom only faith can give us access, but always in agony and doubt.

Greek and Roman antiquity, on the one hand, and Jewish and Christian antiquity, on the other hand, thus brought to light two demands of humanism: that of a rational mastery of the world, and that of an historical and properly human initiative. The problem and the program of humanism in the Western tradition would be henceforth to hold both ends of the chain even if we were to be rent by it. The Renaissance failed to do it, for once again the two were separated. The

[1] Augustine *De anima et ejus origine* iv. 6. 8.

first great synthesis was undertaken by the classical German philosophers, and particularly by Kant and Fichte, bringing the two ends of the chain nearer to unite the necessity of a rational law (without which neither science nor the world can exist) and the freedom of man's creative action (without which there can be neither moral initiative nor responsibility and without which there can be no history). But once more the chain was broken, for the synthesis had not been carried out. The balance of knowledge and liberty wished by Goethe and his Faust remains a dream and a promise, the finest dream and the finest promise of humanity, but still a dream forever reviving and forever postponed. The divergence springs up again with, on the one hand, Hegel's stately rational system of nature and history and, on the other hand, Kierkegaard's claim for a subjectivity fundamental in its peculiarity but a claim at the same time for transcendence.

Transcendence

Christianity, in effect, has juxtaposed the problem of transcendence and the problem of subjectivity (and this is, in fact, its specific way of entering into the problem of subjectivity). Transcendence is a dangerous expression, for its past is heavy with confusions and mystifications. Traditionally this notion means belief in a world beyond, in the supernatural, with the irrationality, the miracles, the mystery, and finally the deception that those notions carry with them. Must we not ask ourselves, before this central aspect of the religious attitude, what need, what question, what experience this faith in transcendence and the supernatural answers to? The claim to transcendence is the actual human experience that man, though belonging to nature, is different from the things and animals and that man, forever able to progress, is never complete.

As Marx explained it, with the appearance of a specifically human work—a work whose law is the prosecuted aim, a project—man rises over all other animal species and begins an historical evolution, the rhythm of which is without any common measure to that of biological evolution.

Here we have a qualitative leap, a real outgrowing, a "transcendency" (in the strictly etymological sense of the term) in relation to nature. Man belongs to nature. But out of him, with culture, a superior level of nature appears. Such is the real human substance of this notion of transcendency: Transcendence is the alienated expression of *nature* outgrowing itself into *culture*. That he who crossed the threshold, man himself, should have been so filled with wonder that he conceived another order of reality from nature, a super-nature, a beyond full of promise and menace—this is the typical process of alienation. To elaborate a conception of transcendency that is not alienated is, therefore, to show—and dialectic materialism allows it—that this possibility of initiative and creation is not the attribute of a God but, on the contrary, the specific attribute of man that differentiates him from all other animal species.

Subjectivity

This conception of transcendency allows us to single out another aspect of the Christian contribution: the sense of subjectivity. If for Greek humanism man was a fragment of the universe and a member of the city, Christianity, following Judaism, laid the stress on the subjective moment of man's life—on the possibility for man to start a new future. Between the action of the external world and the action of man, who goes towards the external world to cope with its threat, stands conscience on its various levels: anguish and effort, search and dream, hope and love, risk and decision. Such is subjectivity. Christianity has accumulated a rich experience on that plane, from Augustine to Kierkegaard, from Pascal and Racine to Claudel; but at the same time, by resuming the Neoplatonic themes of renunciation of the external world, it has developed fatalism and submission.

Love

Along with transcendency and subjectivity, love is one of the most questionable contributions of Christianity to human formation.

If we have not beforehand mutilated man by excluding all subjectivity and true interiority in order to reduce him to the mere product of social structures, entirely determined by them; if on the contrary we have, with Marx, shown that what is stifled and crushed by the structures of capital is precisely a human reality, ever developing historically but not entirely created by the present structures, and which can therefore be a protest against these structures—then we shall be able to understand how such unavailing protest has led to a projection of love that is "the other" of this brutal world, a projection out of this world into another world, into a "beyond." This love has found wonderful artistic forms of expression, from the poetry of courtly love to Tristan and Isolde, from St. Theresa of Avila to Racine, from Marceline Desbordes Valmore to the "Fou d'Elsa," from Eluard to the "Soulier de Satin."

Moreover, the specifically Christian attitude towards love could not be mingled with a variant of Platonism, which opposes "the other world" or "the beyond" to this world and demands that one should part from this world, that one should turn one's back upon it to emigrate towards "the other," towards the "beyond," towards God. This dualism, this idealism, this disembodiment, is on the contrary characteristic of heresies from docetism to the Cathars, whereas the essential Christian teaching, even if often contaminated by Hellenism or gnosticism, is founded upon incarnation and implies very different relations with the other man, the "neighbor": to deal with every human being as if Christ, the living God, were standing before us. The love of man is one with the love of God. That is why the mystics, according to a tradition that dates back to the Song of Solomon, evoke divine love with the very image of human love, as it particularly appears with St. Theresa of Avila.

It is necessary to insist upon this capital aspect of the Christian inheritance. If we distinguish the specific contribution of Christianity from that which, according to Nietzsche's expression, renders it into "a Platonism for the people," then the new dimensions and the meaning that Christianity has given to love constitute the most fruitful contribution ever made to man's continuing creation of himself. At the same time, this is the aspect of Christianity that can be the most deeply integrated with the Marxist conception of the world and of man.

To demonstrate this, it is sufficient to compare the Christian conception of love with the noblest conception of love given by the Greek humanism—to compare Plato's *eros* with the Christian *agape*. The Platonic conception of love, the *eros* of *The Symposium* and the *Phaedras*, is characterized by a movement which lifts us towards the supreme being or good by wresting us from the earthly world. *Eros* makes us rise from the love of the beauty of the bodies to the love of the beauty of the spirits, and hence it leads us by an ascendant dialectic to the love of beauty in itself. Love (*eros*) finally carries us away from the world of other men altogether; it carries us out of time. It is a yearning that nothing in the real world can fulfill, a yearning inconsistent with the everyday world of men. The other is therefore not loved for what he is but for what he conjures up of another reality. In this love there is no "neighbor." The other is only an occasion for rising towards a reality without any common measure with the other himself. Therefore, each loves the other only for himself, or rather what he loves is not another being but love itself.

Before Christianity's teaching had been influenced by Hellenism, Platonism, gnosticism, and later by millenarianism, from the "imitation of Christ" to certain forms of the courtly love—and including the hypocritical condemnation of the flesh or of an interested contempt for the world, which we still find today—before all this, the central experience of the incarnation of Man-God and of God-man meant a radically novel transition *from the love of love to the love of the other*. It consisted in having given an absolute value through that incarnate love to the other and to the world. In the fundamental Christian (that is to say, Christ-centered) doctrine, rising to God in no way implies turning away from the world, since the living God can be met in every being. It is what in the sixteenth century Cardinal Bellarmine called "rising to God by the ladder of creatures," what in the twentieth century Father Teilhard de Chardin called "going beyond by going through," "transcending by traversing." In *Evolution of Chastity* he wrote that it is in carrying the world along with us that we make progress into the "bosom of God," and he suggested that we find a heaven for our natural activity in the faith of Christ. The more lucid Christians have tried to dissociate what is fundamental in their faith from out-of-date conceptions of the world in which their faith was traditionally expressed.

Christianity and the Changing World

More and more, the distinction becomes necessary between, on the one hand, religion as an ideology and a conception of the world, as a cultural form taken by faith at given periods of historical evolution, and, on the other hand, faith itself. A contemporary Protestant philosopher, Paul Ricoeur, writes: "Religion is the alienation of faith."[2] The problem of the distinction between faith and the historical transient cultural form that it has taken is strongly posed by a Catholic philosopher, Leslie Dewart, in his recent book *The Future of Belief*. Dewart first recalls that the universalization, the Catholicization, of Christianity from Paul to Augustine was conditioned by its Hellenization. A new conception of the relations of man and the world arose as Christianity was born from Judaism. But this conception adopted a pre-existing cultural form: that of Greek thought, which introduced into Christianity its own ideal of perfection, that is, "immobility." This Hellenistic influence led to the petrification of the dogma. Centuries later the rediscovery of Aristotle strengthened that trend, and medieval scholasticism emerged as the language in which the Christian faith has been, on the whole, expressed to our own day. The Christian conception of God was always more or less contaminated

[2] Paul Ricoeur, *De l'interprétation: Essai sur Freud* (Paris: Éditions du Seuil, 1965), p. 159.

by Parmenides' conception of true being, whether in the form of Plato's idea of the good, Aristotle's primary cause and unmoved mover, or Plotinus' idea of the One.

This is, no doubt, the reason for the impact of Teilhard de Chardin's works upon so many Christian consciences. He has posed a basic problem for his Church and indeed for all men of our times, the basic problem of our century, the very problem that Marx posed for the first time a century ago and which he began to answer: how to think the law of change and how to master it. Marx's discovery has produced the deepest transformation of the world that history has ever known. The question that Father Teilhard put to the Christians required of them nothing less than an inversion of attitude towards the world. He recalled a basic aspect of Christianity often obscured by a latent Platonism: that ascending to God does not imply turning one's back upon the world but, on the contrary, participating in its transformation and its construction with a more lucid mind, with more intense activity, and with a more vehement passion.

We thus reach the highest level of the dialogue, that of the integration by each of us of that which the other bears in himself, as other. I have said previously that "the depth of a believer's faith depends upon the strength of the atheism that he bears in himself." I can now add: "The depth of an atheist's humanism depends on the strength of the faith that he bears in himself." The dialogue will be truly fruitful insofar as all of us, in common defense of man's basic values, are rendered capable of integrating to ourselves the truth borne by our partner in dialogue.

Evolution, Myth, and Poetic Vision

Walter J. Ong, S.J.

Because the modern poet continues to cling to an out-moded, cyclical view of history and time, his plight is, in the opinion of Walter J. Ong, S.J., "truly extreme." If he wishes to speak for his age the poet must dispense with the imagery of recurrence (though to do so will require a dras-tic reorganization of his psyche and sensibility). "A sense of history, seen as evolutionary development, has now be-come an inevitable dimension of all reflective human exist-ence, and if the very feel of evolutionary development is unassimilable by poetry, then poetry cannot compass one of the most profound and intimate of modern experiences." Father Ong finds an affinity between evolutionary thought and Christianity—both are "anticyclic"—and suggests that the Catholic poet Gerard Manley Hopkins was far ahead of his time in that he possessed a well developed evolu-tionary time-sense. A professor of English at Saint Louis Uni-versity, Father Ong has a lengthy list of writings to his credit; it includes such books as *Darwin's Vision and Chris-tian Perspectives*, *The Barbarian Within*, *In the Human Grain*, and *The Presence of the Word*. His essay originally appeared in *Comparative Literature Studies** (Vol. III, No. 1, 1966), a quarterly formerly published by the University of Maryland and now published by the University of Illinois.

> . . . They say,
> The solid earth whereon we tread
>
> In tracts of fluent heat began,
>   And grew to seeming-random forms,
>   The seeming prey of cyclic storms,
> Till at the last arose the man.
>
>   . . . Arise and fly

* University of Illinois Press, Urbana, Illinois, 61801.

> The reeling Faun, the sensual feast;
> Move upward, working out the beast
> And let the ape and tiger die.
> —(Tennyson, *In Memoriam*, CXVIII)

THE INFLUENCE OF DARWIN upon the poetic and artistic imagination has become a commonplace, documented by a large assortment of studies from Lionel Stevenson's *Darwin among the Poets* (1932) through Georg Roppen's *Evolution and Poetic Belief* (1956). And yet, surveying the work of the creative human imagination today, one is struck by the slightness of creative drive connected with an awareness of evolution, cosmic or organic. It is not that the poets refuse to accept evolution. They render lip service to it. But it does not haunt their poetic imaginations.

One of the great evolutionary philosophers of our day, Father Pierre Teilhard de Chardin, has been accused of writing often as a poet. But we are hard put to find poets who make creative use of evolutionary insights comparable to Teilhard's. Teilhard faces forward, into the future, as, in its brighter moments, does the rest of our world, permeated as it is with evolutionary thinking. But the poets and artists tend to exalt the present moment when they are not facing the past. There is here certainly some kind of crisis concerning the relationship of the poet or artist to time.[1]

The situation is complicated by the fact that today's poets and artists generally are acutely aware of the continuing development of art itself. The existence of a self-conscious *avant-garde* makes this plain enough. Poetry, together with art generally, has a sense of its own domestic time. But cosmic time, as this has been known since the discovery of evolution, is another matter. Most poets and artists are not much interested in it, even when they are most intently concerned with man, who exists in this time. Writers who do deal with larger patterns of development in time tend to slip into thinly veiled sensationalism, as does George Bernard Shaw in *Back to Methuselah*, or sensationalism not so thinly veiled, as in George Orwell's *1984*, or they handle cosmic time not very successfully, as does Hart Crane, or half-heartedly, as does T. S. Eliot. One feels that, in the last analysis, the poet and artist are not very much at home in an evolutionary cosmos.

The basic issue between poetry and evolutionism is seemingly the need in poetry, as in all art, for repetition. The drives toward repetition show in poetry in countless ways—in rhythm, in rhyme, in other sound patterns, in thematic management and plotting (Joyce plots *Ulysses*, which for all practical purposes is a poem in the full sense of this term, to match Homer, as Virgil in a different way plotted the *Aeneid*). Even the key to all plotting, recognition, is a kind of repetition, a return to something already known.

In "Burnt Norton" T. S. Eliot writes:

> And the end and the beginning were always there
> Before the beginning and after the end.[2]

Finnegans Wake is a serpent with its tail in its own mouth, the *ouroboros*: the last words of the book run back into its first words.

The preoccupation of poetry and of art in general with repetition is shown at its deepest level in the constant resort to the natural cycle of the year: spring, summer, autumn, winter. Mircea Eliade has shown the tremendous drive of this cycle within the human consciousness in his book *The Myth of the Eternal Return*. Indeed, the cosmic myth of the seasons, with its lesser parts, its contractions, expansions, and other variations and projections (the succession of day and night, the imaginary Hindu *kalpa* of 4,320,000,000 solar years, Yeats's elaborate hocus-pocus in *A Vision*), dominates the subconscious so thoroughly that one can speak of it simply as natural symbolism—all nature symbolism comes to focus here—or even as *the* myth, for, in effect, there is no other. Professor Cleanth Brooks, distinguishing interest in history from interest in nature, notes that in modern poets "the celebration of nature is not tied to a cyclic theory."[3] It is my conviction that it need not be. But even in the writers Professor Brooks cites, such as Dylan Thomas, there is a discernible hankering for cyclicism; and in others he cites, such as Wallace Stevens, who shows keen interest in non-cyclic change, one finds less than a wholehearted welcome of a truly historic view. As we shall see, in place of the continuities of history one finds in Stevens rather a discontinuous series of states of chaos, each separately resolved by the imagination, each resolution, in a sense, being a kind of repetition of foregoing resolutions, with no recognizable progress.

In a perceptive study Professor Northrop Frye has recognized this fact, proffering a classification of the archetypes of literature based on the natural cycle of the year because "the crucial importance of this myth has been forced on literary critics by Jung and Frazer."[4] Professor Frye's first phase is the "dawn, spring and birth phase," concerned with the hero, revival and resurrection, creation, and the defeat of the powers of darkness, and having as subordinate characters the father and the mother. This, he states, is the "archetype of romance and of most dithyrambic poetry." The second phase is that of "zenith, summer, marriage or triumph." Here we are concerned with apotheosis, the sacred marriage, and entering into Paradise, and with the subordinate characters of the companion and bride. This is the archetype of comedy, pastoral, and idyll. The "sunset, autumn and death" phase is the third, concerned with the dying god, violent death and sacrifice, and the hero in isolation. The traitor and the siren are subordinate characters, and this phase is the archetype of tragedy and elegy. The fourth and last phase is the "darkness, winter and dissolution phase," with its floods, return of chaos, defeat of the hero—the *Götterdämmerung*, accompanied by the ogre and the witch as subordinate characters. This is the archetype of satire, as instanced in the conclusion of *The Dunciad*.

Waiving questions as to the applicability of the details of this structure to the actuality of poetry and art, we can see that Professor Frye is presenting us here with something on the whole both real and powerful. Moreover, as he himself observes in the same place, the natural cycle not only touches poetry in terms of its themes, imagery, and characters, but also in more pervasive terms, such as that of rhythm itself, which appears essential for art, verbal or visual: "Rhythm, or recurrent movement, is deeply founded on the natural cycle, and everything in nature that we think of as having some analogy with works of art, like the flower or the bird's song, grows out of a profound synchronization between an organism and the rhythms of its environment, especially that of the solar year."

Everyone can recognize the actuality of these rhythms, too. Spring does come back each year. Day succeeds night, and night day. Men are born and die. There are, however, certain problems here in establishing rhythmic patterns. The likening of man's life to a cycle, for example, is based on an all too obvious distortion: there is *some* likeness between the helplessness of an old man and that of an infant, but to mistake one for the other one would have to be out of one's mind—here the cyclic myth has asserted its compelling power in consciousness and made plausible in our assessment of human life a pattern which is really not there: the life of an individual actually ends quite differently from the way it began. One can think otherwise only by blotting out certain facts.

The same is true with regard to groups of men taken as groups. In an article a few years ago, I pointed out in some detail that the likening of the "life" of a nation or empire or of a culture or people or tribe to the life even of an individual man, and *a fortiori* to a perfect cycle in which the end is the same as the beginning, is quite indefensible and utterly contrary to fact, although by leaving out of consideration certain obvious facts, by proper selectivity, a certain analogy, very loose, between a nation and an individual and a much feebler analogy between the history of a social group and circular movement can be made out.[5] But, on the whole, these analogies probably deceive more than they inform. The Roman Empire "fell" (returned to the starting point from which it had presumably "risen") only in a very loose sense. It "died" only in a very loose sense, too, for it had never really been conceived and born as a human being is. The institutions of the Roman Empire are still all around us and in us, more widespread today than ever before; the descendants of its citizens are extraordinarily active over a greater expanse of the world than ever before, as mankind becomes more and more unified. Much as a circular area, say, a foot in circumference, can be discerned on an absolutely blank blackboard simply by disregarding the rest of the blackboard, so rise-and-fall or birth-and-death patterns can, of course, be discerned in events in the stream of time by proper selectivity. But what do such patterns explain? We like the rise-and-fall pattern probably less because it informs us about what is actually going on in the world than because it is, after all, a pattern, and the simplest pattern of all, imposed on the field of history, noteworthy for its lack of pattern. The attraction of periodicity operates largely from within the human psyche.

What sort of actuality do the cycles of nature have when we view them in terms of what we know of the universe since the discovery of cosmic and organic evolution? In the last analysis, they do not have much. Rhythms are approximations. Perfect cycles, exact repetitions, recurrences of identical starting points, are not really to be found. Although each winter is succeeded by spring, every year is actually different from every other if we look to details. What lengthier rhythms there may be—several years of drought and several of floods—are not really exact cycles, but approximations of cycles which gradually alter. On the whole, the global climate is changing in some kind of linear-style pattern, for the evolution of the earth is progressing toward an end-point quite different from its beginning. In the cosmos as we now know it, there is no real repetition anywhere, for all is in active evolution. One sees repetition only in the rough, where one does not examine more closely.

But the universe is being examined more closely all the time. Weather patterns, to stay with our example, are being fed into computers to give us the remarkably accurate forecasting which has developed over the past decade or so. Climatic changes are being studied as they really occur over telling expanses of time, not as impressionistic constructions fabricated out of the limited experiences in one man's lifetime, inaccurately recalled.

Of course, there is a human dimension to the universe, and in the dimensions of one life, rhythms of repetition humanly identifiable and humanly satisfying are to be found. But the human dimension today also includes a great deal of abstract, scientific knowledge—for science is nothing if not a human creation, since it exists only within the human mind. Our abstract, scientific knowledge, which is now entering so thoroughly into planning as to be eminently real as well as abstract, includes a knowledge of the evolution of the cosmos and of life. This means that, in conjunction with an immediate experience of approximate recurrence, we experience also, if we are alert to the world in a twentieth-century way, an awareness of the fact that recurrence does not stand up *in detail*. Quite literally, in the modern physical universe, nothing ever repeats itself. Least of all does history.

The classic model for cyclic repetition, when it was rationalized, had been the supposedly immutable path of the sun around the earth. Now we know not merely that the earth moves around the sun, but also that it moves in a path, not circular but elliptical, which is gradually changing its form, in ways which are measurable. The stars are not changeless, but in full evolutionary career. So is our solar system. And the elements themselves are dismembered and reconstituted in the process of cosmic evolution.

One can still project a cyclic model of perpetual repetition upon actuality, pretending that everything now happening happened before an infinite number of times and will happen again an infinite number of times. But study fails to reveal any warrant within actuality itself even for the model. Even if we are living in a so-called "throbbing universe," which expands to a maximum and then over billions of years reverses and contracts to a single, unimaginably hot super-atom only to explode and expand again, all the evidence we have around us from the universe itself suggests that the pattern of events in the second explosion will be different from that in the first. To cap all this anti-repetitiveness is the appearance of human life itself in the cosmic process. For each man is a unique individual, utterly different from his fellows, all of them, no matter how many they are. The difference is not merely genetic. It is conscious, as can be seen in identical twins, who have the same genetic structures but quite different consciousness, the one "I" utterly distinct from the other. Each of us knows he is unique—that no one else experiences this taste of himself which he knows directly, a taste, as Gerard Manley Hopkins put it, "more distinctive than . . . ale or alum." No one in possession of his wits is concerned that one of the other three billion or so persons in the universe today is identical with himself. For each man knows his own induplicability and interior inaccessibility. In simply knowing himself, each knows that his interior landscape is unique and open only to his own mind. With man at the term of the cosmic and organic evolutionary process, we thus are aware of the universe in its entirety as building up to maximum unrepeatability, self-conscious uniqueness, singularity folded back on itself.

With this kind of awareness, what remains of recurrence as a foundation for poetry and art? We are, of course, as we have seen, still acutely conscious of approximate recurrence to a degree: there is, after all, the evident succession of spring, summer, autumn, winter, repeating year after year. But this basic repetition, and all that goes with it, is no longer at the heart of life in the way in which it used to be. It has been displaced. It is now eccentric. A somewhat sentimental account explains the displacement by urbanization and industrialization: large numbers of men now live far from the wilds of nature or the domesticated life close to nature on the farm. But, more radically, the displacement has come about by the intellectual discovery of the cosmic facts, which are known to persons in rural areas as well as in the cities: we live not in a cyclic, perpetually recurring, but in a linear-type time. I say "linear-type" rather than "linear" because time, being nonspatial, is not entirely like a straight line, either. But it is like a straight line rather than a circle in the sense that events in time end at a different point from that at which they begin. (Whether they are really "strung out" like points on a line is another question: in fact, they are not.) My life at its end is different from what it was at its beginning. The universe, even now, is different from what it was five billion years ago and gives evidence of continued progressive differentiation from its initial stage and all subsequent stages.

The displacement of the sense of recurrence as the dominant human awareness is, I believe, a major crisis, and probably *the* major crisis, in the arts today. The displacement does not, of course, affect everyone in society equally. The sensibility of millions of persons, even in highly technologized societies, is doubtless still dominated by a feeling for recurrence which is functionally little different from that of their ancestors two hundred years ago, at least in many areas of life. They do feel the spring, summer, autumn, and winter as a real part of themselves. But even they are undoubtedly affected more radically than they are consciously aware by the psychological structures of society today, particularly by the stress on planning, whether economic or social or industrial or international or interplanetary. Planning means the conscious control of mind over the elements in nature and spells the end of the dominance of quasi-cyclic experience. With planning, matters end up differently from the way in which they began. Moreover, with modern technology, the effect of the seasons—basic to sustaining a sense of recurrence—has been blunted in ways which are sure to be telling, if only subconsciously, for all. A heated and air-conditioned building is pretty much the same in summer and winter, and more and more persons, educated and uneducated, are spending more and more time in such buildings. Transportation, formerly so much affected by the movement of the seasons, is more and more independent of this movement. In technologized societies menus are increasingly the same the year round, or can be. On television one can see skiing in the middle of one's own summer and aquaplaning in midwinter. The difference between night and day, for practical working purposes, has long since disappeared from major areas of human existence. One has to gloss the text "The night cometh when no man can work" to make it comprehensible to a swing-shift worker in an assembly plant. Even the most unreflective are affected by this detachment of life from the rhythms of nature.

A fortiori the poets and artists are affected. And they know it. In accord with their deeply felt desire for up-to-dateness, which is the desire to speak for man in our time and is itself an anti-cyclic or post-cyclic phenomenon, contemporary poets generally will give at least lip service to the eclipse of recurrence as a central human experience. But how far is poetry affected by this lip service? Poets in English and some other languages continue to use rhyme —although it is significant that they no longer use it so often as they once did. They continue to use lines of more or less matching lengths—although again they do so less than they used to. Occasionally, in fits of desperation, they may resort to bongo drums. But here again, although jazz is indeed relevant to modern living precisely because of its apotheosis of rhythm, resort to jazz is regarded more and more as an escape, if a necessary one. Primitive man banged his drums to attune himself to cosmic harmonies. Modern man resorts to jazz to get away from it all.

The real crisis, however, for modern poets occurs in the images of which they can avail themselves and of course in stylistic and structural devices of repetition where these intersect with or otherwise engage the imagery of a poem. The old reliable cosmological imagery of recurrence appears less and less serviceable. What sort of enthusiasm could be brought today, for example, to the creation of a work such as Edmund Spenser's "Epithalamion," where, if we can believe Professor Kent Hieatt's fantastic calculations,[6] the day and year are represented by the twenty-four stanzas and 365 long lines of the poem, the apparent daily movement of the sun relative to the fixed stars is figured in other line-totals, and at one point the ratio of light to darkness at the time of the summer solstice, when the action of the poem takes place, is properly signaled to the reader? One can, of course, cite Joyce's *Ulysses*—but here the relevance of cosmic imagery is indirect. It is maintained by literary allusion rather than by direct feeling for nature. Joyce builds out of Homer, and countless others, not out of "nature" directly. Of course Spenser builds out of other poets, too, for he is filled with literary allusion. But with him cosmology itself is also more directly operative. Milton, here, is a key figure. *Paradise Lost* was built on a cosmology no longer viable in Milton's day, but clung to deliberately by Milton for poetic reasons. My point is that poets and artists generally today are faced with a crisis similar to Milton's, and even deeper than his was. The polarization of literary dispute around the figures of Milton and Joyce in the mid-twentieth century is perhaps symptomatic: both Milton and Joyce face cosmological problems, and both retreat from them.

Awareness of the modern cosmological crisis in poetry has seldom come to the surface of the contemporary sensibility, and a case for modern "cosmic poetry," with some of the marks of the older recurrence-based patterns, has in fact been made in *Start with the Sun*, by James E. Miller, Jr., Karl Shapiro, and Bernice Slote.[7] The authors of this book also show how, more or less in association with the drift to old cosmic themes, another emphasis is capital in many modern poets: the stress on the esthetic moment, on "creativity," on the instant of "epiphany." This emphasis, which has an obvious Coleridgean as well as Symbolist and Imagist background, deserves attention here, for it throws great light on the poet's relationship to the sense of cosmic time itself. Mircea Eliade has shown that the primitive sense of time, particularly of sacred time, involves a psychological need to recover the beginning of things.[8] Early man—and we can assimilate to early man all mankind generally, more or less, until the psychological effect of typography had entered deep into the subconscious and established a new relationship toward records, the past, and time—early man felt time and change as somehow involving degeneration, a moving away from a perfect "time" at the beginning, a time which was really not a time but an extratemporal condition, the so-called "time" of mythological existence. The events of mythology—for example, Athena's springing from the head of Zeus, Dionysus' dismemberment by the Maenads—were not the sort of things for which one could supply dates. (As has frequently been noted by scholars, the Biblical accounts of origins involve a different, contrasting sense of time, even when the Biblical accounts are obviously influenced by extra-Biblical mythology.)

Time poses many problems for man, not the least of which is that of irresistibility and irreversibility: man in time is moved ahead willy-nilly and cannot actually recover a moment of the past. He is caught, carried on despite himself, and hence not a little terrified. Resort to mythologies, which associate temporal events with the atemporal, in effect disarms time, affording relief from its threat. This mythological flight from the ravages of time may at a later date be rationalized by various cyclic theories, which have haunted man's philosophizing from antiquity to the present. In the wake of romanticism, however, we find a new refuge from the pressure of time in the cult of the here-and-now esthetic experience, the esthetically achieved moment which gives a sense of expanded existence and of a quasi-eternity. Georges Poulet, in *Studies in Human Time*, Frank Kermode in *Romantic Image*, and others elsewhere have elaborated various ways in which this sense of escape from time is managed, from the French writers leading up to Proust on through various American writers: Emerson, Poe, Emily Dickinson, T. S. Eliot, and others.

234 / Walter J. Ong, S.J.

Post-romantic estheticism depends in great part on the sense of this esthetic moment, different from and more valuable than experiences in ordinary time. We find this sense particularly acute in the Bloomsbury esthetic growing out of and around G. E. Moore's *Principia Ethica*, which influenced so typical a modern writer as Virginia Woolf. James Joyce's doctrine of "epiphany," of course, belongs in this same setting. And the influence on the New Criticism is evident: the poem as "object" is assimilated to a world of vision, which is a timeless world by comparison with that of words and sound. An esthetic of "objective correlatives," whatever its great merits, to a degree insulates poetry from time. Up to a point all poetry provides an esthetic refuge from "real" time, but earlier poetic theory, even that expounding poetry as divinely inspired and thus different from ordinary talk, generally lacks this exaltation of a moment of "realization" which is so commonplace today.

The stress on the moment of realization, on epiphany, under one of its aspects, can thus actually be a dodge to avoid the consequences inherent in the knowledge we have that we live in an evolving universe. It can provide a means of escaping from the real—that is, from cosmic on-goingness—a latter-day timeshelter, replacing the primitive's mythological refuge. This is not to say that the older attempts to escape from time have been entirely abandoned. The quest for a lost Eden, the "radical innocence," which Professors R. W. B. Lewis, Ihab Hassan, and others have discerned in American writers particularly, revives some of the old mythological routines. But this quest for a lost Eden, although real enough, must today be looked for closely to be found. Writers do not openly advertise that their creative drives are being powered by a quest for a lost Eden. They often do talk openly about the value of the esthetic moment.

Once we are aware of the psychological issues here, it is possible to discern some fascinating perspectives in modern poetry. Those which we shall here employ are related to Professor Cleanth Brooks's division, already adverted to, between poets preoccupied with history (related to evolutionism) and those preoccupied with nature (related, as we have seen, to cyclicism). But they refine this division further, as I believe. We can view poets in three groupings, not always too neatly distinct, but, given the proper reservations, highly informative concerning the poet's problem of relating to the known universe.

There are, first of all, those poets who are consumed with the imagery of the old cosmic mythology to such an extent that it rather effectively dominates their entire outlook. Such would be, for example, D. H. Lawrence, Dylan Thomas, Lawrence Durrell, and Robert Graves. The suggestion of cyclicism takes various forms here, but common to them all is at least preoccupation with fertility (or its opposite, sterility). Indeed, the present cult of sex (often clearly an obsession) in literature appears from the point of vantage we occupy here to be a flight from time comparable to the fertility ceremonials of primitives, but more desperate because our sense of the evolutionary nature of actuality makes time more insistent today than ever before. Radical innocence is sought more frenetically because we are more aware of its inaccessibility.

In the case of Lawrence, the cult of sex and death—which yields such beauties as "Bavarian Gentians"—is linked with a nostalgia for the past and conscious revivals of old chthonic images, such as the serpent, which were supposed to restore modern man to his lost Eden. Dylan Thomas immerses himself more spectacularly in nature imagery. "Fern Hill" runs on in a riot of time and fertility symbols: apple boughs, the night, time, barley, "all the sun long," grass, sleep, owls, the dew, the cock, "Adam and the maiden," the new-made clouds, "in the sun born over and over," sky blue trades, morning songs, "the moon that is always rising," "time held me green and dying." This stirring poem is a litany of life and death, in its cosmology still of a piece with Lucretius. Lawrence Durrell celebrates the mysteries of sex with a sophisticated neopagan fervor, having little to do with a sense of man's present position in the cosmos he is taking over more and more, although Durrell does have some sense of temporal progression in the evolution of social groupings. Graves protracts what he takes to be ancient continuities into the present.

> Is it of trees you tell . . .
>
> . . . .
> Or of the Zodiac and how slow it turns
> Below the Boreal Crown,
>
> . . . . ?
> Water to water, ark again to ark,
> From woman back to woman:
> So each new victim treads unfalteringly
> The never altered circuit of his fate,
> Bringing twelve peers as witness
> Both to his starry rise and starry fall.[9]

Here one notes strong, and doubtless deliberate, suggestions of the old wheel of fortune, so well known to students of the Middle Ages and so revealing of the pagan cyclicism which haunted the medieval mind. Other poets deeply involved in various ways in chthonic, cyclic themes are Edgar Lee Masters and, most of all, Yeats. Indeed, Yeats is so spectacularly and desperately anti-evolutionary that there is little point in discussing him here. But it is worth noting that in *A Vision*, "Byzantium," and elsewhere his cyclicism comes patently and directly from his poetic needs.

The work of poets such as these, deeply involved in sex, fertility rituals, and, by the same token, death, could perhaps be described as Dionysian; and, by contrast, an evolutionary view, which takes full cognizance that history and time do not fold back on themselves but move resolutely forward with the mysterious upthrust evident in the ascent from protozoans to man, could be described as Apollonian. Perhaps all poetry must be in some way Dionysian because of its sources in the subconscious. But one hesitates to make this judgment if only because one suspects that the Nietzschean division into Dionysian and Apollonian is itself the result of a flight from time. Nietzsche's own cyclicism suggests that his thought, whatever its other brilliances, was not relating itself to the full facts of an evolutionary cosmos.

A second group of poets is related to time in another way. These are the poets adverted to above who attempt to solve the problem of time by greater concentration on the pure esthetic moment. In his *Studies in Human Time* Georges Poulet beautifully describes the way in which Emily Dickinson presents in her poetry moments without past and without future except insofar as the future threatens the loss of the moment.[10] Each poem is a moment of experience which releases us from time:

> Safe in their alabaster chambers,
> Untouched by morning and untouched by noon,
> Sleep the meek members of the resurrection,
> Rafter of satin, and roof of stone.[11]

Miss Dickinson does not flee evolutionary time by resort to the seeming endless recurrences associated with a cult of the Earth Mother. She simply dwells in the instant and attempts to protract it. In this, her work is an early example of what would become a regular style, particularly from the Imagists on, a style revived by many poets at the present moment. The cult of the esthetic moment (or epiphany) marks to a greater or lesser degree the poetic performance and beliefs of James Joyce, Edith Sitwell, Conrad Aiken, Wallace Stevens, E. E. Cummings, William Carlos Williams in his more Imagist phases, and countless others. To a greater or lesser degree it permeates the contemporary consciousness from the heights of the New Criticism down to the level of the most unimaginative beatnik writers. Ezra Pound, with his own complicated sense of history, shows its influence, most evidently in his constant cry to "make it new"—although this exhortation has other implications also. In his poetry and poetic theory, Wallace Stevens, despite his predilection for change, bypasses the development of the universe as such and views existence—poetically conveyed—

as a series of disconnected esthetic mergings of imagination and chaos. And the newer generation of poets—James Wright, Robert Bly, Donald Hall, Howard Nemerov, John Knoepfle, and others—may repudiate their predecessors on other scores, but they show, if anything, an even more intense devotion to the esthetic movement, often very intimately conceived.

The drift toward the old chthonic fertility cycles (more noteworthy in the Old World poets, at least until very recently) and the retreat into the esthetic moment (discernible on both sides of the Atlantic) are complemented by a third tendency in modern poetry, a disposition actually to accept linear-type change and even to demand it as a condition of poetic activity. This disposition is more marked among American poets than among British and Irish, a fact which is of course related to the nature of the American experience. Whitman is obviously a striking expositor of this experience, with his attitude of total acceptance toward being and his sense of a dynamic present, diverging toward past and future and uniting and equalizing them. Probably more than the somewhat doctrinaire and clinical acceptance of evolutionism which one meets with in early British writers such as Tennyson, George Bernard Shaw, and H. G. Wells, or even Swinburne, Whitman's sense of participation in the ongoing work of the universe appears to acclimate evolutionism to the poetic world. But does it really succeed? Poulet is quite right in noting that Whitman's is "an enunciation, at once successive and cumulative, of all that has been, and of all that will be."[12] "The universe is a procession with measured and perfect motion," Whitman announces.[13] But, unlike Péguy's comparable procession, which as Poulet again explains, has a termination, Whitman's procession simply advances, occupying worlds and times, but never changing anything, never getting anywhere. In fact, in Whitman we find little if any attention to the inner dynamism of evolution itself; what Teilhard has called the "inwardness" of things, the drive within the evolutionary process which moves from the externally organized original cosmos to the cosmos known and more and more controlled from the interior of man's person,[14] is missing from Whitman.

This is not to say that there is no historicism at all in Whitman. Whitman comes off one of the best in his awareness of the one-directional process of history, for his sense of a dynamic present, diverging toward the past and future and uniting and equalizing them, as well as his sense of the uniqueness of the individual imply a sense of the evolutionary, essentially nonrepetitive movement of time.[15] And yet, Whitman, too, is trapped by the old cyclicism, as, for example, in "Song of the Answerer":

They bring none to his or her terminus or to be content and full,
Whom they take they take into space to behold the birth of the
    stars, to learn one of the meanings,
To launch off with absolute faith, to sweep through the ceaseless
    rings and never be quiet again.[16]

In the last analysis there is little or nothing in Whitman to differentiate past and future. Whitman's is still a cult of the present moment, temporally expanded, with little real anguish. For him the present does not grow out of the past, nor the future out of the present. Past, present, and future simply coexist—and all too peacefully. The universe and Whitman's appetite, as Poulet notes, exactly equal one another. How can anything happen when so much bland satisfaction reigns? Whitman has little of the dissatisfactions of the reformer or the future-oriented man.

But if he is not especially concerned about improving things, other American poets more typically are—William Carlos Williams, for example, who insists, dramatically in his *In the American Grain* and by explicit assertion in many other places, that it is the business of the present in America to reconstitute its past and to improve its poetic language and hence its poetic realization of actuality.[17] It is interesting that Williams does not think much in terms of degeneration or decadence (which often reveal a cyclic model in the subconscious): the plight of Americans is not that they have defected from their past but rather that they are only now in a position to lay hold of it reflectively and effectively for the first time, since it now is old enough really to be a past to them. Williams dedicates *Paterson* to this enterprise of recovery, which in a way does look ahead. Yet the time which Williams deals with does not unfold, nor does it thrust forward. The present is authenticated by the past and the future lies as a potential in past and present, but there is little adventure in facing what is to come, little sense of unattained horizons ahead. Such a sense, of course, is not necessary for the writing of poetry, but it would seem to be something which could be included in poetic awareness.

One discerns comparable attitudes in Hart Crane. Crane's vision, conceived in *The Bridge*, is born of his sense of his own moment in history, in time, at the dawn of the machine age. His reactions are not querulous, but positive, like those of Whitman, whom he eulogizes. Crane's confident assertion of faith in the future of industrial America hints at a feeling for linear, evolutionary time. But his compulsion to create the "American myth" drives him toward more cyclic views to fulfill his need for a pattern, and we find in the "Ave Maria," for example, a fascination with the old cosmic movements and with cyclic patterns in a variety of forms:

> Of all that amplitude that time explores,
> . . . . :
> This disposition that thy night relates
> From Moon to Saturn in one sapphire wheel:
> The orbic wake of thy once whirling feet,
> Elohim, still I hear thy sounding heel!
>
> White toils of heaven's cordons, mustering
> In holy rings all sails charged to the far
> Hushed gleaming fields and pendant seething wheat
> Of knowledge,—round thy brows unhooded now
> —The kindled Crown! acceded of the poles
> And biassed by full sails, meridians reel
> Thy purpose—still one shore beyond desire![18]

The fascination with cyclic patterns echoes in the last line of "To Brooklyn Bridge": "And of the curveship lend a myth to God."

Crane's representation of history is more interiorized than Whitman's expansive canvases, but his quest for a stabilizing myth, a symbolic structure which will somehow catch the historical process in poetic toils, draws him back at times into something like primitive cyclicism. Crane had read Oswald Spengler. At other times, perhaps under the influence of P. D. Ouspensky, he retreats from the flow of time into a mythical eternal present which alone exists but is parceled out to man piecemeal.

Crane is typically American in his determination to try to make poetic sense of history. Other Americans show a similar concern. Allen Tate, Robert Penn Warren, William Carlos Williams, Archibald MacLeish, and Robert Lowell, for example, have felt compelled at least from time to time to build poetry around historical events which have appeared to them as part of their own life-worlds—the Civil War for Tate and Warren, the New Jersey city of Paterson for Williams, for MacLeish American *miscellanea*, New England for Robert Lowell. All these poets evince a distinctly open-end or linear-type view of time. They are helped by the fact that the American past they turn to is a recorded, truly historical past, free to all intents and purposes of prehistory and of prehistory's cyclic tow. (The exception which must be made for the native American Indian prehistory is relatively minor.) Another American, Robert Frost, shows the same open-endedness in his own less explicitly historical, more anecdotal concerns. There is little if any mythical reconstruction in Frost. No cyclic nostalgia shows, for example, in the typically courageous, forward-looking poem "An Old Man's Winter Night." Nevertheless, in the particular perspectives we are considering here, it appears that the achievements of these poets are often limited. Their historical mood is predominantly retrospective. It may seem strange to suggest that history can be anything other than retrospective, and yet we know so much history now that we rightly feel the knowledge of the past driving us into the future. I am not saying that these or other poets should be obliged to treat history otherwise than as they have, for they have done exceed-

242 / Walter J. Ong, S.J.

ingly well in following each his own genius. Nor do I intend to suggest that anyone should opt for a fatuous view of pure progress as man's destiny in his earthly future. I am only saying that these poets cannot be cited as having caught up in their poetry the entirety of present-day man's real time sense.

Even Pound and Eliot, whose personal and poetic journey from the United States back into Europe was a quite conscious re-entry into history, have not provided a point of view in which one can assimilate a full historical and evolutionary vision to a poetic one. Pound piles historical incident on historical incident. His "Cantos" read as a vast pastiche of eye-witness accounts, overheard conversations, and reflections from everywhere out of the past, with Ecbatana and the ancient Near East jostling what Pound in "Canto XXVIII" styles "solid Kansas." But the impression one gets is not of the development of history so much as it is of a present in which all this history is caught up and somehow moved out of time. "Time is the evil. Evil," "Canto XXX" cries. Eliot's great essay on "Tradition and the Individual Talent," with its sensitive description of the relationship of past, present, and future, provides one of the purest examples of truly historical thinking in our century, and the line from "Burnt Norton" which states, "Only through time time is conquered," is a gnomic expression of the condition of both history and transcendence. And yet, the same "Burnt Norton" opens with a quotation from Heraclitus which states, "The way up and the way down are one and the same," focuses, especially in its part II, on the image of whirling movement ("There is only the dance"), and concludes with the lament, "Ridiculous the waste sad time/Stretching before and after." It is noteworthy that the Heraclitian fragment, "The way up and the way down are one and the same," strongly suggests cyclic fatalism (return to point of departure or inability to leave it) and by no means says the same thing as does Eliot's much advertised other source, St. John of the Cross, or the Gospel source on which St. John relies, "He who exalts himself will be humbled, and he who humbles himself will be exalted."

The words of Jesus incorporate a dialectical movement missing in this somewhat paralyzing quotation from the Greek sage. All in all, in his poems and plays (for example, *Murder in the Cathedral*, Acts I and II) Eliot interlaces references to historical, evolutionary time with references to cyclic patterns so frequent and intense as virtually to immobilize the historical. Geoffrey Bullough has pointed out Eliot's preference for "formal patterns" over Bergson's open-ended *élan vital*.[19]

In a sense the point thus far made in this study might be seen as predictable. The poetic theorists from Aristotle through Sir Philip Sidney and beyond always knew that poetry and history were at root incompatible—despite the fact that, as we are well aware today, the poetic imagination has often been stimulated by historical events, proximate or remote. But the point here is precisely that such theory is no longer adequate. The incompatibility of poetry and history is today a more desperate matter than it used to be. A sense of history, seen as evolutionary development, has now become an inevitable dimension of all reflective human existence, and if the very feel for evolutionary development is unassimilable by poetry, then poetry cannot compass one of the most profound and intimate of modern experiences.

A sense of history, which is of a piece with a sense of an evolutionary cosmos, is a sense of the present as growing out of a past with which we are in some kind of verifiable contact, and a sense that the present differs from this past with which it connects and that the future will differ from both present and past. It is a sense of continuity and difference, each reflecting the other, such as Eliot so well expounds in "Tradition and the Individual Talent." We have seen the basic reason why such a sense poses a problem for poets: it undercuts structures dear to them, first by downgrading recurrence as such, making what repetition there is only approximate and somewhat incidental, and secondly by making the present not only a present but also a sequel and a prelude. The problem may not appear pressing when we experience only a single poem, but when we look at the entire body of work of a poet, either in its larger themes or images or in the theory which it at times consciously—perhaps often too consciously—shows forth, the problem, as we have seen, is urgent indeed. A significant drift toward either cyclicism or the isolated moment is unmistakable in modern poetry.

The poet has always been ill at ease, to some degree, in the world of actuality. Poetry is imitation, as the ancients well knew. Admittedly, poetry as such cannot be history. But it must be human, and the urgent question today is whether it must write off the modern experience of evolutionary historicity, whether it can even talk about this experience without betraying itself as poetry. This unresolved question, I believe, is what, deep in the subconscious, in great part underlies the *malaise* of poets and their friends today, occasioning the complaint that poets are outsiders more than they used to be, discarded by "modern society," a seemingly unrealistic complaint, since it appears probable that never have poets been more read and more courted than in our present technological United States. The basic question is: Can poetry face into continuous nonrecurrence as such and assimilate it without distorting it? Can it be that the poet (and the artist generally) feels himself an outsider today less because he has been actively expelled from modern society than because he has failed to make his own one of its deepest insights, its sense of historical time and its drive into fulfillment in the future?

We have noted above the American poets' share in the American sense of drive into the future. This sense holds some promise of change. Further promise of change is to be found in the Christian world view itself, which calls for specific attention here because it has been the source of so much of modern man's sense of history. For the Christian, both the universe and the life of the individual man end in quite different states from those in which they began. Time makes a difference. Time tells. Christian teaching urges no one to try to recover a lost Eden. Salvation lies ahead, at the end of time. And Adam's sin, which drove man from the Garden of Eden, is even hailed in the Holy Saturday liturgy of the

Roman Catholic Church as *felix culpa*, "happy fault," because it gave God occasion to send His Son Jesus Christ to redeem man. The promise of the future is thus greater than that of the past. Christian (and Hebrew) teaching underlines the nonrepetitiveness of actuality and by the same token the importance of the unique, unrepeatable, human self, the human person. Christianity, like evolutionary thinking, is anticyclic.

Many of the modern poets who espouse an open-end view of time also give evidence of more or less explicit Christian influence—Allen Tate, Robert Lowell, Richard Wilbur, and W. H. Auden would be examples in point, although I do not believe that any of them has fully solved the problem of assimilating our modern sense of time to the artistic medium. There is however another poet generally classified as modern who is especially worth looking into here for the directness—and precocity—with which he has faced into the problem of time, historicity, and the human person living in time. The grounds on which he faces the problem may be too explicitly Christian to solve the problem for some. Yet there is, I believe, something to learn from him. This poet is Gerard Manley Hopkins, an artist who, although he apparently had read little if any Darwin, is still, I believe, more at home in history and in an evolutionary cosmos than most other modern or near-modern poets, although he is not quite aware of his own entire at-homeness here. His Catholic dogmatic background simply fitted him for an evolutionary time-sense despite the fact that the initial steps toward evolutionary thinking caused no little consternation in Catholic and other religious circles.

The key passages in Hopkins for our present purposes are in "The Wreck of the Deutschland." In this poem Hopkins is dealing with the significance of a horrifying event, a wreck in which a German ship, the *Deutschland*, outward bound from Bremen, foundered on shoals in the North Sea during a storm and was stranded for thirty hours without help, with great loss of life and with the most horrible suffering and distress. In one rescue incident, a seaman, lowered on a rope from the rigging to help a woman or child drowning on the deck, was dashed by a wave against the bulwarks and decapitated. The next morning, according to the *Times* report, "when daylight dawned, his headless body, detained by the rope, was swaying to and fro with the waves."[20] Among the details which he picked up from the *Times* accounts, Hopkins focuses on one particularly: "Five German nuns, whose bodies are now in the dead-house here, clasped hands and were drowned together, the chief sister, a gaunt woman 6 ft. high, calling out loudly and often, 'O Christ, come quickly!' till the end came."[21] The central movement in Hopkins' thought in his poem turns on his inquiry into what this nun meant in her cry, "O Christ, come quickly!" He explores many possibilities—was she asking for rescue? For death as a relief for herself and all those around? —and finally settles for the cry as one of recognition and acceptance. This horrible visitation, this agonizing, not even private but involved with the agony of all those around her, was the real advent of Christ Himself in this nun's life: here she would meet Him in her death, and she called out for Him to come and take her "in the storm of his strides." She sees Christ not as an avenger, but as God, her Lover, and in his love as "the Master/*Ipse*, the only one, Christ, King, Head:/He was to cure the extremity where he had cast her;/Do, deal, lord it with living and dead." This was the point—unknown until now—to which her life had been building up, and she was ready, for she had known that God's coming need not be gentle, that He is present not only in "the stars, lovely-asunder" or in "the dapple-with-damson west," but in all the events in history, even the most horrible, out of which He can bring joy. Hers was a faith which could see God in everything—in disaster as well as joy, indeed most of all in her own death—and never waver in its confidence in Him. Had not St. Paul asked in the *Epistle to the Romans* (8:35, 37), "Who shall separate us from the love of Christ? Shall tribulation, or distress, or persecution, or hunger, or nakedness, or danger, or the sword? . . . But in all these things we overcome, because of Him who has loved us."

What we note here is a sense of history at perhaps its highest possible pitch. Hopkins, as we find in his theoretical observations, was devoted to the "instress" of things, to uniqueness itself, to what made each thing itself only, other, different from all else. His poetry everywhere testifies to the intensity of his love for variety, for "all things counter, original, spare, strange," as he puts it in "Pied Beauty." Hopkins connected his interest in the uniqueness of things with the thought of his thirteenth-century predecessor at Oxford, Duns Scotus, but interest in the unique was beyond a doubt far more intense and explicit in the post-romantic Englishman than in his medieval compatriot, who was necessarily far less sensitized to history by his age than Hopkins by his. Hopkins, in fact, is clearly a proto-existentialist in his preoccupation with the singular and the singularity of existence, with "my selfbeing, my consciousness and feeling of myself, that taste of myself, of *I* and *me* above all and in all things, which is more distinctive than the taste of ale or alum."[22] His sonnet "As kingfishers catch fire, dragonflies draw flame" announces a kind of self-definition in action: "Whát I dó is me." But his fascination with the unique and his sense of historicity is shown perhaps most strikingly by the way in which in the "Deutschland" he has fixed on the consciously accepted death of a human being—the utterly unique culmination of an utterly unique existence—as the very focus of existence and meaning.

He relates this death to the action of God's grace—the free gift of God which establishes the unique relationship between each unique individual and God. But grace itself, Hopkins insists, is an historical event. It does not come from heaven, direct from God's existence beyond time. Hopkins knows this will shock but presents it as a central Catholic teaching:

> Not out of his bliss
>   Springs the stress felt
> Nor first from heaven (and few know this)
>   Swings the stroke dealt—
> Stroke and a stress that stars and storms deliver,
> That guilt is hushed by, hearts are flushed by and melt—
>   But it rides time like riding a river
> (And here the faithful waver, the faithless fable and miss).[23]

It is clear from the preceding lines of the poem that the "stress" is God's grace, the pressure he exerts on man's life (firm, delicate, mysterious, in Hopkins' image, like the pressure of the streams trickling down from the surrounding hills which hold the head of water in a well up to its level). This grace, "delivered" through the universe in the violence of storms as well as in the interior movements of consciousness which bring the sinner to repentance and hope, does not come directly from God in eternity ("his bliss") but only in history through Jesus Christ, who was and is both God and man, and as man a real material figure identifiable in actual cosmic time. Hopkins goes on about grace:

> It dates from day
>   Of his going in Galilee;
>   Warm-laid grave of a womb-life grey;
>   Manger, maiden's knee;
> The dense and the driven Passion, and frightful sweat;
> Thence the discharge of it, there its swelling to be,
>   Though felt before, though in high flood yet.

The grace at work in the world today comes into the present through the historical life of Jesus Christ—His Incarnation, birth, and, most of all, His passion and death. Even the grace given fallen man antecedent to Christ was given in view of Christ's coming into historical time.

"It dates." This is the scandal. Hopkins' uncanny appreciation of the drives in the human psyche which make it want to dissociate itself and what it values from time is evident in the fact that he recognizes the scandal of time, which creates difficulties even for believers. "Here the faithful waver." For it seems indecent that an Almighty God would tie Himself so firmly into the flux of things, focusing His definitive visitation of man at one single brief period, the lifetime of Jesus Christ, and spreading all out from there. Equally uncanny is Hopkins' deep appreciation of the psychological mechanism of the old cosmic mythologies. Far ahead of his time, writing as though he had read Professor Eliade, he states with precocious insight that myths are nothing less than an attempt to escape from time, to make significance dateless. "The faithless fable and miss." They do not see the movement of grace in life as something that "rides time like riding a river." They try to find meaning by escaping from time.

Written in 1875, only sixteen years after the appearance of *The Origin of Species* and without any discernible direct Darwinian influence, "The Wreck of the Deutschland" actually makes use of a theme assimilable to an evolutionary sense of time, an "open-end," developmental structuring of events more explicitly and downrightly than any other poem of comparable size or importance which I know of since Darwin. The presence of grace has proved, in the Christian sense of history, to be a presence curiously of a piece with the presence which man himself feels in the universe since knowledge of cosmic and organic evolution has shaped his deeper attitudes toward his life-world. Hopkins' open-end view of time is focused in the world of the human person and of grace, which lives in persons, rather than in the more material world of cosmic and organic evolution. To this degree his view remains underdeveloped. Hopkins was not greatly taken with Darwin's discoveries, although perhaps he would have been had he lived longer. But his world is open to them; indeed, it would welcome them, with the sense of the uniqueness of things to which these discoveries can give and have given rise.

Hopkins is certainly not the only poet who is influenced by a Christian sense of God's grace operating in real historical time on persons each of whom is unique. Many other poets, most of them far less consciously, are influenced by the same open-ended historicism, as Professor Brooks has pointed out in *The Hidden God*. Such open-ended historicism is part of the Hebreo-Christian heritage, which in fact was perhaps a necessary condition for Darwin's seeing what he saw: it appears unlikely that a sensibility overconditioned by cyclic views would have been gripped, as Darwin was, by evolutionary patterns. But to say that open-ended historicism and the related evolutionary outlook are at home in the

Christian world view is not to say that earlier poets, even the most Christian, entirely succeeded in accommodating a truly Christian sense of time to their poetic sensibilities. Professor Brooks has suggested that "with the breakup of the Christian synthesis, nature and history have tended to fall apart."[24] We have to be careful about imputing to past ages a Christian synthesis. If such a synthesis should include a sense of man's real place in the real physical universe of time and space, as apparently it should, there has been not only no valid Christian synthesis in the past but not even a moderately good synthesis. You cannot have a valid Christian synthesis based on a false cosmology or even on a notably defective one. We must face the fact that earlier cosmologies were both defective and, in many crucial points, false. Nature was never until recent times effectively conjoined with history. The problem today is not to restore an old union but to implement a new one. This problem, the present study suggests, is not particularly distressing to the Christian who understands his heritage in the depths at which it can now be understood. But it is a grievously distressing problem for the poet and artist of our time as poet or artist—whether he be Christian or not—and one from which most poets and artists, consciously or subconsciously, retreat. In other words, it is easier for the Christian as such than for the poet or artist as such to subscribe in the depths of his being to an evolutionary universe. It is also easier, *mutatis mutandis*, for the Jew, since the Old Testament sense of time and the New Testament sense of time are of a piece, although the entry of God into time and history is less intense without the New Testament doctrine of the Incarnation.

The plight of the modern poet and artist is truly extreme. The poet or artist is acutely ill at ease in our present life-world. The earlier life-world belonged to the poets largely because it was so largely constructed out of the archetypal images which poetry and art tend to favor. If to a degree the modern world has rejected the poet, the poet also often has rejected the modern world because it demands a reorganization of his sensibility which is utterly terrifying. If the poet speaks for his age, he tends to speak for those who turn away from the characteristic awarenesses of modern man concerned with history and time.

With some exceptions, in his sense of time and history and of the succession of events, the poet thus has tended to be an aborigine, a primitive. Some maintain that the poet or artist must continue always to be such. I do not believe that he can afford to do so. Of course, no one can prescribe how a poet must speak. If, however, the poet is going to speak for modern man, he is going to have to take into account somehow man's total consciousness, even though this entails a reorganization of his own psyche and of the entire tradition of poetry so drastic as to fill us with utter terror. Very possibly the archetypes in the psyche are themselves in process of being reorganized under pressure of present discoveries. How subconsciously archetypal can archetypes be when they are the objects of knowledge as conscious as that which we bring to them today? Let us be honest in facing the future of poetry and art and man. What will poetry be like ten thousand or one hundred thousand years from now? Will man be able still to live with his once fascinating little dreams of recurrence?

Notes

[1] In another context, but using some of the material used here, I have treated this subject in the study "Myth or Evolution? Crisis of the Creative Imagination," *McCormick Quarterly*, XVIII, Special Supplement (Jan., 1965), 37–56. This previous study was read as a paper at a colloquium on "Myth and Modern Man" sponsored by McCormick Theological Seminary in Chicago on October 22, 1964, with other papers by Paul W. Pruyser, Mircea Eliade, and Schubert M. Ogden. The present study is a revised and enlarged version of a lecture given on May 11, 1964, for the Thirty-First Peters Rushton Seminar in Contemporary Prose and Poetry at the University of Virginia. For material in both these studies I wish to acknowledge help from papers and discussion by members of a 1964 St. Louis University graduate seminar on modern poetry and evolutionism: John K. Crane, Sister Mary Ruth Gehres, O.S.U., Elaine K. Halbert, Judith Hoemeke (Mrs. Gerald A.), Leah Jansky (Mrs. Radko K.), Barbara Lawrence, Lannie LeGear, Young Gul Lee, Catherine Manore, John A. Marino, Sister Mary Joan Peters, O.S.F., Barbara Quinn, Mary Slackford, Sister Dorothy Marie Sommer, C.PP.S., Norman J. Stafford, Doris Stolberg, and Alice Zucker.

[2] T. S. Eliot, *Collected Poems 1909–1962* (New York, 1963), p. 180.

[3] Cleanth Brooks, *The Hidden God: Studies in Hemingway, Faulkner, Yeats, Eliot, and Warren* (New Haven, 1963), p. 130.

[4] Northrop Frye, "The Archetypes of Literature," in *Myth and Method*, ed. James E. Miller, Jr. (Lincoln, Neb., 1960), p. 155.

[5] Walter J. Ong, "Nationalism and Darwin: A Psychological Problem in Our Concept of Social Development," *Review of Politics*, XXII (1960), 466–481.

[6] *Short Time's Endless Monument: The Symbolism of Numbers in Spenser's "Epithalamion"* (New York, 1960). See also Alastair Fowler, "Numerical Composition in *The Faerie Queene*," *Journal of the Warburg and Courtland Institutes*, XXV (1962), 199–239, and the same author's *Spenser and the Numbers of Time* (New York, 1964).

[7] *Start with the Sun: Studies in Cosmic Poetry* (Lincoln, Neb., 1960).

[8] Mircea Eliade, *The Myth of the Eternal Return* (New York, 1954), *passim*; cf. the same author's *The Sacred and the Profane* (New York, 1957) and *Patterns in Comparative Religion* (New York, 1958).

[9] Robert Graves, "To Juan at the Winter Solstice" (1946), *Collected Poems 1959* (London, 1959), p. 212.

[10] Georges Poulet, *Studies in Human Time*, trans. Elliott Coleman [with an Appendix, "Time and American Writers," written for the translated edition] (Baltimore, 1956), pp. 345–350.

[11] *The Poems of Emily Dickinson*, ed. Thomas H. Johnson (Cambridge, Mass., 1955), p. 151 (n. 216).

[12] *Studies in Human Time*, p. 344.

[13] *The Complete Poetry and Prose*, ed. Malcolm Cowley (New York, 1948), I, p. 120.

[14] Pierre Teilhard de Chardin, *The Phenomenon of Man* (New York, 1959) and *The Divine Milieu* (New York, 1960), *passim*.

[15] See *Studies in Human Time*, pp. 342–345.

[16] Quoted by Bernice Slote in *Start with the Sun*, p. 238.

[17] See, for example, his "Author's Note" contributed to *Modern Poetry: American and British*, ed. by Kimon Friar and Malcolm Brinnin (New York, 1951), p. 545.

[18] Hart Crane, *Collected Poems*, ed. Waldo Frank (New York, 1946), p. 8.

[19] Geoffrey Bullough, *Changing Psychological Beliefs in English Poetry* (Toronto, 1962), pp. 226–227.

[20] "The Historical Basis of 'The Wreck of the Deutschland' and 'The Loss of the Eurydice,'" Appendix [giving the text of the *Times* reports], in *Immortal Diamond: Studies in Gerard Manley Hopkins*, ed. by Norman Weyand (New York, 1949), p. 368.

[21] *Ibid.*, pp. 367–368.

[22] I have pointed out this existentialist strain in Hopkins in a review in *Victorian Studies*, III (1960), 305–308.

[23] "The Wreck of the Deutschland," in *Poems of Gerard Manley Hopkins*, ed. W. H. Gardner, 3d ed. (New York, 1948), p. 57.

[24] Cleanth Brooks, *The Hidden God*, p. 129.